Lecture Notes in Computer Science   13105

More information about this subseries at http://www.springer.com/series/7412

Patrick Bourdot · Mariano Alcañiz Raya ·
Pablo Figueroa · Victoria Interrante ·
Torsten W. Kuhlen · Dirk Reiners (Eds.)

Virtual Reality
and Mixed Reality

18th EuroXR International Conference, EuroXR 2021
Milan, Italy, November 24–26, 2021
Proceedings

Editors
Patrick Bourdot (iD)
University Paris-Saclay
Orsay, France

Pablo Figueroa
Los Andes University
Bogota, Colombia

Torsten W. Kuhlen
RWTH Aachen University
Aachen, Nordrhein-Westfalen, Germany

Mariano Alcañiz Raya (iD)
Universitat Politècnica de València
Valencia, Valencia, Spain

Victoria Interrante (iD)
University of Minnesota
Minneapolis, MN, USA

Dirk Reiners
University of Central Florida
Orlando, FL, USA

ISSN 0302-9743   ISSN 1611-3349 (electronic)
Lecture Notes in Computer Science
ISBN 978-3-030-90738-9   ISBN 978-3-030-90739-6 (eBook)
https://doi.org/10.1007/978-3-030-90739-6

LNCS Sublibrary: SL6 – Image Processing, Computer Vision, Pattern Recognition, and Graphics

This Springer imprint is published by the registered company Springer Nature Switzerland AG
The registered company address is: Gewerbestrasse 11, 6330 Cham, Switzerland

Preface

We are pleased to present in this LNCS volume the scientific proceedings of EuroXR 2021, the 18th EuroXR International Conference, organized by CNR-STIIMA, Italy, which took place during November 24–26, 2021. Due to the COVID-19 pandemic, EuroXR 2021 was held as a virtual conference to guarantee the best audience while maintaining the safest conditions for the attendees.

This conference follows a series of successful international conferences initiated in 2004 by the INTUITION Network of Excellence in Virtual and Augmented Reality, supported by the European Commission until 2008. Embedded within the Joint Virtual Reality Conference (JVRC) from 2009 to 2013, it was known as the EuroVR International Conference from 2014 and until last year.

The focus of these conferences is to present, each year, novel Virtual Reality (VR) through to Mixed Reality (MR) technologies, also named eXtended Reality (XR), including software systems, immersive rendering technologies, 3D user interfaces, and applications. These conferences aim to foster European engagement between industry, academia, and the public sector, to promote the development and deployment of XR in new and emerging, but also existing, fields.

Since 2017, EuroXR (https://www.euroxr-association.org/) has collaborated with Springer to publish the papers of the scientific track of our annual conference. To increase the excellence of this applied research conference, which is basically oriented toward new uses of XR technologies, we established a set of committees including Scientific Program chairs leading an International Program Committee (IPC) made up of international experts in the field.

Eight scientific full papers have been selected to be published in the proceedings of EuroXR 2021, presenting original and unpublished papers documenting new XR research contributions, practice and experience, or novel applications. Five long papers and three medium papers were selected from 22 submissions, resulting in an acceptance rate of 36%. Within a double-blind peer reviewing process, three members of the IPC with the help of some external expert reviewers evaluated each submission. From the review reports of the IPC, the Scientific Program chairs took the final decisions. The selected scientific papers are organized in this LNCS volume according to four topical parts: Perception and Cognition, Interactive Techniques, Tracking and Rendering, and Use Case and User Study.

Moreover, with the agreement of Springer and for the third year, the last part of this LNCS volume gathers scientific poster/short papers, presenting work in progress or other scientific contributions, such as ideas for unimplemented and/or unusual systems. Within another double-blind peer reviewing process based on two review reports from IPC members for each submission, the Scientific Program chairs selected four scientific poster/short papers from nine submissions (an acceptance rate of 44%).

Along with the scientific track, presenting advanced research works (scientific full papers) or research works in progress (scientific poster/short papers) in this LNCS volume, several keynote speakers were invited to EuroXR 2021. Additionally, an application track, subdivided into talk, poster, and demo sessions, was organized for participants to report on the current use of XR technologies in multiple fields.

We would like to thank the IPC members and external reviewers for their insightful reviews, which ensured the high quality of the papers selected for the scientific track of EuroXR 2021. Furthermore, we would like to thank the Application chairs, the Demo and Exhibition chairs, and the local organizers of EuroXR 2021.

We are also especially grateful to Anna Kramer (Assistant Editor, Computer Science Editorial, Springer) and Volha Shaparava (Springer OCS Support) for their support and advice during the preparation of this LNCS volume.

September 2021

Patrick Bourdot
Mariano Alcañiz Raya
Pablo Figueroa
Victoria Interrante
Torsten W. Kuhlen
Dirk Reiners

Organization

Conference General Chairs

Luca Greci   STIIMA, CNR, Italy
Hideo Saito   Keio University, Japan
Bruce H. Thomas   University of South Australia, Australia

Scientific Program Chairs

Patrick Bourdot   Université Paris-Saclay, CNRS, VENISE team, France
Mariano Alcañiz Raya   Universidad Politécnica de Valencia, Spain
Pablo Figueroa   Universidad de los Andes, Colombia
Victoria Interrante   University of Minnesota, USA
Torsten W. Kuhlen   RWTH Aachen University, Germany
Dirk Reiners   University of Central Florida, USA

Application Program Chairs

Jérôme Perret   Haption, France and Germany
Kaj Helin   VTT, Finland
Andrey Lunev   XR Insight Europe, The Netherlands
Lorenzo Cappannari   AnotheReality, Italy
Krzysztof Walczak   Poznań University of Economics and Business, Poland
Sara Arlati   STIIMA, CNR, Italy

Demo and Exhibition Chairs

Matthieu Poyade   Glasgow School of Art, UK
Giannis Karaseitanidis   ICCS, Greece
Arcadio Reyes-Lecuona   University of Malaga, Spain
Vera Colombo   Politecnico di Milano - STIIMA, CNR, Italy

International Program Committee

Mariano Alcañiz Raya   Universidad Politécnica de Valencia, Spain
Angelos Amditis   ICCS, Greece
Ferran Argelaguet Sanz   Inria, France
Sara Arlati   STIIMA, CNR, Italy
Pierre Boulanger   University of Alberta, Canada
Patrick Bourdot   Université Paris-Saclay, CNRS, VENISE team, France

Lorenzo Cappannari	AnotheReality, Italy
Weiya Chen	Huazhong University of Science and Technology, China
Vera Colombo	Politecnico di Milano - STIIMA, CNR, Italy
Manfred Dangelmaier	Faunhofer IAO, Germany
Angelica De Antonio	Universidad Politecnica de Madrid, Spain
Thierry Duval	IMT Atlantique, Lab-STICC, France
Vincenzo Ferrari	EndoCAS Center, Italy
Pablo Figueroa	Universidad de los Andes, Colombia
Cédric Fleury	IMT Atlantique, Lab-STICC, France
Jakub Flotynski	Poznan University of Economics and Business, Poland
Kaj Helin	VTT, Finland
Victoria Interrante	University of Minnesota, USA
Daisuke Iwai	Osaka University, Japan
Ioannis Karaseitanidis	ICCS, Greece
Torsten W. Kuhlen	RWTH Aachen University, Germany
Domitile Lourdeaux	UTC, France
Katerina Mania	Technical University of Crete, Greece
Anne-Hélène Olivier	Université Rennes 2 /Inria, France
Jérôme Perret	Haption, France and Germany
Alexander Plopski	University of Otago, New Zealand
Wendy Powell	Tilburg University, The Netherlands
Matthieu Poyade	Glasgow School of Art, UK
Dirk Reiners	University of Central Florida, USA
Arcadio Reyes-Lecuona	University of Malaga, Spain
James Ritchie	Heriot-Watt University, UK
Marco Sacco	STIIMA, CNR, Italy
Hideo Saito	Keio University, Japan
Christian Sandor	City University of Hong Kong, Hong Kong
Stefania Serafin	Aalborg University, Denmark
Agata Marta Soccini	Università degli Studi di Torino, Italy
Jeanne Vézien	Université Paris-Saclay, CNRS, VENISE team, France
Krzysztof Walczak	Poznan University of Economics and Business, Poland
Tim Weissker	Bauhaus-Universität Weimar, Germany
Gabriel Zachmann	University of Bremen, Germany

External Reviewers

Markos Antonopoulos	ICCS, Greece
Daniel Eckhoff	City University of Hong Kong, Hong Kong
Fotios Konstantinidis	ICCS, Greece
Eleftherios Ouzounoglou	ICCS, Greece
Qiaochu Wang	City University of Hong Kong, Hong Kong
Pui Chung Wong	City University of Hong Kong, Hong Kong

Organization Team

Daniele Dalmiglio   STIIMA, CNR, Italy
Francesca Sacchini   STIIMA, CNR, Italy
Marco Sacco   EuroXR
Beatrice Palacco   EuroXR
Patrick Bourdot   EuroXR

Sistemi e Tecnologie Industriali Intelligenti
per il Manifatturiero Avanzato
Consiglio Nazionale delle Ricerche

Contents

Perception and Cognition (Scientific Session 1)

Comfort and Sickness While Virtually Aboard an Autonomous Telepresence Robot

Markku Suomalainen[1]($\boxtimes$), Katherine J. Mimnaugh[1], Israel Becerra[2],
Eliezer Lozano[2], Rafael Murrieta-Cid[2], and Steven M. LaValle[1]

[1] Center for Ubiquitous Computing, University of Oulu, Oulu, Finland
{markku.suomalainen,katherine.mimnaugh,steven.lavalle}@oulu.fi
[2] Centro de Investigacion en Matematicas (CIMAT), Guanajuato, Mexico
{israelb,eliezer.lozano,murrieta}@cimat.mx

Abstract. In this paper, we analyze how different path aspects affect a user's experience, mainly VR sickness and overall comfort, while immersed in an autonomously moving telepresence robot through a virtual reality headset. In particular, we focus on how the robot turns and the distance it keeps from objects, with the goal of planning suitable trajectories for an autonomously moving immersive telepresence robot in mind; rotational acceleration is known for causing the majority of VR sickness, and distance to objects modulates the optical flow. We ran a within-subjects user study (n = 36, women = 18) in which the participants watched three panoramic videos recorded in a virtual museum while aboard an autonomously moving telepresence robot taking three different paths varying in aspects such as turns, speeds, or distances to walls and objects. We found a moderate correlation between the users' sickness as measured by the SSQ and comfort on a 6-point Likert scale across all paths. However, we detected no association between sickness and the choice of the most comfortable path, showing that sickness is not the only factor affecting the comfort of the user. The subjective experience of turn speed did not correlate with either the SSQ scores or comfort, even though people often mentioned turning speed as a source of discomfort in the open-ended questions. Through exploring the open ended answers more carefully, a possible reason is that the length and lack of predictability also play a large role in making people observe turns as uncomfortable. A larger subjective distance from walls and objects increased comfort and decreased sickness both in quantitative and qualitative data. Finally, the SSQ subscales and total weighted scores showed differences by age group and by gender.

Keywords: Telepresence · Robotics · VR sickness

This work was in part supported by Business Finland project HUMOR 3656/31/2019, in part by Academy of Finland project PERCEPT 322637, in part by European Research Counsil project ILLUSIVE 101020977, in part by the US National Science Foundation under Grants 035345 and 1328018, and in part by the Secretaría de Innovación, Ciencia Y Educación Superior SICES under Grant SICES/CONV/250/2019 CIMAT.

P. Bourdot et al. (Eds.): EuroXR 2021, LNCS 13105, pp. 3–24, 2021.
https://doi.org/10.1007/978-3-030-90739-6_1

1   Introduction

In immersive robotic telepresence, as seen in Fig. 1, a user wearing a Head-Mounted Display (HMD) embodies a physical robot in a distant location. Besides the visual input through the HMD, the user can communicate with people around the robot through bidirectional audio, and can command the robot to move. This technology creates opportunities to visit museums or nature for people with limited mobility or who otherwise cannot, or grandparents attending grandchildren's birthdays far away. Overall, the technology enables meetings which mix physically present and remotely attending people, such that, for example, a single remote participant can join a physical meeting and actually feel as if she was really there. The robot also allows for touring real facilities or office buildings, helps join physical conferences remotely and facilitates the important impromptu corridor discussions during remote work [50].

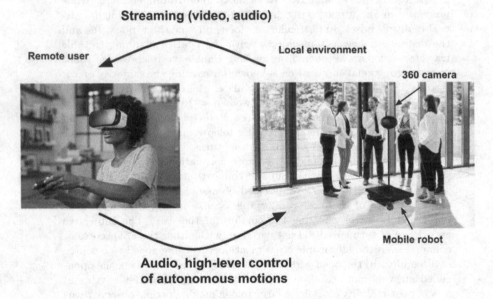

Fig. 1. Immersive robotic telepresence.

There is evidence that telepresence robot users prefer the robot to handle low-level motions autonomously, such that the users only choose the target location for the robot to move in a map or within visible area [1,41]. Most of current commercial telepresence robots (with standard camera streaming into a standard screen, in other words, not employing an HMD) have a joystick or similar as the main control method, with autonomy functionalities only being rolled out at the moment in products such as the Double 3 robot. However, with the increased immersion and embodiment of an HMD-based telepresence robot, any autonomous path is not suitable but the motions the robot makes must be carefully planned to avoid adversarial effects; pure Virtual Reality (VR) research and applications usually enable and encourage the use of teleportation to avoid VR sickness, often caused by sensory mismatch rising from seeing motion in the HMD while staying stationary. Thus, there is a very limited amount of research on how an immersive telepresence robot should move to make the embodied user feel comfortable.

It is unclear which aspects of autonomous motions make an HMD user feel uncomfortable or experience VR sickness [5,26], besides the known result of rotations causing more sickness than translations [22]. For example, distance to walls and objects modulates the optical flow linked to sickness, but simply staying as far as possible from objects and walls is often not a suitable path planning strategy for a robot in complex environments. Also, even though there is evidence that performing turns faster may reduce cybersickness [2,51], such fast motions may not feel comfortable for the immersed users and there may be more factors in turns besides the speed that modulate comfort and sickness.

In this paper we make an attempt to disentangle comfort and VR sickness experienced by subjects aboard an autonomous immersive telepresence robot and advise what aspects in the trajectory of such a robot should be paid attention to. First, we present an unexpected result: the amount of VR sickness suffered by users does not affect their choice of most comfortable path, even though paths are shown to induce different amounts of VR sickness. As there is a correlation between experienced VR sickness and comfort, it was expected that people who suffer more from sickness would prefer paths that are more comfortable. Then, we present several results regarding the robot's turns; the Likert-scale answers show that perceived turn speed does not correlate with VR sickness or perceived comfort. However, turns are very often mentioned in open-ended questions as reason for discomfort or the choice of most comfortable path; further analysis of the open-ended questions reveals that even though turn speed was the most mentioned keyword, predictability and length of turn also play major roles in making a turn comfortable or uncomfortable. Additionally, distances to walls and objects were weakly correlated with comfort and sickness, which was also reflected in the open-ended questions, meaning that distance should be kept whenever possible. Finally, we report the effect of age, gender and gaming experience on the results, as well as the Simulator Sickness Questionnaire (SSQ) subscales, finding that women in our study experienced higher levels of sickness on average than men, adding to the currently conflicting results on the topic [13,39]. Contrary to a recent meta-analysis [45], in this study older subjects suffered more from the effects of VR sickness. We discuss why subjects in our experiments suffered more from VR sickness when compared to roller coaster studies and find ways to reduce the VR sickness caused by VR-based telepresence to make it a viable option for the general population.

The main contributions of this paper are 1) quantitative analyses of the relation between sickness, comfort, and other variables related to immersive telepresence, with suggestions on turn lengths and speeds, and 2) in-depth analysis of open-ended questions regarding turns, leading to findings that turn predictability and length play major roles in making turns comfortable while retaining the non-sickening abilities of performing the turns fast. Additionally, we present results on VR sickness; carryover effects, effect of demographics and comparison to similar studies, to contribute to the literature on the topic from the perspective of autonomous motions in VR. We note that we performed the experiments purely in VR to avoid confounding factors (such as shaking of the robot) that would arise from using a physical robot. However, we are planning to test the results also on a physical robot to confirm the results.

2 Related Work

Telepresence, a term originally coined by Minsky [33] and sometimes referred to as tele-embodiment [38], is classically, and in this paper, defined as embodying a robot in a remote location. Most of the work on robotic telepresence considers seeing the remote environment through a standard naked-eye display [11,28,35,40,41]; these works present the potential of telepresence robots in, for example, conferences and classrooms, with also medical applications being an often researched topic [16,47]. Additionally, there is research for more personal, intimate, and extensible use cases, such as sharing outdoor activities [15] or more personal long-distance relationships [52].

There is an increasing number of works that demonstrate the potential of increased immmersion created by an HMD in telepresence, such as better task performance [12] and situational awareness [30]. An interesting motivator is also the finding that in a group work task, users telepresent through a traditional display speak less and perceive tasks as more difficult than the physical participants [48]; this is exactly the sort of issue that the increased feeling of presence by the user [44], facilitated by the increased immersion of an HMD, can remedy. A few other researchers have also noticed the importance of robotic telepresence using an HMD: Baker et al. [1] let the user choose the destination similarly as in teleporting and then make the robot move to the destination autonomously. Zhang et al. [53] explored using redirected walking on a telepresence robot. Finally, Oh et al. [36] used such a robot on a tour with several pre-selected destinations.

However, as always when using an HMD, VR sickness can severely deteriorate the experience for many users. A major cause for VR sickness is a conflict between the visual and vestibular senses when self-motion is seen through the HMD but not sensed by the vestibular organs in the ears [5,42]. In virtual environments, the use of teleportation is frequently used to avoid VR sickness [3], but in telepresence teleportation would have a significant delay and is thus not a realistic option. Thus, in virtual environments, continuous autonomous motions are often avoided, with perhaps the notable exception of roller coasters often used in sickness studies due to their more sickening effects [8,18,31,34]. Though there is a recommendation that VR sessions should not last longer than 55–70 min to avoid overwhelming sickness levels [25], in the roller coaster studies many people could not even complete a 15 min session. A meta-analysis found that 15.6% of participants across 46 VR studies dropped out due to sickness effects [45].

Even though sickness plays a major part in the comfort of an embodied telepresence user, it should not be the only criterion considered when designing motions for a telepresence robot. Becerra et al. [2] showed that the use of piecewise linear paths (meaning that the robot is only rotating in place, and during forward motions there was no rotation) can decrease the VR sickness on embodied participants and make the path more comfortable when compared to a traditional robot path where the robot can rotate and move forward simultaneously; however, they did not explore more detailed questions on why such turns were preferred, or other path aspects such as speeds and distances to objects. Moreover, due to the varying susceptibility to VR sickness [43], other aspects should not be completely ignored in favor of reducing VR sickness, as some methods to reduce VR sickness (such as driving extremely slowly) also deteriorate the overall experience. To the knowledge of the authors, there are no studies that would consider aspects such as closeness to objects and speeds as factor in immersive telepresence robots motion planning.

To collect results from VR studies that give a more accurate reflection of effects in the general population, demographic information and individual differences must be taken into account. Though there have been conflicting findings in the VR literature regarding gender differences in response to VR sickness [13], a recent meta-analysis found that SSQ effects were systematically associated with the number of men and women in the study [39], such that when there are fewer women participants, SSQ scores tend to be higher. In regards to age differences in VR sickness effects as measured by the SSQ, a 2020 meta-analysis of 55 VR articles analyzing VR sickness across types of content and individual factors found that older subjects had lower SSQ scores, and in particular older subjects had significantly lower SSQ scores on the disorientation subscale as compared with younger subjects [45].

3 Methods

3.1 Setup and Test Paths

The study was run on a university campus in February 2020 before COVID-19 caused any local restrictions. The users were seated during the study, as shown in Fig. 2, and shown pre-recorded panoramic videos with an Oculus Rift S using the Virtual Desktop application; as the video was recorded as a 360 video, the users were able to look around in the virtual environment as the virtual robot was moving. The test environment was designed with Unity. To create a more realistic optical flow and experience for the users, there were various paintings on the walls and statues in the gallery of the museum.

Three paths were considered, presented in Fig. 3. Two of the paths, Pareto Least Turns (PLT) and Pareto Shortest Path (PSP), were piecewise linear, and in [2] they were shown to be less sickening and more comfortable than the third path, the Rapidly-exploring Random Trees (RRT) path. PLT and PSP were paths chosen from a Pareto front across multiple criteria; the Pareto front of a multiobjective optimization problem is the set of solutions from which any

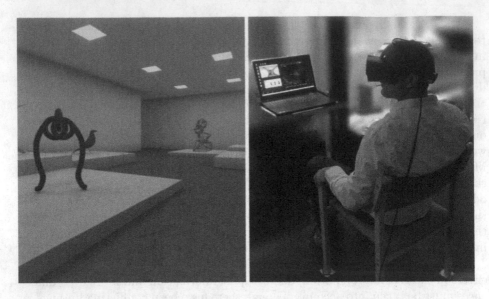

Fig. 2. A participant in the user study watches one of the panoramic videos in the Oculus Rift S (right). A screenshot of the gallery inside the virtual museum (left).

objective score cannot be improved without deteriorating another objective. The Pareto front was computed with the objectives of minimizing the number of turns, minimizing the distance to goal and minimizing the amount of time an object was closer than 2 m from the subject.

The first path, the PLT, (duration 76 s, length 72 m, min distance to walls 1 m), minimized the number of turns along a piecewise linear path (2 turns), and the second path, the PSP, (67 s, 62.6 m, 0.4 m), minimized the length of the path (4 turns). Both the PLT and PSP had a constant turn speed of 90 deg/s and mean forward speed of 1 m/s. The RRT path had smooth turns and was generated by the RRT algorithm [27], widely used in robot motion planning. This algorithm respects the dynamics of the Differential Drive Robot (DDR) base, which means that the actual path exists in a 5-D space, from which only two dimensions are plotted here; this is why simply curating the path to avoid unnecessary curves, or finding a more optimal path, is infeasible. As the RRT is a sampling-based algorithm and does not provide an optimal path, the algorithm was run 1000 times and the path with the least amount of changes in direction was chosen as the third path (129 s, 67.2 m, 0.3 m, avg. turn speed 18.8 deg/s, avg. forward speed 0.52 m/s).

3.2 Participants

Subjects were recruited from a university campus and the surrounding community. Of the 45 participants, altogether nine subjects were excluded; three quit the experiment due to excessive sickness symptoms (we will discuss possible

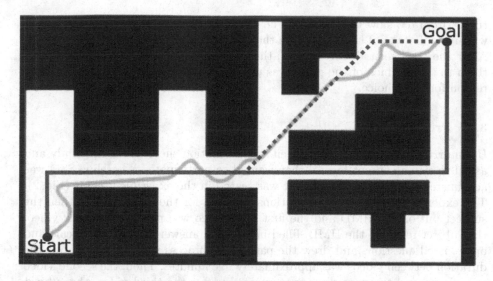

Fig. 3. The paths presented to the subjects in the user study: blue is the Pareto Least Turns (PLT), dotted red the Pareto Shortest Path (PSP) and yellow the RRT path. (Color figure online)

reasons for this high number of dropouts in Sect. 5), and the rest were excluded due to technical failures, not completing questionnaires, or for feeling severe sickness symptoms before the study began. Thus, the results are from 36 subjects, age 20–44 with mean 28.25, divided equally between men (n − 18) and women (n − 18). Regarding video game use, 25% of the subjects (n = 9) reported that they never played video games on PC, mobile, or console, 14% (n = 5) rarely played them, 28% (n = 10) played them weekly or often, 19% (n = 7) played them daily, and 14% (n = 5) did not respond.

3.3 Measures

The Simulator Sickness Questionnaire (SSQ) [21] was used as a measure of VR sickness symptoms. Before seeing any of the path videos, subjects completed a baseline SSQ which was used for screening purposes. They also filled out SSQ's immediately after seeing each video; the order in which the videos were shown to users was counterbalanced to avoid order effects. Then, the subjects completed a questionnaire created for this study after each path. The questionnaire consisted of several questions that were rated on a six-point Likert scale, followed by some open-ended questions asking why they gave that rating. The Likert-rated questions asked subjects how comfortable their experience was on the path (from very uncomfortable to very comfortable), how well they could find their way back to where they started in the museum (from not easily at all to very easily), how they felt about the distance between themselves and the walls or objects in the museum (from too close to too far), and how they felt about the speed of the turns (from too slow to too fast). The open-ended questions asked why a path was uncomfortable if they had given that rating, and if they had any comments. After they had seen all three paths, they answered additional questions asking them to select which of the paths was preferred and most comfortable, and the reason for that choice.

3.4 Procedure

Upon arrival, each subject was given an information sheet about the study and asked to sign a consent form if they wanted to participate. A baseline SSQ was administered, and then the subject was seated in the experiment chair (Fig. 2). The experimenter read the instructions out loud for the subjects, and then the subject put on the HMD and the first path video was played. After the video, the subject removed the HMD, filled in an SSQ, answered the Likert scale and open-ended questions and drew the path. This process was not timed, but the duration between videos was approximately five minutes. Then, the second video was played and the procedure was repeated. After the third video, the subject completed the final questionnaire comparing the paths, and then reported demo-graphic information and gaming experience. Once they had completed this, they were given a debriefing about the study, copies of the consent forms to take home, and a coupon worth €2 for a coffee from the local cafe.

4 Results

Data from the same experiment has earlier been used in [2,32], where the focus has been on both the technical implementation, comparison of the paths and the naturalness and preference of the user. In contrast, in this paper we do not focus on comparing the paths and path-planning methods, but instead analyze other interesting results accross all paths. The main focus is about perceived user com-fort, to present the community more information about the use of autonomous motions in VR-based telepresence. The total number of comments on turns and distances for the "why was the path uncomfortable" question have been reported in [32], but without the more detailed analysis presented in this paper regarding the actual contents of the open-ended comments. Also, even though individ-ual results on questions regarding comfort across paths have been reported, the relationship analyses between variables reported here have not been presented. Finally, we note that [2] found PSP and PLT causing less VR sickness and being rated more comfortable than the RRT.

Exploratory analyses were conducted with two-tailed significance levels for alpha set at 0.05 and confidence intervals set at 95%. When multiple tests were run, Bonferroni correction within each test was used. Post-hoc power analyses and observed effect sizes [6] were calculated using G*Power [10], Psychometrica freeware [29], or by hand [49]. Thematic analysis with an inductive approach [37] was used to classify the responses to open-ended questions by two independent coders. Results from Likert-scale questions, forced-choice questions and SSQ are first presented in Sect. 4.1, after which responses to the open-ended questions are analyzed in Sect. 4.2.

4.1 Quantitative Data

Sickness Had a Negative Correlation with Comfort. The more the subjects suffered from VR sickness, the less comfortable they felt. A Spearman's rank-order correlation test was run between the Likert comfort ratings, from very uncomfortable (1) to very comfortable (6), and the total weighted SSQ scores after each path. There was a statistically significant moderate, negative correlation $(rs(108) = -.400, p < .001)$; as the total SSQ scores increased, the Likert comfort ratings decreased.

High Sickness Scores Did Not Influence People's Choice of Preferred or Most Comfortable Path. The motivation for checking for this relationship is the assumption that people who suffer more from VR sickness would put a higher weight on how comfortable the path is. To crudely rank the sickness sensitivity of the participants, the highest of the three total SSQ scores for each individual was selected as an index. These scores were then separated into three equal-sized groups of 12 people. Highest total weighted SSQ scores under 15 were in the low sickness group, between 15 and 40 in the medium sickness group, and over 40 in the high sickness group. The relationship between sickness groups and choice of most comfortable path was analyzed using crosstabulation and a Fisher's exact test (two-sided) to account for the small sample size. There was no statistically significant association in choice of the most comfortable path by sickness group, $p = .164, w = 0.85$. Similarly, there was no statistically significant association between choice of preferred path and sickness group, $p = .873, w = 0.58$.

Increase in Perceived Distance to Walls and Objects Had a Weak Correlation with Sickness and Comfort. The distance to walls and objects in virtual museum from 1 (too close) to 6 (too far) was compared to Likert ratings for comfort (higher numbers mean greater comfort) and total weighted SSQ scores (higher scores mean more sickness symptoms) using a Spearman's rank-order correlation test. There was a statistically significant weak, positive correlation $(rs(108) = .302, p = .002)$ between the distance to walls and objects and comfort. The closer to walls and objects the paths were rated, the less comfort subjects reported experiencing. Compared to the SSQ scores, there was again a statistically significant weak, negative correlation $(rs(108) = -.277, p = .004)$. The closer to walls and objects the paths were rated, the more sickness symptoms subjects reported experiencing.

The Perceived Speed of Turns Did Not Influence Comfort or Sickness. There was no statistically significant correlation between the speed of the turns, rated from too slow (1) to too fast (6), and the Likert ratings of comfort ($rs(108) = -.157, p = .105$) or the total weighted SSQ scores ($rs(108) = .117, p = .228$).

There Were No Carryover Effects on Sickness with 5 min Breaks Between Videos. The videos of the museum were counterbalanced by gender and by the order that they were seen in. This counterbalancing was used to allow comparison between paths regardless of whether carryover effects had an impact or not. However, to see if there were carryover effects, a Friedman's test on the SSQ total weighted scores after each video by order was run. There was no statistically significant difference in the distributions of total weighted SSQ scores after the first, second, and third videos, $\chi^2(2, 36) = .775, p = .679, W = 0.01$. Thus, the recovery time subjects had with the headset off, involving answering questionnaires for about five minutes after each video, appears to have been sufficient for participants to recover from these VR sickness effects. In one extreme case, for example, the subject's total weighted SSQ score after their second video was 153.34, and the score after their third video was zero. Whereas several papers report longer carryover effects (for example [46]), a large variation across studies has been observed, with lowest recovery times being 10 min [9].

Older People Suffered More from VR Sickness. Age differences in sickness were examined by splitting the subjects into three similar-sized groups for analysis (small variance in group sizes result from not splitting same-aged subjects to different groups): Under 26 (13 subjects), 26 to 30 (12 subjects), and Over 30 (11 subjects), collapsing across paths, and testing the difference between these groups on each of the SSQ subscales and total weighted scores. A Kruskal-Wallis test showed for the nausea subscale (NS), $\chi^2(2, 108) = 19.02, p < 0.001, \eta^2 = 0.16$, the disorientation subscale (DS), $\chi^2(2, 108) = 9.23, p = 0.010, \eta^2 = 0.07$, and the total weighted score (TS), $\chi^2(2, 108) = 11.48, p = 0.003, \eta^2 = 0.09$, there were statistically significant differences in scores between the age groups. Post-hoc pairwise comparisons all showed the same pattern, with the Over 30 age group significantly higher than the 26 to 30 group (NS $p = .001$, DS $p = .019$, TS $p = .012$), and the Over 30 group significantly higher than the Under 26 group (NS $p < .001$, DS $p = .030$, TS $p = .007$), but no difference between the Under 26 group and the 26 to 30 group. The exception to this pattern was on the oculomotor subscale, where there was no statistically significant difference between the age groups, $\chi^2(2, 108) = 4.296, p = 0.117, \eta^2 = 0.02$. Mean SSQ subscales and total scores for each age group are shown in Fig. 4.

Previous VR Experience Did Not Influence VR Sickness. Subjects were split into three groups based on how often they used virtual reality to test whether or not previous virtual reality experience had an impact on sickness.

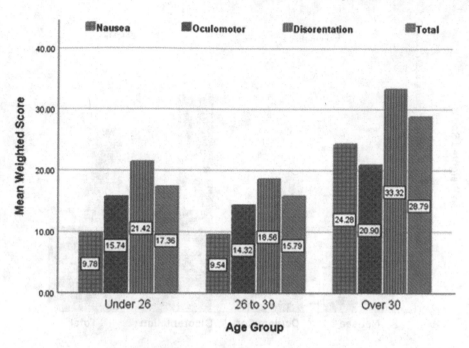

Fig. 4. Mean weighted SSQ subscales and total scores from all paths by age group.

Ten subjects had never tried a VR HMD (28% of the sample), 15 subjects had tried VR between one and nine times or a few times (43% of the sample), and 10 subjects tried ten or more times or used VR regularly (28% of the sample). One subject did not give a response about his previous VR use and was excluded from these analyses. There were no statistically significant correlations between VR usage frequency and the nausea subscale ($rs(105) = .011, p = .915$), the oculomotor subscale ($rs(105) = -.030, p = .764$), the disorientation subscale ($rs(105) = .038, p = .697$), or the total weighted SSQ score ($rs(105) = .008, p = .933$).

Women Suffered More from VR Sickness. To investigate potential differences in sickness by gender, scores across paths were collapsed and compared each with a Mann-Whitney U test. Women had statistically significantly higher SSQ scores than men on the nausea subscale ($U = 746.00, z = -4.55, p < .001, r = 0.44$), the oculomotor subscale ($U = 1037.50, z = -2.63, p = .008, r = 0.25$), the disorientation subscale ($U = 904.50, z = -3.51, p < .001, r = 0.34$), and the total weighted score ($U = 827.50, z = -3.90, p < .001, r = 0.38$), as presented in Fig. 5.

Subjective Wayfinding Ability Was Weakly Correlated with Comfort. The idea for testing this correlation is reports that loss of wayfinding ability can

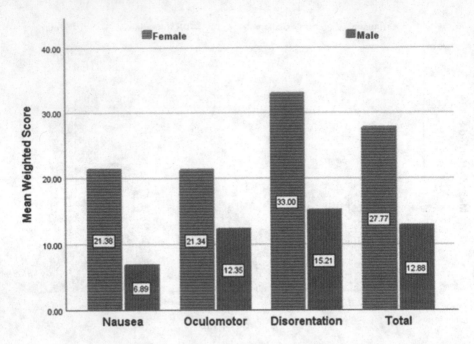

Fig. 5. Mean weighted SSQ subscales and total scores from all paths by gender.

cause discomfort [7]. Likert ratings for comfort (higher numbers mean greater comfort) were also tested against the Likert ratings for subjective wayfinding (answer to the question "If you had to go back to where you started in the museum, how well do you think you could find your way back?", with a high number meaning more likelihood of finding the way back) using a Spearman's rank-order correlation test. There was a statistically significant weak, positive correlation $(rs(108) = .205, p = .034)$. The better that subjects believed they could find their way back to the beginning of the museum, the greater the comfort experienced.

4.2   Qualitative Data

Turns Was the Most Commented Aspect Making a Path Uncomfortable, with Fast Turns Being the Most Commented Within Turns but Unexpectedness and Length of Turns Also Playing Major Roles. After the Likert-rated question regarding how comfortable each path was, subjects were asked an open-ended question, "if it [the path] was uncomfortable, why?" Their answers were coded with keywords based on the text that they provided. A full breakdown of the distribution of all codes for each path can be seen in Fig. 6. The largest group of comments was in relation to the turns, with 59 comments across all paths; fast turns had the greatest number of individual comments, with surprising turns, sharp turns and many turns also getting at least several mentions. This is in contrast to turn speed not being correlated with the Likert-scale value for comfort.

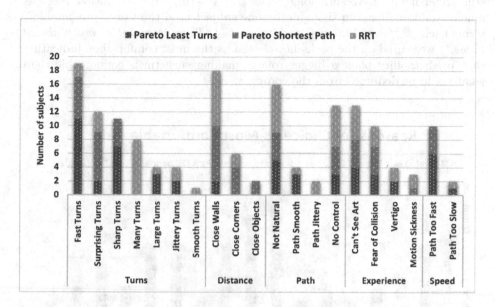

Fig. 6. The frequently found codes from the question "If the path was uncomfortable, why?" which was asked after each path that a each user watched.

Whereas fast and surprising turns are quite evident, looking closely into the comments saying "sharp turns" reveals that the word "sharp" is often associated with the "length" of the turn. For example, the comments *"SHARP (90 DEGREE)TURNS ARE VERY UN REALISTIC"* and *"The turn is very sharp and rapid. Turn is like 90 degree, so I feel uncomfortable"* were typical. Moreover, the degrees of the turn were mentioned also when turns were classified as "fast", such as *"The 90 degrees turns felt very fast."*. It is likely that because there is no clear and concise everyday word, especially within non-native speakers, to talk about the degrees a turn makes, the "large turns" category is in fact larger than it appears to be in these results (Fig. 6).

Turns Also Had the Largest Influence on the Choice of the Most Comfortable Path. The "size", Speed and Predictability of the Turn Seem to Have a Large Effect. The largest number of individual comments were under the code "good turns". However, it become evident that people had varying preference of turns when looking at the responses together with the chosen path. For example, subjects chose the PSP because *"It was smoother, there were not so many forced turns"* and *"The walking speed was not too high, and again, the number of uncomfortable turns was not too high."* and *"Turn is not rapid and sharp. The distance is also OK."*, even though PSP had the same amount of 90° turns as PLT, and additionally two 45° turns. This implies that, even though long turns at once should make people less sick, users would still prefer not to have such long turns and 45° turns do not bother users as much. Additionally, even though only one subject used the word "predictable", terms such as *"forced"* (above) and *"abrupt"* (*"There were not so much abrupt turns."*) were used on the paths not chosen as the most comfortable, indicating that predictability plays a bigger role in making such turns comfortable than what could be deduced from the coding alone.

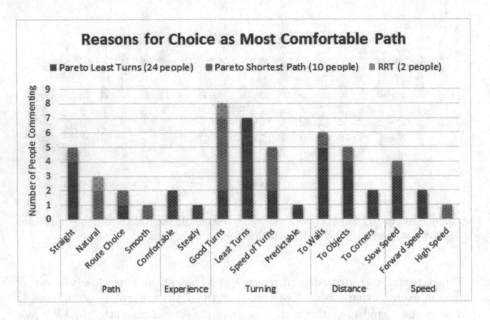

Fig. 7. The frequently found codes from the question "Of the three paths, which one was the most comfortable? Why?" which was asked after the subject had seen all three paths.

Small Distances to Walls and Objects Were Considered a Major Source of Discomfort, and an Important Factor When Choosing the Most Comfortable Path. There were 26 comments across all paths regarding the distance group of responses in the "why uncomfortable" question, most of which were related to close walls (18) or corners (6), with only two responses mentioning being too close to objects. A very related category is fear of collision (10 mentions), where most quotes were related to distance to walls (*"Sometimes it felt I would bump into the walls"*); these responses were detected in all paths, with PSP and RRT being most mentioned but also PLT gathering several mentions, even though PLT had a larger minimum clearance (1 m) than the other two paths (0.3 m and 0.4 m). The responses reveal that it was considered problematic that the 1m clearance was at a 2m wide corridor, which was deemed too narrow (*"in the end when we went trough a very narrow path, it felt like the*

walls were closing in."); indeed, a good distance to objects or walls was often
mentioned as a favorable property when choosing the most comfortable path
(Fig. 7), with almost all mentions being together with the PL. When inspecting
the comments regarding most comfortable path, the distance to objects is mentioned as often as distance to walls. However, from the five mentions of "distance
to objects", only one considered that the objects were close enough (*"going near
to the objects"*), whereas another one simply stated that distance was "good"
and the rest preferred staying as clear from objects as from walls and corners.

5   Discussion

We expected to find a stronger link between the perceived comfort and SSQ
scores than what the results showed (no relationship between the SSQ and the
choice of "most comfortable path," and a moderate correlation between the SSQ
and the Likert-scale comfort); we expected people with higher SSQ scores to
prefer paths that, in general, caused less sickness (PLT and PSP). The lack of
this connection shows that there are more facets to a user's comfort than only
the often used SSQ; even though experiencing VR sickness can have the most
impact on users, sickness symptoms may not be the most significant part of
the VR experience for the users. Several subjects stated this outright, such as
"It was not sickening but not comfortable in the way the (virtual) robot moves".
The importance of this is highlighted by a strong relationship between perceived
comfort and preference reported in [32], meaning that people can like things that
make them a little sick. Also, comfort is a more subjective feeling than sickness,
and discomfort does not necessarily equal sickness; all of this should be taken
into account when designing VR experiences and new methods for quantifying
the sickness effects and comfort of VR exposure.

We were also expecting that perceiving a fast turn speed would not have an
effect on the SSQ, based on [51] finding that performing the same turn faster
than slower makes people less sick; the data confirmed this. However, it came
as a surprise that even though the turns were most frequently mentioned in the
open-ended questions regarding why users felt a particular path was uncomfortable, there was no statistically significant correlation between Likert-scale turn
speed ratings and comfort. A likely reason is that we specifically asked about
the turn speeds in the Likert-scale question; thus, the Likert-scale question did
not consider any other aspects of the turn besides speed. Besides the earlier
mentioned quotes where the 90° turns were specifically mentioned, also other
quotes with fast turns had additional adjectives hinting towards the surprise
element, such as *"the movement was slow but, the turns were fast a jarring"*.
Another subject, who chose PSP as the most comfortable path, stated that PSP
"Didn't contain sharp turns and lot's of unreasonable moves.", even though it
contained the same amount of 90° turns as PLT, and additionally two 45° turns;
this suggests that the 45° turns were not considered as uncomfortable as the
longer turns. These findings indicate that there could be even a contradiction
between perceived comfort and experienced VR sickness during turns; long turns

are considered uncomfortable, even though they reduce sickness. We believe this should be taken into account when designing the motions of a telepresence robot, and make a more controlled experiment about turn speeds and lengths in VR, where besides sickness also comfort is queried. Even though the results are only preliminary, we suggest avoiding 90° turns at once and making the turns more predictable. We still suggest keeping the turns fast, at least close to the 90 deg/s, since there is known evidence of effect on VR sickness but contradictory evidence with comfort.

Distance to walls and objects had a correlation with both comfort and sickness, even if weak, and was also mentioned frequently in the open-ended questions. This was expected, as a closer passing distance increases the optical flow, which is linked to increase in VR sickness. Additionally, fear of collision was mentioned a few times, which, as a strong feeling causing anxiety, may have a strong effect on comfort and sickness [14]. Based on the results, 1m passing distance did not cause users any discomfort unless in a narrow corridor, but such a passing distance would make robot motion planning complicated. However, it would be beneficial to verify the result on a real robot in a real environment, with more variance of passing distance.

The observed relationship between subjective wayfinding ability and comfort is not surprising, since there is evidence in the literature that loss of wayfinding ability can cause discomfort [7]. The environment used in this study was too simple to test objective wayfinding ability, and the correlation is only weak, with also the possibility that this is only a coincidence; however, the observed connection and evidence in literature indicates that a more focused study would be useful to explore whether the wayfinding ability can be increased by careful planning of the robot's motions.

The subjects succumbed to VR sickness quickly considering that the videos were not very long (67 s–129 s) and the robot moved slowly (0.5 m/s–1 m/s); however, the subjects also recovered faster than suggested by earlier literature. For example, Kourtesis et al. [25] state that VR sessions can be comfortable up to 55 to 70 min, but we experienced three dropouts (two during their first videos, which were RRT and PLT, and one while watching RRT as second video after already finished PLT) with videos lasting less than two minutes. This supports the proposition that continuous motions, without a visual, stationary cue that moves with the user, are a significant contributor to VR sickness. However, the surprisingly fast recovery time (no carryover effects detected with 5 min breaks, whereas the lowest suggested required recovery time from literature is 10 min [9]) balance this; these results hint that VR sickness with continuous motions raises fast but also decreases fast. However, more focused research on VR sickness for continuous motions would be required to confirm this.

Comparing to the SSQ scores caused by roller coasters in two other studies (both using HTC Vive), the results from this study were comparable or slightly higher when adjusted for the duration of the stimuli; Islam et al. [18] had no dropouts in a 15-min roller coaster ride with a mean SSQ of 55.45, and McHugh et al. [31] had no dropouts in a 5 min 50 s exposure with a mean SSQ of 34 (visually approximated from figure), whereas our mean SSQ was 20.3; thus, it seems that the telepresence experience provided a higher variance of sickness to test subjects than a roller coaster, since in our study there were more dropouts but less average sickness. In fact, there are a few considerable differences between telepresence and a roller coaster, both adding and reducing the potential for VR sickness. A roller coaster moves much faster, which increases the optical flow and the probability for sickness, but it has a constant frame of reference (the car) which is known to decrease VR sickness [4]. Also, most of the scenery does not move with the speed of the roller coaster if it travels higher than on ground level, reducing the optical flow; a reduction of sickness has been reported when a plane flies higher above the ground [20]. Additionally, the turns are predictable - the user can always see the track ahead, which has also been shown to reduce VR sickness [24]. We also observed individual comments in open-ended questions on turns being unpredictable ("*the turns were too fast, but thankfully pretty predictable this time.*") and, in regards to why the path was uncomfortable, "*The turns were very strong (sudden)*" and "*It was not sickening but not comfortable in the way the (virtual) robot moves. Sudden turns very close to the corners of the walls.*" Thus, future ways to combat VR sickness in autonomous telepresence motions could be visualizing the path to the user so that movements are less unexpected and providing a constant frame of reference, such as visualizing the robot.

Women experienced greater sickness symptoms during the study than men, which has been found previously in VR research [43]. In this study, previous VR experience did not influence the severity of VR sickness, which is in agreement with [25], even though such an effect through habituation [17] has been reported elsewhere [43]. Regarding higher sickness in older subjects, we were unable to find similar work in the literature, and in fact found conflicting results [45]. One explanation could perhaps be related to differences in lens flexibility in the eye across the lifespan, making it easier to focus on things very close to your face when you're younger and sometimes resulting in the need for reading glasses later in life. It will be an interesting topic for future research whether there is something specific in continuous motions that causes this discrepancy.

5.1 Limitations and Future Work

We established in this study that the design of the robot's turns are very important for increasing comfort and reducing VR sickness. Based on the results, we can provide initial suggestions for designing robot motions, but to draw decisive conclusions more research is needed. For example, it seems that a Likert-scale question about the length of the turns should have been asked, to pinpoint with more accuracy which aspect of the turn makes them so uncomfortable. Moreover, we want to test how big a role predictability plays, to make the experience closer to a slow speed roller coaster. The predictability could be done either explicitly, such as using arrows or a path on the ground, or by modifying the velocity profile of the turns; for example, the common trick used in animation to employ high-order derivatives of speed, such as jerk, could be useful to increase predictability by making the turn start slower but then increase the speed to take advantage of the less-sickening nature of performing turns fast [51].

The different durations of the videos could have had an effect on the SSQ measures. However, as the travelled distance was still similar, this means that the higher speed had less of an impact on the experienced VR sickness. The slower RRT path made some unnecessary turns, but it is a de facto standard robot motion planning algorithm, and therefore we believe this to be a useful comparison. However, a more direct comparison between a path similar to the PSP but with smooth turns could also be useful to pinpoint the effect of rotation in place. We did not measure head motions, but as they have been successfully used in predicting VR sickness [19], it would have been interesting to test their correlation to VR sickness; ad-hoc observations from the study instructors indicate that an increase in sickness was observable by a decrease in the subjects' head motions.

We intentionally had art in the museum to make the study more realistic, both in terms of ecological validity and optical flow. Besides an expected effect on the subjects' preferences, the art also affected the perceived comfort; users reported in open-ended questions issues such as how comfortably they could see the art (*"Many times I was just facing the wall and couldn't see the displayed items"*). Whereas it is important to acknowledge the effect that the situation and environment have on comfort, it is difficult to quantify. In the future we plan to run another study in an empty museum and compare the results; this will give us a proper, quantifiable metric on the importance of context, at least between the cases of museum and a simple path from A to B.

The study was run in a virtual environment, even though the ideas are meant for a telepresence robot streaming real video footage. Although there is some evidence that 360° videos make people more sick than virtual environments [45], there is no single study comparing these two cases on sickness (although it has been shown that teleoperation increases stress over a virtual environment, which in turn can increase discomfort and sickness [23]); moreover, as there is no reason to believe that the mechanisms causing sickness would work differently in a 360 video than in a virtual environment, we expect our results to extend to real video capture. Nevertheless, we will also run a study with a real telepresence robot to verify these results.

The number of subjects in the study was small. We tried to account for this by using statistical tests that are more sensitive for small samples when appropriate, and by calculating the effect sizes and then running post-hoc power analyses. One final limitation was the choice of a six point Likert scale rating instead of a standard five or seven point scale. This scale was selected so that subjects would need to make a decision either way on the ratings and could not simply select a neutral choice. In future studies, a more traditional scale will be used.

6   Conclusion

We presented an analysis focusing on the interplay between and possible causes of comfort and sickness of VR telepresence users with regards to the path taken by the robot. In essence, discomfort and sickness are distinct yet overlapping concepts, and more focus should be put on addressing the comfort of the user instead of simply targeting VR sickness since reducing only sickness may cause other issues that degrade the whole experience. As autonomous motions are rarely considered in virtual worlds, this paper will hopefully spark further interest in research from other investigators both in telepresence and in autonomous continuous motions in virtual worlds.

References

1. Baker, G., Bridgwater, T., Bremner, P., Giuliani, M.: Towards an immersive user interface for waypoint navigation of a mobile robot. In: The Second International Workshop on Virtual, Augmented and Mixed Reality for Human-Robot Interaction (2020)
2. Becerra, I., Suomalainen, M., Lozano, E., Mimnaugh, K.J., Murrieta-Cid, R., LaValle, S.M.: Human perception-optimized planning for comfortable VR-based telepresence. IEEE Robot. Autom. Lett. **5**(4), 6489–6496 (2020)
3. Buttussi, F., Chittaro, L.: Locomotion in place in virtual reality: a comparative evaluation of joystick, teleport, and leaning. IEEE Trans. Vis. Comput. Graph. **27**, 1–12 (2020)
4. Cao, Z., Jerald, J., Kopper, R.: Visually-induced motion sickness reduction via static and dynamic rest frames. In: 2018 IEEE Conference on Virtual Reality and 3D User Interfaces (VR), pp. 105–112 (2018). https://doi.org/10.1109/VR.2018.8446210
5. Chang, E., Kim, H.T., Yoo, B.: Virtual reality sickness: a review of causes and measurements. Int. J. Hum. Comput. Interact. **36**(17), 1–25 (2020)
6. Cohen, J.: Statistical Power Analysis for Behavioral Sciences, 2nd edn. Routledge, New York (1988)
7. Darken, R.P., Peterson, B.: Spatial orientation, wayfinding, and representation. In: Handbook of Virtual Environments. CRC Press (2014)
8. Davis, S., Nesbitt, K., Nalivaiko, E.: Comparing the onset of cybersickness using the oculus rift and two virtual roller coasters. In: Proceedings of the 11th Australasian Conference on Interactive Entertainment (IE 2015), vol. 27, p. 30 (2015)
9. Dużmańska, N., Strojny, P., Strojny, A.: Can simulator sickness be avoided? A review on temporal aspects of simulator sickness. Front. Psychol. **9**, 2132 (2018)
10. Faul, F., Erdfelder, E., Lang, A.G., Buchner, A.: G*power 3: a flexible statistical power analysis program for the social, behavioral, and biomedical sciences. Behav. Res. Methods **39**(2), 175–191 (2007)
11. Fitter, N.T., Raghunath, N., Cha, E., Sanchez, C.A., Takayama, L., Matarić, M.J.: Are we there yet? Comparing remote learning technologies in the university classroom. IEEE Robot. Autom. Lett. **5**(2), 2706–2713 (2020)
12. García, J.C., et al.: A natural interface for remote operation of underwater robots. IEEE Comput. Graphics Appl. **37**(1), 34–43 (2015)

13. Grassini, S., Laumann, K.: Are modern head-mounted displays sexist? A systematic review on gender differences in HMD-mediated virtual reality. Front. Psychol. **11**, 1604 (2020)
14. Guna, J., Geršak, G., Humar, I., Song, J., Drnovšek, J., Pogačnik, M.: Influence of video content type on users' virtual reality sickness perception and physiological response. Futur. Gener. Comput. Syst. **91**, 263–276 (2019)
15. Heshmat, Y., et al.: Geocaching with a beam: shared outdoor activities through a telepresence robot with 360 degree viewing. In: Proceedings of the 2018 CHI Conference on Human Factors in Computing Systems, pp. 1–13 (2018)
16. Hilty, D.M., et al.: A review of telepresence, virtual reality, and augmented reality applied to clinical care. J. Technol. Behav. Sci. **5**, 1–28 (2020)
17. Howarth, P.A., Hodder, S.G.: Characteristics of habituation to motion in a virtual environment. Displays **29**(2), 117–123 (2008)
18. Islam, R., Lee, Y., Jaloli, M., Muhammad, I., Zhu, D., Quarles, J.: Automatic detection of cybersickness from physiological signal in a virtual roller coaster simulation. In: 2020 IEEE Conference on Virtual Reality and 3D User Interfaces Abstracts and Workshops (VRW), pp. 649–650. IEEE (2020)
19. Jin, W., Fan, J., Gromala, D., Pasquier, P.: Automatic prediction of cybersickness for virtual reality games. In: 2018 IEEE Games, Entertainment, Media Conference (GEM), pp. 1–9. IEEE (2018)
20. Johnson, D.M.: Introduction to and review of simulator sickness research. Technical report, Army Research Inst Field Unit Fort Rucker Al (2005)
21. Kennedy, R.S., Lane, N.E., Berbaum, K.S., Lilienthal, M.G.: Simulator sickness questionnaire: an enhanced method for quantifying simulator sickness. Int. J. Aviat. Psychol. **3**(3), 203–220 (1993)
22. Keshavarz, B., Hecht, H.: Axis rotation and visually induced motion sickness: the role of combined roll, pitch, and yaw motion. Aviat. Space Environ. Med. **82**(11), 1023–1029 (2011)
23. Khenak, N., Vézien, J., Bourdot, P.: Spatial presence, performance, and behavior between real, remote, and virtual immersive environments. IEEE Trans. Visual Comput. Graphics **26**(12), 3467–3478 (2020)
24. Kolasinski, E.M.: Simulator sickness in virtual environments, vol. 1027. US Army Research Institute for the Behavioral and Social Sciences (1995)
25. Kourtesis, P., Collina, S., Doumas, L.A.A., MacPherson, S.E.: Validation of the virtual reality neuroscience questionnaire: maximum duration of immersive virtual reality sessions without the presence of pertinent adverse symptomatology. Front. Hum. Neurosci. **13**, 417 (2019)
26. LaValle, S.M.: Virtual Reality. Cambridge University Press, Cambridge (2021)
27. LaValle, S.M., Kuffner, J.J., Jr.: Randomized kinodynamic planning. The Int. J. Robot. Res. **20**(5), 378–400 (2001)
28. Lee, M.K., Takayama, L.: Now, i have a body: uses and social norms for mobile remote presence in the workplace. In: Proceedings of the SIGCHI Conference on Human Factors in Computing Systems, pp. 33–42. ACM (2011)
29. Lenhard, W., Lenhard, A.: Calculation of effect sizes (2016)
30. Martins, H., Ventura, R.: Immersive 3-D teleoperation of a search and rescue robot using a head-mounted display. In: 2009 IEEE Conference on Emerging Technologies & Factory Automation, pp. 1–8. IEEE (2009)
31. McHugh, N., Jung, S., Hoermann, S., Lindeman, R.W.: Investigating a physical dial as a measurement tool for cybersickness in virtual reality. In: 25th ACM Symposium on Virtual Reality Software and Technology, pp. 1–5 (2019)

32. Mimnaugh, K.J., Suomalainen, M., Becerra, I., Lozano, E., Murrieta-Cid, R., LaValle, S.M.: Analysis of user preferences for robot motions in immersive telepresence. In: 2021 IEEE/RSJ International Conference on Intelligent Robots and Systems (IROS). IEEE (2021)
33. Minsky, M.: Telepresence (1980)
34. Nesbitt, K., Davis, S., Blackmore, K., Nalivaiko, E.: Correlating reaction time and nausea measures with traditional measures of cybersickness. Displays 48, 1–8 (2017)
35. Neustaedter, C., Singhal, S., Pan, R., Heshmat, Y., Forghani, A., Tang, J.: From being there to watching: shared and dedicated telepresence robot usage at academic conferences. ACM Trans. Comput. Hum. Interact. (TOCHI) 25(6), 1–39 (2018)
36. Oh, Y., Parasuraman, R., McGraw, T., Min, B.C.: 360 VR based robot teleoperation interface for virtual tour. In: Proceedings of the 1st International Workshop on Virtual, Augmented, and Mixed Reality for HRI (VAM-HRI) (2018)
37. Patton, M.Q.: Qualitative research. Encyclopedia of statistics in behavioral science (2005)
38. Paulos, E., Canny, J.: Social tele-embodiment: understanding presence. Auton. Robot. 11(1), 87–95 (2001)
39. Peck, T.C., Sockol, L.E., Hancock, S.M.: Mind the gap: the underrepresentation of female participants and authors in virtual reality research. IEEE Trans. Visual Comput. Graphics 26(5), 1945–1954 (2020)
40. Rae, I., Mutlu, B., Takayama, L.: Bodies in motion: mobility, presence, and task awareness in telepresence. In: Proceedings of the 32nd Annual ACM Conference on Human Factors in Computing Systems, pp. 2153–2162. ACM (2014)
41. Rae, I., Neustaedter, C.: Robotic telepresence at scale. In: Proceedings of the 2017 CHI Conference on Human Factors in Computing Systems, pp. 313–324 (2017)
42. Reason, J.T., Brand, J.J.: Motion Sickness. Academic Press, London (1975)
43. Rebenitsch, L., Owen, C.: Individual variation in susceptibility to cybersickness. In: Proceedings of the 27th Annual ACM Symposium on User Interface Software and Technology, pp. 309–317 (2014)
44. Sanchez-Vives, M.V., Slater, M.: From presence to consciousness through virtual reality. Nat. Rev. Neurosci. 6(4), 332–339 (2005)
45. Saredakis, D., Szpak, A., Birckhead, B., Keage, H.A., Rizzo, A., Loetscher, T.: Factors associated with virtual reality sickness in head-mounted displays: a systematic review and meta-analysis. Front. Hum. Neurosci. 14, 96 (2020)
46. Singer, M.J., Ehrlich, J.A., Allen, R.C.: Virtual environment sickness: adaptation to and recovery from a search task. In: Proceedings of the Human Factors and Ergonomics Society Annual Meeting, vol. 42, pp. 1506–1510. SAGE Publications Sage, Los Angeles (1998)
47. Soares, N., Kay, J.C., Craven, G.: Mobile robotic telepresence solutions for the education of hospitalized children. Persp. Health Inf. Manage. 14(Fall) (2017)
48. Stoll, B., Reig, S., He, L., Kaplan, I., Jung, M.F., Fussell, S.R.: Wait, can you move the robot? examining telepresence robot use in collaborative teams. In: Proceedings of the 2018 ACM/IEEE International Conference on Human-Robot Interaction, pp. 14–22 (2018)
49. Tomczak, M., Tomczak, E.: The need to report effect size estimates revisited. An overview of some recommended measures of effect size. Trends Sport Sci. 1(21), 19–25 (2014)
50. Tsui, K.M., Desai, M., Yanco, H.A., Uhlik, C.: Exploring use cases for telepresence robots. In: 2011 6th ACM/IEEE International Conference on Human-Robot Interaction (HRI), pp. 11–18. IEEE (2011)

51. Widdowson, C., Becerra, I., Merrill, C., Wang, R.F., LaValle, S.: Assessing postural instability and cybersickness through linear and angular displacement. Hum. Factors **63**, 296–311 (2019)
52. Yang, L., Neustaedter, C.: Our house: living long distance with a telepresence robot. Proc. ACM Hum. Comput. Interact. **2**(CSCW), 1–18 (2018)
53. Zhang, J., Langbehn, E., Krupke, D., Katzakis, N., Steinicke, F.: Detection thresholds for rotation and translation gains in 360 video-based telepresence systems. IEEE Trans. Visual Comput. Graphics **24**(4), 1671–1680 (2018)

Can You Perceive the Size Change? Discrimination Thresholds for Size Changes in Augmented Reality

Liwen Wang[1]([✉]) [iD] and Christian Sandor[1,2] [iD]

[1] City University of Hong Kong, Kowloon, Hong Kong
`liwen.wang@my.cityu.edu.hk`
[2] Laboratoire Interdisciplinaire des Sciences du Numérique (LISN), Université
Paris-Saclay, Gif-sur-Yvette, France
`christian.sandor@universite-paris-saclay.fr`

Abstract. Existing psychophysical experiments show that size changes of objects could influence the human perception of objects properties (e.g., shape or weight) in the physical surroundings. On the other hand, Augmented Reality (AR) is an interactive toolkit that allows the integration of virtual objects and real-world environments. However, the absolute detection threshold of size changes on virtual objects is not clear in AR, limiting human perception and experience in AR. In this paper, we designed a pilot study and two psychophysical experiments to explore the humans' ability towards the range of the detection threshold of size changes on virtual objects in AR. Our experimental results show that the range of the detection threshold of size changes is 3.10%–5.18% (reference is a $10 * 10 * 10\,\mathrm{cm}^3$ cube). We also calculated the value of the point of subjective equality (PSE = 4.00%), which means that users react 'same' with 50% probability upon the given stimulus.

Keywords: Augmented Reality · Size discrimination

1 Introduction

A number of studies have recently investigated object perception in Virtual Reality (VR) [10] and Augmented Reality (AR) [4]. Size perception is critical for users to understand the virtual environments [22], which enhances the interaction between humans and virtual objects in both the virtual and physical surroundings. In addition, size changes of virtual objects could induce some illusions in AR, such as weight [17] or satiety [15]. Such illusions [21] have the potential to help us understand virtual object perception.

To further investigate the effect of size perception on virtual objects, Helbig and Marc explored the human's ability of size discrimination [13] by utilising a distortion lens to change the heights of objects. Their experimental results demonstrate that changing the visual stimuli could influence size discrimination performance when visual and haptic shape information was available. However,

© Springer Nature Switzerland AG 2021
P. Bourdot et al. (Eds.): EuroXR 2021, LNCS 13105, pp. 25–36, 2021.
https://doi.org/10.1007/978-3-030-90739-6_2

they did not calculate or measure any thresholds in their experiments. Hence, Thomas conducted several studies [22] on users' ability of spatial size perception (i.e., width and height) for virtual objects with different colours in VR. The results reveal that the users could perceive the height and width of the virtual object very close to the reference object (height: less than 1.5 mm, width: less than 2.3 mm). These works show that even though human eyes are susceptible to size changes on objects, there still exists a noticeable difference in size on human observation, and those tiny differences could influence people interactive experience.

Even though some works have studied the detection threshold of size perception in virtual or physical environments, there is no current work exploring humans' ability to discriminate size in AR. However, understanding the tolerance of virtual objects size could benefit the stakeholders to help create and evaluate virtual object prototype design in AR. For example, an AR modeller or designer could design an adequate and reasonable 3D virtual push-button for users to perceive the significantly changeable size during different statuses (e.g., on/off). Hence, this paper tries to explore the humans' ability of size perception in AR. Specifically, this article investigates the following research questions:

RQ1: Is there exist some different size changes but human eyes could not distinguish in AR?

RQ2: What value or range is the detection threshold of size changes that human could not identify in AR?

To solve these two questions, we proposed two psychophysical experiments to investigate size discrimination in AR. Specifically, we designed one pilot user study and two different user-perception experiments based on the two-alternative forced-choice (2AFC) method: one experiment for narrowing down the interval of users' size discrimination gain and another experiment designed for more delicate unity gain. Our experimental results show that the point of subjective equality (PSE) value is 4.00%, indicating that the user at this point has a 50% chance to estimate the size difference.

2   Related Work

2.1   Size Perception Augmented Objects

AR could provide a direct link between physical reality and virtual information about the real world [3]. Still, the measuring perception level would become an essential indicator of how AR integrates into human life. Meanwhile, size as a very significant indicator is often defined as a study variable. Ahn et al. compared whether different AR-HMDs can affect human perceived object size [2]. Their results showed that users tend to overestimate the size of objects when using handheld displays, and people could have an estimating bias on the object size in AR scenarios. In addition to directly changing the graphics in the HMD, it is also possible to influence the size perception by controlling the depth of the virtual object. Dey et al. demonstrated that visual clutter in AR reduces the discernibility of occluded objects and decays depth judgment [11]. Moreover, Diaz et al.'s work show that changes in object depth could influence the user's judgment of object size in AR [12]. However, in recent years, due to innovations in hardware such as LIDAR, influencing the subjective feelings of objects directly by changing the depth of the graphics has become less mainstream. Another example [14] is that the user's perception of the virtual object's size can also manipulate by distortions of FOV (field-of-view) in a video see-through AR-HMD. However, the notable disadvantage of this approach is that it could affect the user experience and even cause sickness.

2.2 Two-Alternative Forced-Choice Method

Researchers always use three classical psychophysical methods [6] (e.g.: adjustment, serial exploration and constant stimuli) to study thresholds in psychophysical experiments. Since the subject cannot specify the threshold himself in the constant stimulus approach, the experimenter calculates the threshold based on his response probability. Therefore constant stimulus method is more respected. As a typical representative of the constant stimulus, the two-alternative forced-choice (2AFC) [7] method is well suited to explore thresholds in our experimental condition. 2AFC is that subjects were given two independent stimuli within the same trial, and they were forced to choose one between two stimuli at the end of the trial. The observer was not allowed to say "I do not know", "I am not sure", or "I did not see anything". The two-alternative forced-choice (2AFC) method could more closely approximate indistinguishable thresholds. It minimizes subjective judgments (e.g., expectations), and the series of randomly ordered, discrete values of the stimulus provides a more honest probability of the stimulus. Rolland et al. utilized the 2AFC method [18] to render virtual objects in a binocular HMD with a depth-aware manner. Their results showed that the accuracy was 2 mm and precision was 8 mm when rendering depth in the HMD. The results of those above experiments show that the 2AFC method could get relatively accurate thresholds for virtual objects.

3 Psychophysical Experiment

In this section, we performed one pilot study and two user perception experiments to identify the minimal height increase for the virtual cube and determine the detection threshold for height perception of virtual objects in augmented reality. Those two studies aimed to fit the psychometric functions that describe the detection thresholds of height increase.

We used an HTC Vive HMD with Stereolabs ZEDmini camera to observing an augmented world, and utilised a hand controller as our grasping proxy (Fig. 1). The virtual scene was developed by Unity (2018.4.30f) and running on a desktop (AMD Ryzen9 3950X 16-core 3.49 GHz, NVIDIA GTX 3080, Windows 10 Pro).

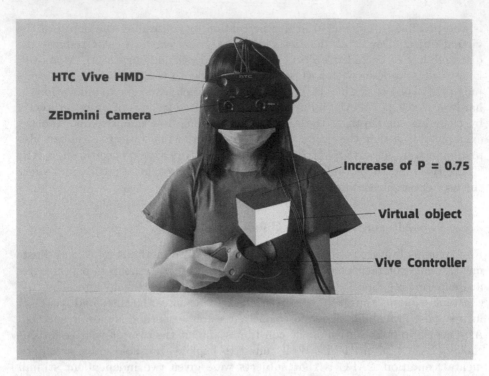

Fig. 1. The user is holding a hand controller with a virtual object above it. The blue part in the cube is the 5.18% increment, denoted as the discrimination threshold's upper boundary. (Color figure online)

The Vive HMD display resolution is 2160×1200 pixels and the field of view is $110°$ with 90FPS. The physical scene of surroundings was capture by a ZED mini camera with 60FPS at its default setting of 720P.

3.1 Pilot Study

In this pilot study, we applied the aforementioned two-alternative forced-choice task in [19] to test the validity of size discrimination in the augmented virtual objects. Following the experiment setup in [22], we also define changing height as the size discrimination variable.

Two participants, one male and one female, all right-hand, were recruited for this experiment. The average age was 22 years old. They both have limited AR using experiences. The experiment task was to answer whether two virtual objects are the same by grasping and rotating the hand controller. The order of two virtual objects shown in each trail is one in standard $10 * 10 * 10$ size cube and another in $10 * 10 *$ height-changed cube. The range of height-changing is from 1%–20%. Each height-changed trial was repeated three times. Therefore, each participant should discriminate in 20 stimuli $\times$ 3 repetitions = 60 comparison trials. The order of comparison trials is entirely random. Observation time and interval time were consistent for every trial throughout this study. The entire experiment lasted approximately one hour.

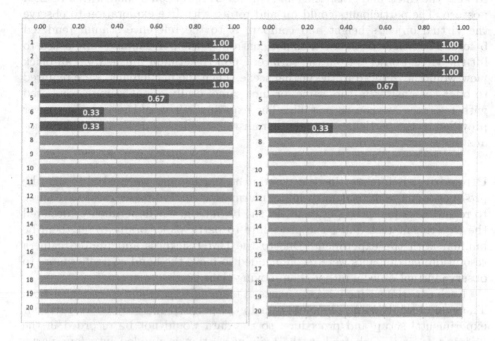

Fig. 2. The image is the analysis result of two users. The green parts are users think the probability of two objects have the same height, and the blue parts are users think the probability of two objects have different heights. (Color figure online)

The result were shown in Fig. 2. We observed that the phenomenon of size discrimination happened in all subjects, which responded to RQ1. All subjects could easily distinguish between the two virtual objects when the growth height was more than 8%. This result supports our continued exploration of RQ2 and allows us to narrow the increasing range to 0%–7%.

3.2   Experiment 1: 0–7 Range Increasing

This experiment applied a two-alternative forced-choice method to measure the participants' ability of size discrimination towards a specific range for virtual objects in AR. Meanwhile, we want to narrow the increased range for precise threshold and determine an accuracy step through Experiment 1.

Participants and Task. Five participants, all males, all right-hand, were recruited for this experiment. The average age was 26.8 years old (SD = 0.837). We define the score of AR experience in 0-None, 1-seldom, 2-often, 3-always. Thus, the average score of AR experience is 1.8 (SD = 1.304).

The experiment task was to distinguish the height change of virtual objects through grasping and rotating the hand controller. Each participant was required to wear the HMD and grasp the hand controller, sitting on a chair with a relaxed posture. The participants could lift and rotate with free exploration to observe the virtual object's height and compare it to the reference stimuli rendered before. The height of the lift was not controlled; the participants were asked to lift the virtual objects from the surface. Upon the stimuli finished, an all-black view would be induced to the virtual scene. Then the participants were required to offer the answer in the 'same' or 'not same' orally about stimuli compared with reference as soon as possible. The experimenter would record the answer provided by the participants, and other answers, such as 'I don't know'/'I cannot answer' is not allowed.

Procedure. Before starting the experiment, participants were asked to sign the pre-questionnaire with demographic information for the experiment and agree to record data for the experiment. In the beginning, the experimenter declared the experiment task and basic procedure to participants orally to let them be familiar with the experiment. Due to the HMD sickness and limited camera resolution, participants were recommended to move the hand controller more to observe virtual objects rather than moving their heads.

Each experiment includes two parts, a training session and a testing session. The goal of the training session is to help the participants fully understand our experimental setup and procedure, so the data would not be recorded in the training session. Each trial in the training section is divided into four parts: reference observing, rest, new-stimuli observing, and end-trail rest. The reference observing section asked the users to memorize the size of virtual objects; therefore, the time is no limit. After the participants think they remembered the virtual object size, the all-black view was rendered in the virtual scene to allow the participants to rest for 5 s and then a new stimulus would appear on the hand controller. The participants were allowed to observe the new stimulus for only 5 s, and after 5 s, the all-black view would back. Next, the experimenter would ask the participants, "Do you think this stimulus is the same with reference?" After got the 'same' or 'not same' answer from participants, they were allowed to rest for 10 s until the subsequent trial. The training section would repeat six trials. After the 6-trials training section, Participants still have the right to repeat it until they agree to enter the testing section. The procedure of each trial in the testing section is the same as the training section. The only difference is that the 'same' or 'not same' answer would be recorded.

Stimuli. In this study, we provided eight different visual (from 0 to 7) stimuli for object sizes to users and allowed them to compare with the reference cube size. The reference size set as 10 cm, and the other seven virtual cube size augmented in 1%-step levels of extends (i.e., from 1% to 7%). In addition, we implemented six repetitions for each of the eight stimuli. Therefore, each participant should discriminated in total 8 stimuli × 6 repetitions = 48 comparison trials.

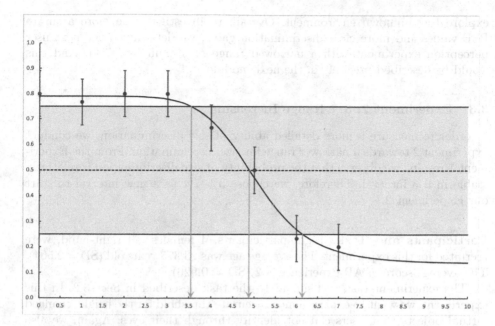

Fig. 3. The result of our pilot study. The size of referenced cuboid is 10 cm and the stimuli with augmented size is from 1% to 7% with 1% as the interval. The error bars show the standard deviation. The dashed line shows equivalent probability (50%) for the perceived stimuli were reacted by the participants as 'same' or 'not same', comparing to the reference. The yellow shady shows the range of 25%–75% discrimination gain for size discrimination by the participants. (Color figure online)

The order for stimuli was randomized, and the total duration of the experiment was approximately 30 min.

Results and Analysis. Based on our above experiment, the results are showing in Fig. 3. The x-axis shows the percentage of virtual object size increased from 0% to 7%. The y-axis shows the probability that subjects perceive the stimuli as the same as the reference, denoted as P_s. The solid line shows the fitted symmetrical psychometric function. The average of $P_s = 0.596$ (SD $= 0.255$), and the PSE value is 4.88%. The blue shady part in the figure shows that the range of 25%–75% for the possible discrimination gains is 3.55%–6.14%.

Based on the results of our Experiment 1, we noticed that the previous four stimuli (0%, 1%, 2% and 3%) yield similar level in some extent. Specifically, the probability of perceived stimuli were reacted by the participants as 'same' among four stimuli are: Stimuli 0%: $P_s = 0.800$, Stimuli 1%: $P_s = 0.767$, Stimuli 2%: $P_s = 0.800$, Stimuli 3%: $P_s = 0.800$ (All of them are over than 75%.). Although both subjects in the pilot study could give all 'same' answers in the interval 0%–3%, there is missing a common consent on the size perception results. This result could be due to the fatigue or uncertainty from users when they explore the unknown environment. Overall, to investigate the more accurate PSE values and more clear discrimination gains, we determined the next user perception experiment with a narrowed range of stimuli (3%–7%). And this would be described precisely in the next module.

3.3   Experiment 2: 3–7 Range Increasing

In order to measure a more detailed ability of size discrimination, we conduct experiment 2 towards a narrower range for size discrimination. From the Experiment 1 results, we observe that the probability of size discrimination is relatively stable in 0–3 interval. Therefore, we choose 3%–7% as a new interval to start our Experiment 2.

Participants and Task. Eight participants, 4 females, all right-hand, were recruited for this experiment. The average age was 23.375 years old (SD = 2.504). The average score of AR experience is 2 (SD = 0.926).

The experiment task was similar to the task described in Sect. 3.2. In this experiment, we want to explore a more accurate threshold for the height-changed virtual objects that users can not identify through their eyes. Again, we also used the VIVE controller as a rotating handle to display the virtual object and applied it in the same VST(video-see-through)-HMD. And also present the same virtual object in the actual physical scene. Subjects were seated and kept the controller in the same analogue to the setup described in Sect. 3.2. The experiment process in Experiment 2 also keeps the 2AFC method to continue the experiment. Questions and answers are also setting in the same way with Sect. 3.2.

Procedure. The procedure of Experiment 2 was similar to Sect. 3.2. We still divided the experiment into two parts, training session and testing session. Each trial in both sessions also included four same order rounds as Sect. 3.2: observation period for reference, 5-s rest, height-changed stimuli watching period, answer and end-trial rest. In the training stage, compared with Sect. 3.2, we also told users that using cheating methods (e.g., always keep the controller in the same position or use a body part as a reference to measure height) to judge the height changes of objects is not allowed in our experiment. And this will cause the experiment to restart directly. Due to the tiny changes of virtual objects in the testing stage, we would ask participants whether to rest more times to avoid fatigue or being over-skilled. The remainder of the process remains the same as in Sect. 3.2.

Stimuli. This experiment provided nine different visual (from 3% to 7%) stimuli for height-changed objects to users. It allowed them to compare stimuli with the reference cube. The reference height was set as 10 cm, and the nine virtual cube heights augmented in 0.5% as step-level extends the increase from 3% up to

7%. In addition, we still implemented six repetitions for each of the nine stimuli. Therefore, each participant should discriminate in total 9 stimuli × 6 repetitions = 54 comparison trials. The order for stimuli was randomized, and the total duration of the experiment was approximately 50 min.

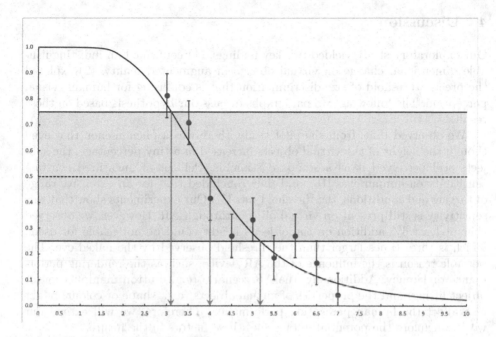

Fig. 4. The result of our Experiment 2. The size of referenced cuboid is 10cm and the stimuli with augmented size is from 10.3–10.7 cm with 0.05 cm as the interval. The error bars show the standard deviation. The dashed line shows the equivalent probability (50%) for the perceived stimuli reacted by the participants as 'same' or 'not same', compared to the reference. The yellow shady shows the range of 25%–75% discrimination gain for size discrimination by the participants. (Color figure online)

Results and Analysis. Figure 4 illustrates the results of our Experiment 2. The psychometric function reveals the specific discrimination boundaries of virtual object size increment. Similar to the analysis of the previous results, the x-axis shows the increasing percentage of virtual cube height and started from 3%. The y-axis shows the probability that subjects perceive the virtual cube as the same as the reference. The solid line shows the fitted sigmoid function that could match the data. We determined a value from the sigmoid function for the point of subjective equality (PSE). The probability of perceived the stimuli as same as the reference P'_s, is 0.36 (SD = 0.254), and the PSE value is 4.00. The detection thresholds were at gains of 3.10 and 5.18 for responses in which subjects judged the virtual objects rendered with height-increased has a high probability of similarity compare with reference. The detection thresholds were at gains of 3.10 and 5.18 for responses. Subjects judged the virtual objects rendered with the larger height as same as a reference. These results show that gain differences within this range cannot be reliably estimated when the height increases between 3.10%–5.18%. Moreover, subjects were able to discriminate against size discrimination reliably and efficiently when the size exceeded 5.18%.

4   Discussion

Our exploratory study yielded two key findings. (1) confirmed an indistinguishable dimensional change on virtual objects in augmented reality. (2) explored the precise threshold of size discrimination that is confusing for humans' visual perception. The following two paragraphs discuss our hypothesis based on these results.

We observed that, from the pilot study, there was a phenomenon that even though the height of the virtual objects increased in a tiny percentage, the subjects still perceived it as a standard stimulus. Pelli et al. measured contrast sensitivity on human eyes [16], and they concluded that for an extensive range of targets and conditions, the threshold was 1%. Our experiments show that this sensitivity is still present on virtual objects through AR. However, we observed that at least 3% addition on the object's height could be noticeable for users, which is three times larger than the threshold observed by the naked eye. The possible reason is the influence of the AR device, such as the rendering performance or latency. Additionally, the AR scenario (e.g., button manipulation or object lifting) and the properties of virtual objects (e.g., shape or colour) might also affect the human perception performance. Therefore, we will extend our work to explore the potential influence of these factors in the future.

Our experimental results show that users could identify these two different objects with height increasing over 5.18% and consider two objects identical with a size change of less than 3.10%. Comparing to the previous studies about size perception/discrimination on virtual objects in VR [22], our results demonstrate a little different threshold for size discrimination. One possible reason is that we adopted different experimental methods. Thomas's work conducted an experiment [22] that allowed users to adjust the height of a virtual object by a game controller with the visible reference object. At the same time, we adopted a similar method from [19], allowing users to determine the size discrimination indirectly. Based on the effectiveness of the 2AFC method in other areas, such as image classification [1], we adopted this in our experiment. Additionally, in the process of our experiments, we have also noticed that users might become tired and over-skilled, thus we will also consider choosing other experimental designs which could avoid those phenomenons and also support accurate measurement of thresholds.

Last but not least, our work could also inspire the future follow-ups in the object perception in AR/VR, such as size-weight illusion [8,20], resize grasping in VR [5,9]. In our future work, we will further investigate the relationships between size and other physical cues (e.g., weight, shape). And we also want to integrate other modalities (e.g., audio, haptic) to explore the multi-modal effects on object perception. Furthermore, we will also explore the detection thresholds corresponding to the size-reduction objects, which replies to diminished reality.

5   Conclusion

In this paper, we performed one pilot study and two user perception experiments to explore and evaluate the humans' ability of size discrimination. The experimental results show that the users could not perform considerably on size discrimination when the object size increases below 5.18%. Our work could potentially benefit those AR designers or developers to help design and evaluate the virtual content with interacting virtual objects, such as picking up or touching the objects. In addition, the probability range of 25%–75% for the size increasing discrimination is 3.10%–5.18%, which denotes above 5.18% increasing has over 75% [19] probability that the participants can reliably determine the changeable height.

Acknowledgments. The authors wish to thank all the participants' helping in all user study. And also want to thank Shaoyu CAI for selfless sharing his psychophysical experiment experience.

References

1. Abbey, C.K., Eckstein, M.P.: Classification image analysis: estimation and statistical inference for two-alternative forced-choice experiments. J. Vis. **2**(1), 5–5 (2002)
2. Ahn, J., Ahn, E., Min, S., Choi, H., Kim, H., Kim, G.J.: Size perception of augmented objects by different AR displays. In: Stephanidis, C. (ed.) HCII 2019. CCIS, vol. 1033, pp. 337–344. Springer, Cham (2019). https://doi.org/10.1007/978-3-030-23528-4_46
3. Azuma, R.T.: A survey of augmented reality. Presence Teleop. Virt. Environ. **6**(4), 355–385 (1997)
4. Ban, Y., et al.: Augmented endurance: controlling fatigue while handling objects by affecting weight perception using augmented reality. In: Proceedings of the SIGCHI Conference on Human Factors in Computing Systems, pp. 69–78 (2013)
5. Bergström, J., Mottelson, A., Knibbe, J.: Resized grasping in VR: estimating thresholds for object discrimination. In: Proceedings of the 32nd Annual ACM Symposium on User Interface Software and Technology, pp. 1175–1183 (2019)
6. Blackwell, H.R.: Studies of psychophysical methods for measuring visual thresholds. JOSA **42**(9), 606–616 (1952)
7. Bogacz, R., Brown, E., Moehlis, J., Holmes, P., Cohen, J.D.: The physics of optimal decision making: a formal analysis of models of performance in two-alternative forced-choice tasks. Psychol. Rev. **113**(4), 700 (2006)
8. Buckingham, G., Goodale, M.A.: Lifting without seeing: the role of vision in perceiving and acting upon the size weight illusion. PLoS ONE **5**(3), e9709 (2010)
9. Cai, S., Ke, P., Jiang, S., Narumi, T., Zhu, K.: Demonstration of ThermAirGlove: a pneumatic glove for material perception in virtual reality through thermal and force feedback. In: SIGGRAPH Asia 2019 Emerging Technologies, pp. 11–12 (2019)

10. Cai, S., Ke, P., Narumi, T., Zhu, K.: ThermAirGlove: a pneumatic glove for thermal perception and material identification in virtual reality. In: 2020 IEEE Conference on Virtual Reality and 3D User Interfaces (VR), pp. 248–257. IEEE (2020)
11. Dey, A., Sandor, C.: Lessons learned: evaluating visualizations for occluded objects in handheld augmented reality. Int. J. Hum. Comput. Stud. **72**(10–11), 704–716 (2014)
12. Diaz, C., Walker, M., Szafir, D.A., Szafir, D.: Designing for depth perceptions in augmented reality. In: 2017 IEEE International Symposium on Mixed and Augmented Reality (ISMAR), pp. 111–122. IEEE (2017)
13. Helbig, H.B., Ernst, M.O.: Integration of visual-haptic shape information. In: 1st Joint Worldhaptic Conference and Symposium on Haptic Interfaces for Virtual Environment and Teleoperator Systems (WorldHaptics 2005) (2005)
14. Kruijff, E., Swan, J.E., Feiner, S.: Perceptual issues in augmented reality revisited. In: 2010 IEEE International Symposium on Mixed and Augmented Reality, pp. 3–12. IEEE (2010)
15. Narumi, T., Ban, Y., Kajinami, T., Tanikawa, T., Hirose, M.: Augmented perception of satiety: controlling food consumption by changing apparent size of food with augmented reality. In: Proceedings of the SIGCHI Conference on Human Factors in Computing Systems, pp. 109–118 (2012)
16. Pelli, D.G., Bex, P.: Measuring contrast sensitivity. Vision. Res. **90**, 10–14 (2013)
17. Rohrbach, N., Hermsdörfer, J., Huber, L.-M., Thierfelder, A., Buckingham, G.: Fooling the size-weight illusion—using augmented reality to eliminate the effect of size on perceptions of heaviness and sensorimotor prediction. In: Virtual Reality, pp. 1–10 (2021)
18. Rolland, J.P., Meyer, C., Arthur, K., Rinalducci, E.: Method of adjustments versus method of constant stimuli in the quantification of accuracy and precision of rendered depth in head-mounted displays. Presence **11**(6), 610–625 (2002)
19. Steinicke, F., Bruder, G., Kuhl, S.: Realistic perspective projections for virtual objects and environments. ACM Trans. Graph. (TOG) **30**(5), 1–10 (2011)
20. Stevens, J.C., Rubin, L.L.: Psychophysical scales of apparent heaviness and the size-weight illusion. Percept. Psychophys. **8**(4), 225–230 (1970)
21. Tang, X., Hu, X., Fu, C.-W., Cohen-Or, D.: Grabar: occlusion-aware grabbing virtual objects in AR. In: Proceedings of the 33rd Annual ACM Symposium on User Interface Software and Technology, pp. 697–708 (2020)
22. Thomas, B.H.: Examining user perception of the size of multiple objects in virtual reality. Appl. Sci. **10**(11), 4049 (2020)

Interactive Techniques (Scientific Session 2)

Tangible Interactions to Navigate Through Space and Time Inside a Virtual Environment

Pierre Mahieux[1]([✉]), Sébastien Kubicki[1], Sylvain Laubé[2], and Ronan Querrec[1]

[1] Lab-STICC, CNRS, ENIB, Technopôle Brest-Iroise, Brest, France
{Pierre.Mahieux,Sebastien.Kubicki,Ronan.Querrec}@enib.fr
[2] Université de Bretagne Occidentale, 20 rue Duquesne, Brest, France
Sylvain.Laube@univ-brest.fr

Abstract. In order to present the results of their work to the general public, historians of science and technology represent technical systems, the activities associated to them and their temporal evolutions in Virtual Reality. The immersed user can then navigate spatially to observe the studied technical systems and temporally according to 2 time scales to observe the temporal evolution of these systems. The different concepts and scales of navigation make this task complex. We therefore propose a model for representing time in an activity model and a tangible user interface allowing a user to navigate spatially and temporally within a Virtual Environment.

Keywords: Tangible user interface · Virtual Reality · Cultural heritage

1 Introduction

Virtual Reality (VR) allows for immersive cultural mediation applications improving acceptability and learning [4]. In the context of history mediation, researchers can reconstruct past places in order to allow users to navigate between the different eras simulated. One of the main issue is to propose to the user an intuitive way to navigate in time in those environment.

In this context several techniques has been proposed. *TimeMachine Oulu* [13] is a mobile application for viewing reconstructions of the city of Oulu in Finland. This application uses a PDA to geolocate the user and display a graphical interface (Fig. 1(a)) showing a 2D representation of the city of Oulu and allowing the user to select the year he or she wishes to observe. In 2017, Koebel *et al.* propose *Biennale 4D* [10], a Virtual Environment (VE) representing the Swiss pavilion at the "Biennale di Venezia". This VE allows the user to access the archives of the different exhibitions that took place in the Swiss pavilion over time. The user can move spatially in the VE by teleporting and can navigate temporally by interacting with a virtual cube, each face of the cube representing a year (Fig. 1(b)). *Evoluson* [6] offers a VE to explore the history of Western music.

© Springer Nature Switzerland AG 2021
P. Bourdot et al. (Eds.): EuroXR 2021, LNCS 13105, pp. 39–50, 2021.
https://doi.org/10.1007/978-3-030-90739-6_3

The user can listen to musical compositions based on Bach's "Art of the Fugue" in 8 eras from antiquity to the present day. Each era is represented by a room or a landscape and the user can change era by moving spatially (Fig. 1(c)). All these techniques are based on the fact that the number of periods to visit is limited and doesn't take into account hierarchy in the periods (century, years, days...). Their generalisation on complex navigation over time in virtual environments for cultural mediation aplication is not feasible.

(a)   (b)   (c)

Fig. 1. Left: graphical user interface of *TimeMachine Oulu*. Middle: virtual cube used to navigate temporally in *Biennale 4D*. Right: rennaissance era hall in *Evoluson*.

More precisely, in the domain of cultural heritage, History of Science and Technology (HST) studies technical systems and the activities associated with them. In order to test their hypotheses and present their work, historians use VR to reconstruct the systems studied and simulate technical activities. When immersed in a VE the user can navigate spatially to observe the technical systems, temporally in the short term to observe the effects of the activities on the environment and temporally in the long term to observe the effects of technological developments or historical events.

The multiple concepts and scales of navigation make the task complex for the user. Therefore, based on the theoretical benefits of tangible interfaces [8,9,14,17], we hypothesise that using a tangible interface would facilitate spatio-temporal navigation and improve the understanding of temporal evolutions of technical systems and activities represented in a VE. We derive 3 research questions from this hypothesis:

1. How to represent technical systems, activities and their temporal evolutions in VR?
2. Which interaction metaphors should we propose to allow a user to navigate spatially and temporally in VR?
3. Which tangible interactor should we use to support these interactions?

In this article we will first present our model of time representation in Sect. 2. We will then expose the functionalities we propose to navigate spatially and temporally in the Sect. 3. Finally, we will present our proposal for an interactor and the associated interaction situations in Sect. 4.

2   Spatio-Temporal Representation

In order to interact with the activities it is necessary to represent them. Several models propose to represent these activities and to execute them.

2.1   Temporal Representation in Activity Models

Activity models such as *CTTE* [12], *K-MADE* [3], *HAMSTER* [2] represent activities with a hierarchical architecture of actions. They base their representation of time on the use of *LOTOS* (Language of Temporal Ordering Specification) operators (e.g. parallelization of actions, choice between several actions etc.) and on the expression of the duration of an action. However, these models are only interested in the simulation of activities and do not allow the representation of technical systems involved.

However, other models allow the execution of activities in VE. *Mascaret* [15] is an extension of the UML meta-model for VR. This model allows technical systems and activities to be represented and simulated in VR. *Mascaret* describes activities, in the form of UML activity diagrams, as a hierarchical sequence of actions with associated resources. The flow of activities and their impact on technical systems is simulated and represented in the VE. However, *Mascaret* does not allow the representation and description of long-term evolutions due to technological evolutions or historical events. We therefore propose to add those concepts in *Mascaret* based on the works proposed next section.

2.2   Models of Temporal Representation in the History of Science and Technology

In order to describe and represent the results of their work, historians use ontology models. These models allow them to characterise periods of time according to criteria depending on their case of application.

PeriodO [16] is an ontology model whose objective is to simplify the indexing and listing of historical periods. A period is described as being composed of a temporal and a spatial extent. But *PeriodO* does not allow for the representation of activities, unlike *CIDOC-CRM* [5]. This ontology model was designed to facilitate exchanges between historians on cultural heritage by providing a common and extensible semantic framework. The temporal representation of *CIDOC-CRM* is based on 3 notions: periods, events and activities. Periods are sets of coherent phenomena or cultural manifestations linked in time and space. They are therefore defined by a temporal extent and a spatial extent. The combination of a temporal extent and a spatial extent constitutes a time-space volume. Events are changes in the state of cultural, social or physical systems. At a low level of detail events can be seen as having an instantaneous effect, but every process has a temporal and spatial extent. This implies that, at a finer level of detail, events can be considered as periods. Activities are intentional events conducted by actors leading to changes of state. Their difference from events is that they are intentional. Activities can be associated with a procedural document (e.g. a diagram or a plan). However, *CIDOC-CRM* does not allow for the description of the sequence of actions to carry out the activity.

ANY-Artefact [11] is an ontology model based on *CIDOC-CRM*, focused on the representation of industrial cultural landscapes [7]. *ANY-Artefact* represents time on two scales: a long-term scale represented by landscapes and a short-term scale represented by activities.

In order to represent the long-term evolution of technical systems and associated activities, we propose to use the notion of landscape and to align the temporal notions of *ANY-Artefact* and *Mascaret*.

2.3   Proposal for a Spatio-Temporal Representation Model for the Activities

In *Mascaret*, a system is described on two levels. The first level corresponds to the classes, grouped together in a model, allowing the structural aspect of the system to be represented. The second level corresponds to the concrete entities forming the system and instances of the classes declared in the model. These two levels are also used to describe the organisational structure and their instances. An organisational structure describes roles and resources which participate in the realisation of procedures. The organisational instances make it possible to assign the agents of the environment to the roles and the entities to the resources for an effective realisation of the procedures. An alignment between the notions of entities, organisational structures, roles and procedures and ANY-Artefact has been proposed in [1].

Mascaret represents procedures as a set of actions in the form of a UML activity diagram. However, it does not allow to represent the temporal evolutions on the long term of technical systems and procedures. We propose to integrate in *Mascaret* (Fig. 2) the notions of landscape, spatio-temporal volume and spatio-temporal event from ANY-Artefact.

A landscape (class *HumanActivityLandscape*) contains the semantic model (class *Model*) of the environment and the organisational structures (and thus the procedures), a set of spatio-temporal events (class *SpatioTemporalEvent*) and a spatio-temporal volume (class *SpatioTemporalVolume*). These volumes are composed of a temporal extent (class *TemporalScope*) delimited by 2 dates and a spatial extent (class *Area*) containing the entities of the model.

Let's take the example of a cultural mediation application dealing with the history of two bridges spanning a military arsenal and succeeding each other in time. Each of these bridges is emblematic of a specific landscape, so in this application we will study two landscapes, each corresponding to the duration of use of each bridge. Because the second bridge was built to replace the older one the 2 landscapes share the same spatial extent. Within these landscapes we find the two bridges as technical systems. The bridges spanning the military arsenal need to be able to open to allow ships to pass. This leads to an opening and closing procedure for each bridge. Therefore, in our application, we find 2

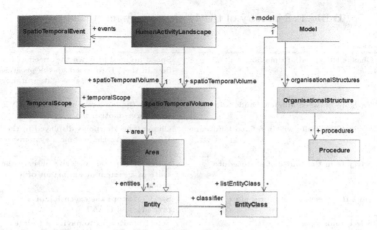

Fig. 2. Class diagram of our model. In blue the classes we integrate to *Mascaret*; in yellow the original structure of *Mascaret*. (Color figure online)

landscapes, each corresponding to a space-time volume. Each landscape includes 1 entity (the bridges) and 2 procedures.

This spatio-temporal representation model allows us to represent and interact with technical systems, the activities related to these systems and the temporal evolutions induced by technological changes or historical events. The following section presents the functionalities we implement to allow a user to navigate spatially and temporally within a VE.

3   Spatio-Temporal Navigation

3.1   Identification of the Functionalities

In order to identify the different functionalities necessary for spatio-temporal navigation, we organised a workshop with 12 experts (8 women and 4 men) in cultural mediation, history of science and technology and cultural heritage. On average the experts had 15 years ($SD = 8.05$) of experience working on building cultural mediation scenarios or working with the general public. The objectives of this workshop were, firstly, to identify and define the user profiles likely to be concerned by spatio-temporal navigation in VR within a cultural mediation framework and then to identify the functionalities to implement in order to allow a user immersed in VR to navigate spatio-temporally.

These profiles then enabled us to write user stories allowing us to identify the spatio-temporal navigation functionalities. 69 stories were written by the experts, from which we drew 23 functionalities that we then grouped into 11 elementary functionalities (see Table 1). For example, the elementary functionality "navigate between different landscapes" can be done either by selecting a date or by selecting an event.

In these 11 functionalities, the first 7 are directly linked to spatio-temporal navigation, functionalities n°8 and 9 are not about navigation but allow to bring

Table 1. Summary of the 11 elementary functionalities

Id	Name	Features
F1	Change the speed of time flow	Speed up or slow down the speed of time flow in the VE to speed up the progress of a procedure or observe a step in more detail
F2	Navigate between different landscapes	Change the landscape shown in the VE to observe another place or time
F3	Navigate spatially within a fixed landscape	Change the viewpoint displayed in the VE to observe the technical systems represented
F4	Navigate in the course of a procedure	Select an action in order to observe the state of a system at an instant of a procedure
F5	Start the execution of a procedure	Start (or stop) the execution of a procedure in the VE
F6	Select landscapes	Select landscapes to navigate to later
F7	Select procedures	Select procedures to obtain information and initiate execution
F8	Access information relating to the selected landscape	Display information characterising the selected landscape (e.g. start and end dates, milestones...)
F9	Superimpose several temporal states	Display several landscapes at the same time in the VE (navigate in several landscapes simultaneously)
F10	Define time scales	Define or redefine the time scales used to perform activities or represent landscapes
F11	Create a landscape according to 2 dates	Create and add a new landscape in the application

additional information to the user. The functionalities n°10 and 11 are functionalities of control of the environment and instantiation of data, because they do not concern the spatio-temporal navigation or give the user access to informations, they are not essentials for our usecase.

This set of functionalities allows us to interact with the model in order to navigate spatially and temporally on 2 time scales. In order to achieve these functionalities we propose to design a tangible interface.

4   Interactions for Spatio-Temporal Navigation

The third step of our work consists in designing a tangible interface allowing a user to navigate spatio-temporally. To do this, we first organised an ideation and prototyping workshop. We then asked experts in cultural mediation to evaluate the proposals made during the workshop in order to determine which one to implement.

4.1   Ideation and Prototyping Workshop

The objective of our ideation and prototyping workshop was to design low-fidelity prototypes presenting tangible interactors and associated interactions.

The workshop lasted 4h30 and involved 16 participants (6 women and 10 men). Because our objective is to propose, design and build a tangible interactor for cultural mediation applications we invited people with competences in mechanical design, electronics and mediation. Among our participants we had researchers in computer science specialised in virtual reality and human-computer interaction, teachers in mechatronics and computer-aided design, historians of science and technology, cognitive psychologists, ergonomists and designers. These different profiles allowed us to obtain results focusing on different aspects of the design of an interactor. The participants were separated randomly into 2 groups and first took part in a brainstorming session around 2 questions: how to represent time in a tangible way? What kind of interactions to associate to each functionality? Following this brainstorming session, the participants took part in a design workshop, the objective of which was to propose tangible interactors taking up the elements discussed during the brainstorming session. The participants were given materials (paper, play dough, coloured crayons, Lego blocks) to design a low-fidelity prototype of their proposals and could work as they wanted, alone or in groups. 7 participants decided to work alone, 3 groups of 2 and 1 group of 3 were formed, either by affinity or because the participants proposed similar ideas. At the end of this session 11 low-fidelity prototypes and their respective interactions were proposed (Fig. 3).

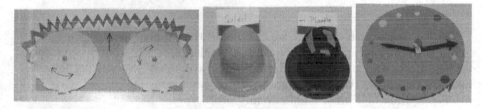

Fig. 3. Examples of interactors prototype. Left: prototype n°1. Middle: prototype n°6. Right: prototype n°3.

4.2   Evaluation of the Proposed Interactors

To evaluate the interactors proposed during the ideation and prototyping workshop, we asked 10 experts (5 women and 5 men) in cultural mediation to fill in a scoring table according to two criteria: usability and affordance. All of the participants had more than 5 years of experience in building cultural heritage applications or using them to show the results of their work.

The affordance criterion makes it possible to evaluate whether the shape of the interactor (i.e. the low-fidelity prototype) suggests its use. The usability criterion has been divided into 3 sub-criteria (ISO 9241-11 standard):

Effectiveness does the interactor enable the user to achieve his objective, to carry out the intended task?
Efficiency is the interactor easy to use, does it require much Effort to use?
Satisfaction is the interactor pleasant to use?

Each criterion and sub-criterion was evaluated on a scale from 1 to 5, with 1 being the worst and 5 the best. The affordance criterion was to be evaluated for the whole interactor and the usability sub-criteria were to be evaluated for each of the functionalities handled by the interactor.

Due to the health situation this evaluation was carried out remotely, we sent each participant a document explaining each feature, each interactor and each criterion. As a result, we were not able to make an objective measurement of the use of the prototypes, so we focus our analysis on the most subjective criteria, namely affordance and satisfaction.

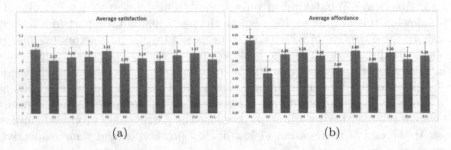

(a)   (b)

Fig. 4. Top: average satisfaction with 95% confidence interval. Bottom: average affordance with 95% confidence interval.

For the satisfaction criterion, we calculated the average satisfaction for each functionality and compared these results considering a 95% confidence interval (see Fig. 4(a)). The affordance criterion is the average of every experts evaluation (see Fig. 4(b)). We did not observe any significant difference between the prototypes, thus we cannot eliminate any prototype.

The expert evaluation did not allow us to designate an interactor with certainty. Therefore, we have also completed this evaluation by adding engineering criteria such as, for example, technical feasibility and manufacturing cost. The interactor that emerges from our evaluation as being the best compromise between affordance, user satisfaction and engineering criteria is the prototype n°4. It is an hourglass-shaped interactor (cf. Figure n°5(a)).

4.3   Implementing the Interactor

The interactor we decided to implement has the shape of an hourglass, 16 cm high and 12 cm in diameter (Fig. 5(b)). It is composed of 3 parts, an hourglass-shaped core and bases that can be changed according to the object tracking system used.

The interactor contains a Rapsberry Pi Zero board, a gyroscope, 12 inductive sensors (6 per side), 84 LEDs (72 in the core and 6 per side) and is powered by

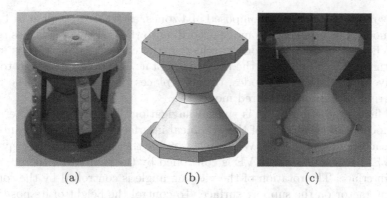

(a)   (b)   (c)

Fig. 5. Left: low-fidelity prototype of our proposed interactor. Middle: 3D representation of our interactor. Right: implementation of our proposition.

an 11.1 V battery. The Rapsberry Pi Zero board allows communication with the computer, retrieving data from the sensors and controlling the LEDs.

The gyroscope is used to determine the tilt of the interactor and whether it is lying or standing. The inductive sensors are arranged in a circle under the bases of the interactor, they can be used as a circular slider or as a capacitive button. The driver we have developed differentiates the use of the slider and the button according to the number of sensors activated simultaneously. If the user wants to use the slider he will activate the sensors one by one, while to use the button he will activate several at the same time. We also propose to use the position and rotation of the interactor to interact with the system. By changing the bases we can adapt our interactor to the interaction scenario and the tracking system used.

4.4   Interaction Scenarios

In order to verify the genericity of our interactor we deploy it in 2 configurations on a case of cultural mediation application around a technical system. The first configuration is based on a CAVE while the second one uses an Mixed Reality (MR) device.

In the first configuration the user is immersed in a VE through a CAVE-type system. Within this CAVE we place a white surface on which we place the interactor and project a graphical interface. The position of the interactor is tracked using the CAVE system.

The second configuration uses a see-through HMD to immerse the user. The use of a see-through HMD allows the user to see the virtual world and the real world at the same time and therefore be able to interact with the interactor while immersed in the VE. In this situation we replace the white surface with an interactive tangible interactive table. The graphical interface is displayed by this interactive table which is also used to track the position of the interactor.

The graphical interface is composed of 4 zones, each corresponding to 1 interaction mode. The user changes mode according to the task he/she wishes to perform. When an interaction mode is selected, the corresponding zone is spread out on the interface to occupy the major part of it. The other areas fold to their respective sides. To change modes, the user places the interactor on the folded area corresponding to the desired mode.

The first interaction mode is spatial navigation. The associated interaction zone is located in the middle of the graphical interface (Fig. 6(a)). The interface contains a top view of the VE. While in this mode the user can navigate spatially in the VE. His position in the VE is controlled by the position of the interactor on the interface. The rotation of the viewing angle is controlled by the rotation of the interactor on the support surface. To control the height of its position in the VE the user uses the circular slider on the top of the interactor (clockwise to move up, counter-clockwise to move down).

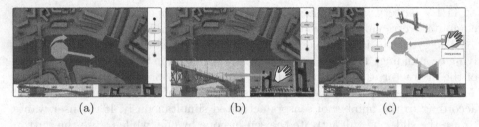

(a)   (b)   (c)

Fig. 6. Left: representation of our proposed interface with the interactor and the possible interactions in the spatial navigation mode. Middle: representation of our proposed interface with the interactor and the possible interactions in the temporal navigation between landscapes mode. Right: representation of our proposed interface with the interactor and the possible interactions in the temporal navigation on the procedures mode.

The second mode of interaction is the one for temporal navigation between landscapes. The corresponding interaction zone is located at the bottom of the graphical interface (Fig. 6(b)). This area contains a timeline representing the temporal sequence of landscapes. In this timeline each landscape is represented by a photo or an image. The user selects landscapes by placing the interactor on their representative image and validating their choice by using the capacitive button at the top of the interactor. When landscapes are selected they are displayed in the VE, thus the user can overlay multiple observed landscapes.

The third mode of interaction is the one of temporal navigation on procedures. The interaction zone displays the list of executable procedures and, when a procedure is selected, the flow and the 3D models of the resources of this procedure (Fig. 6(c)). To select a procedure, the user places the interactor on the element of the list of procedures that he wants, the choice is validated when the user removes the interactor from the list. To start or stop the execution of the selected procedure the user presses the button located on the top of the interactor. To navigate through the procedure step by step the user rotates the interactor on its vertical axis. The procedure navigation mode also allows the user to control the speed at which the time flows by using the circular slider on the top of the interactor. When used clockwise the speed of time increases, when used counter-clockwise the speed decreases. The tilt of the interactor also allows to control the speed of time flow, when it is vertical the speed is maximum and when it is horizontal the time is paused. Between these two positions, the evolution of the speed of time flow is linear.

The last interaction mode allows the exploration of iconographic resources resulting from the work of historians. In this interaction mode, the corresponding interface zone displays all the iconographic resources and documents enabling historians to define and describe the current landscapes. We do not implement this mode of interaction because it does not concern spatio-temporal navigation.

5 Conclusion

To allow a user to navigate spatially and temporally within a VE we propose a spatio-temporal representation model, a tangible interactor and a graphical interface. In order to evaluate the usability of our interface (interactor + GUI) we will carry out a comparative evaluation between our proposal and the use of a classical VR controller in the hardware configuration using a CAVE. This evaluation will take place in the context of a cultural mediation application for the general public. We will use the SUS questionnaire to measure perceived usability and will take objective measures such as task completion time.

References

1. Abiven, M.M.: Humanités Numériques et méthodes de conservation et de valorisation des patrimoines maritimes. L'exemple des arsenaux de Brest et Venise. PhD Thesis, Universite de Bretagne Occidentale (2019)
2. Barboni, E., Ladry, J.F., Navarre, D., Palanque, P., Winckler, M.: Beyond modelling: an integrated environment supporting co-execution of tasks and systems models. In: Proceedings of the 2nd ACM SIGCHI symposium on Engineering interactive computing systems, pp. 165–174. Association for Computing Machinery, Berlin, Germany (2010). https://doi.org/10.1145/1822018.1822043
3. Baron, M., Lucquiaud, V., Autard, D., Scapin, D.: K-MADe: un environnement pour le noyau du modèle de description de l'activité. In: Proceedings of the 18th international conference on Association Francophone d'Interaction Homme-Machine - IHM 2006, pp. 287–288. ACM Press, Montreal, Canada (2006). https://doi.org/10.1145/1132736.1132786
4. Ch'ng, E., Li, Y., Cai, S., Leow, F.T.: The effects of VR environments on the acceptance, experience, and expectations of cultural heritage learning. J. Comput. Cult. Heritage 13(1), 1–21 (2020). https://doi.org/10.1145/3352933
5. Doerr, M.: The CIDOC conceptual reference module: an ontological approach to semantic interoperability of metadata. AI Mag. 24, 75–92 (2003). https://doi.org/10.1609/aimag.v24i3.1720

6. Gaugne, R., et al.: Evoluson: walking through an interactive history of music. Presence: Teleoperators and Virtual Environ. **26**(3), 281–296 (2018)
7. HERITAGE, I.C.F.T.P.O.T.W.C.A.N.: Operational Guidelines for the Implementation of the World Heritage Convention. Tech. rep., UNESCO, Paris, France (2008)
8. Hornecker, E.: Beyond affordance: tangibles' hybrid nature. In: Proceedings of the Sixth International Conference on Tangible, Embedded and Embodied Interaction, pp. 175–182. TEI 2012, ACM, New York, NY, USA (2012). https://doi.org/10.1145/2148131.2148168
9. Ishii, H.: Tangible bits: beyond pixels. In: Proceedings of the 2nd international conference on Tangible and embedded interaction - TEI 2008, pp. 15–25. ACM Press, Bonn, Germany (2008). https://doi.org/10.1145/1347390.1347392
10. Koebel, K., Agotai, D., Arisona, S., Oberli, M.: Biennale 4D — a journey in time: Virtual reality experience to explore the archives of the Swiss pavilion at the "Biennale di Venezia" art exhibition. In: 2017 23rd International Conference on Virtual System & Multimedia (VSMM), pp. 1–8. IEEE, Dublin, Ireland (Oct 2017)
11. Laubé, S., Garlatti, S., Querrec, R., Rohou, B.: ANY-ARTEFACT-O: an ontology developed for history of industrial cultural landscape. In: 2nd Data for History workshop, Pôle histoire numérique (Digital history department) of the LARHRA laboratory, Lyon, France (2018)
12. Mori, G., Paterno, F., Santoro, C.: CTTE: Support for developing and analyzing task models for interactive system design. IEEE Trans. Softw. Eng. **28**(8), 797–813 (2002). https://doi.org/10.1109/TSE.2002.1027801
13. Peltonen, J., Ollila, M., Ojala, T.: TimeMachine Oulu – dynamic creation of cultural-Spatio-temporal models as a mobile service. In: Chittaro, L. (ed.) Mobile HCI 2003. LNCS, vol. 2795, pp. 342–346. Springer, Heidelberg (2003). https://doi.org/10.1007/978-3-540-45233-1_25
14. Petrelli, D., O'Brien, S.: Phone vs. tangible in museums: a comparative study. In: Proceedings of the 2018 CHI Conference on Human Factors in Computing Systems, pp. 1–12. CHI 2018, Association for Computing Machinery, New York, NY, USA (2018). https://doi.org/10.1145/3173574.3173686 event-place: Montreal QC, Canada
15. Querrec, R., Vallejo, P., Buche, C.: MASCARET: creating virtual learning environments from system modelling. In: Dolinsky, M., McDowall, I.E. (eds.) The Engineering Reality of Virtual Reality 2013, vol. 8649, pp. 21–31. SPIE, Burlingame, California, USA (2013). backup Publisher: International Society for Optics and Photonics
16. Rabinowitz, A.: It's about time: historical periodization and linked ancient world data. ISAW Papers **7**, 7 (2014)
17. Zuckerman, O., Gal-Oz, A.: To TUI or not to TUI: evaluating performance and preference in tangible vs. graphical user interfaces. Int. J. Hum. Comput. Stud. **71**(7), 803–820 (2013). https://doi.org/10.1016/j.ijhcs.2013.04.003

Continuous-Touch Text Entry for AR Glasses

Chao Mei[1,2]([⊠]), Buyi Xu[2], and Yi Xu[2] [iD]

[1] Kennesaw State University, Marietta, GA 30060, USA
chao.mei@kennesaw.edu
[2] OPPO US Research Center, InnoPeak Technology, Inc., Palo Alto, CA 94303, USA

Abstract. The emergence of Augmented Reality (AR) has brought new challenges to the design of text entry interfaces. When wearing a pair of head-mounted AR glasses, a user's visual focus could be anywhere 360 °C around her. For example, a technician is looking up at an airplane engine, meanwhile sharing her view with remote technicians through the sensors on the AR glasses. In such a scenario, the technician has to keep her gaze at the parts and look away from input devices such as a wireless keyboard or a touchscreen. Thus, she will have limited ability to input text for tasks like taking notes about a certain engine part. In this work, we designed and developed two innovative text entry interfaces: Continuous-touch T9 (CTT9) and Continuous-touch Dual Ring (CTDR). Our methods employ a smartphone touchscreen and a projected text entry layout in AR space to help the users input texts without looking at the smartphone. Our user studies suggest the effectiveness of CTT9 and CTDR and provide clues on how to optimize them. Based on the user study results, we provide insights about applying the proposed Continuous-touch (CT) paradigms to text entry for AR glasses.

Keywords: AR glasses · Text input · Touchscreen

1 Introduction

Text entry is one of the most basic human-computer interaction tasks, and it has kept evolving with computing devices. Text entry interfaces such as physical keyboards for PCs, virtual keyboards and handwriting for mobile touchscreens, and voice recognition for smartwatches and speakers, leverage available hardware features (e.g., touchscreens or microphones) and mitigate the limitations of the targeted hardware. The emergence of Augmented Reality (AR) glasses has brought new challenges to the design of text entry interfaces. With a traditional computing devices, such as PCs and smartphones, user's areas of interest are mostly limited to a screen. Physical and virtual keyboards are at least within a user's peripheral vision. However, when wearing a pair of head-mounted see-through AR glasses, a user's point of interest is extended to anywhere 360 °C around her. For example, a technician is looking up at an airplane engine, meanwhile sharing her view with remote technicians through the sensors on the AR

P. Bourdot et al. (Eds.): EuroXR 2021, LNCS 13105, pp. 51–64, 2021.
https://doi.org/10.1007/978-3-030-90739-6_4

glasses. The technician has to keep her gaze at the engine and look away from input devices such as a wireless keyboard or a touchscreen. If she wants to enter text to make a note about an engine part or instructions from remote experts, she has to shift her gaze from the engine to the input device which interrupts the view sharing, or hold up a keyboard/smartphone in the direction she is look- ing at, which is tiring and not even feasible at certain situations. Users need text entry methods that can support the separation of the input device and her view. Recently, many new text entry methods have been proposed and studied for Head-Mounted Displays (HMDs) especially Virtual Reality (VR) headsets. These methods have shed some light on designing device-view-separated text entry methods for AR glasses. However, some of these methods still require the presence of tracked controllers or their metaphors in the user's view, such as laser pointers and virtual drums [2]. Others such as virtual pads [6] can separate the input device from a user's view, but requires specific controllers, keys or buttons to complete the tasks. Smartphones with touchscreens, which are arguably the most dominant personal computing devices in the current mobile computing age, were minimally considered in previous designs. With smartphone manufactur- ers having recently released or soon to release smartphone-tethered AR glasses, smartphone is becoming an essential part of AR experience. Given such a con- venience, the question of how to take advantage of smartphone touchscreens in the design of device-view-separated text entry methods is yet to be explored.

The main purpose of this paper is not to improve the performance of any existing text entry method, but rather to design and study an AR glasses text entry method that separates the input device from a user's view, and leverages the accessibility of smartphone that is tethered to the glasses. In this work, we first project the touchscreen to the AR space of the HMD. Then, to compensate for the lost visual cues of hands and fingers, we propose two innovative keyboard layouts and two Continuous-touch (CT) interaction paradigms that can pro- vide continuous feedback to the users. More specifically, this paper presents the designs and the user studies of two innovative text entry interfaces: Continuous- touch T9 (CTT9) and Continuous-touch Dual Ring (CTDR). CTT9 employs a two-stage mechanism, in which one finger selects a multi-character key and another finger of a different hand confirms a specific character within the multi- character group. CTDR lets the user swipe within two rings continuously to select a single-character key and confirm it by moving in and out of an area des- ignated for each key. Overall, the results show that novice users achieved average 7.64 Words per Minute (WpM) with CTDR and 6.43 WpM with CTT9. The main contributions of this paper include: 1) the designs and implementations of CTT9 and CTDR; 2) the user studies that explore the usability and possi- ble optimizations of CTT9 and CTDR; and 3) generalizable guidelines on using Continuous-touch paradigms for text entry tasks in Head-Mounted AR glasses.

2   Related Work

In this section, we survey related work in the area of text entry for HMDs and methods that use smartphones as an input device for AR/VR interactions.

2.1   Text Entry for HMDs

Inputting text for HMDs, especially VR devices, has been a long standing problem. With different input devices, various methods have been proposed. Walker et al. [17] augmented a desktop keyboard with a virtual assistant to enable typing in a VR HMD. Grubert et al. [4] studied different strategies for using desktop and touchscreen keyboards in VR, and they used an external camera or finger tracking device to provide visual feedback to the user. Fashimpaur et al. [3] developed PinchType which uses the QWERTY keyboard layout with thumb and finger interaction gestures.

Body gestures can also be used for text entry. Yu et al. [20] studied various commit methods for head-based text input, where a user controls the pointer on a virtual keyboard using head motion. RingText [19] provides a circular layout with two concentric circles, where a head-pointing movement is used to select letters and/or words. DigiTouch [18] uses a glove-based input device that enables typing by thumb-to-finger touch sensing. Misra et al. [14] presented a vision-based hand gesture recognition to input alphabets. Although these gesture-based methods are innovative, social acceptability and accessibility for certain users are still major concerns.

Controllers are an important part of VR devices, some of which employ an aim-and-shoot style virtual keyboard. DayDream VR [2] utilizes a drum-like metaphor for virtual keyboard typing. Vitty [7] adds individual finger buttons to a normal controller to mimic ordinary typing on a QWERTY keyboard. PizzaText [21] uses dual thumbsticks of a game controller and leverages a circular multi-character layout. One thumbstick traverses the multi-character slices and the other thumbstick selects a target character. However, game controllers are not readily available for HMDs, especially for lightweight AR glasses. HiPad [6] employs the touchpad of certain VR controller devices and uses a circular virtual keyboard layout, enabling one-hand text entry for HMDs.

Smartphone touchscreens have not yet been sufficiently explored as tools for text input for HMDs. How to leverage users' existing habits with the touchscreen remains a question to be addressed.

2.2   Smartphones as an Input Device

Using smartphones as an input device for HMDs has also been explored previously. An early work by Budhiraja et al. [1] investigated how a smartphone could be used as an input device to interact with AR content in HMDs. They focused on interaction techniques using smartphone touchscreens for selection tasks in HMDs. In DualCAD [13], a smartphone is used as an alternative input device for 3D object interaction. More object interaction techniques using a hand-held device were explored in the work of TabletInVR [16]. A design space of cross-device interactions between smartphones and AR HMDs was proposed by Zhu and Grossman [22]. FaceTouch [5] attaches a touchscreen to the back side of an HMD and allows the user to type on the touchscreen with both hands. It provides visual feedback of finger position to the user and using *lift-off* as the character confirmation method. However, no formal user study was performed to evaluate the usability of this text input method. Although using smartphones as input devices has been studied in these previous works, using a touchscreen for text input tasks has not been formally explored. This is the focus of our study.

3   Interface Design

The intention is to build text entry methods that separate the input device and a user's view for AR glasses leveraging the easily-accessible smartphone touchscreens. We designed two virtual keyboard layouts that use continuous-touch gestures for text entry. Users can select and confirm the input characters by continuously touching/swiping on the screen, without "tap" or "lift-off" from the smartphone touchscreen. When a layout is being used for text entry, it is projected to the AR space, so that users will be able to interact with the layout without bringing the touchscreen device into her view.

The designs choose "continuous-touch" over "tap" and "lift-off" mainly because "continuous-touch" enables uninterrupted feedback of where the finger(s) is(are) touching. When the view is separated from the input device, a user cannot see the device and her finger(s). In our designs, a user can monitor the projected virtual keyboard layout in AR spaces. She can see the touching point(s) on the layout as the visual cues about where her finger(s) is(are) touching. In comparison, "tap" will still require the user to monitor her real fingers, which is against our intention of separating device and view. "Swipe" plus "lift-off" paradigm, may also provide feedback of where the user's finger(s) is(are) touching, but lifting the fingers will interrupt the feedback.

Although predictive text input has been a common functionality of input methods, the predictive features are not within the scope of this paper. We wanted to focus on the layouts and interaction paradigms, therefore we did not include the predictive features for any input methods studied in this paper in order not to bias the performance results.

3.1   Continuous-Touch T9 (CTT9)

The CTT9 is inspired by the classic T9 input method. We wanted to leverage a user's familiarity with this popular touchscreen virtual keyboard. We enhanced it with a bimanual operation to eliminate the need for "tap" or "lift-off", thus allowing continuous-touch and feedback in AR environments.

In this design, the screen is divided into two panels. On one panel, it is a keyboard with multi-character keys following the classic T9 layout. On the other side, it is a confirmation panel where a user can commit the character selection among multiple characters (Fig. 1). We assume the keyboard is on the left side during subsequent discussion in this section.

The operation of CTT9 utilizes a bimanual two-stage mechanism. The user slides her left thumb (or any finger of choice) over the T9 keyboard area continuously. The right side of the touchscreen displays the set of multiple characters

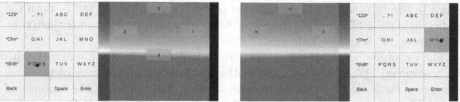

Fig. 1. CTT9 layout   Fig. 2. CTT9-2 layout

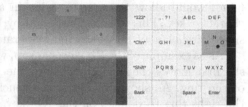

Fig. 3. CTT9-3 layout   Fig. 4. CTT9-4 layout

according to the selection of the left thumb. For example, in Fig. 1, the letters "P", "Q", "R", and "S" are displayed when the left thumb touches the multi-character key "PQRS". To select one of the characters, the user simply swipes their right thumb (or any finger of choice) within the right side of the touchscreen. For example, in Fig. 1, a swipe-up gesture selects and confirms the letter "Q" for input. The individual characters are arranged in four directions aligned with screen edges in the confirmation panel, allowing the user to swipe accurately along any intended direction. For single selection keys (e.g., Backspace, Space, Enter key, etc.), swiping along one fixed direction (e.g., left) confirms the input. Using CTT9, both hands are used collaboratively to enter text, thus enabling a user to perform continuous-touch interaction without using line of sight on the touchscreen and hands.

The keyboard is projected into the display of HMD for visual feedback. In addition, a visual indication (e.g., a black dot) showing the position of the finger touch can be displayed on the virtual keyboard in HMD.

3.2   Continuous-Touch Dual Ring (CTDR)

Our proposed solution CTDR has an innovative dual-circle layout and a "Refined In-and-Out" (RIO) selection mechanism to enable continuous-touch text input. Figure 5 shows the layout of the innovative CTDR input method. There are two rings, each of which is equally divided into 15 sub sections. The 26 letter keys, Space, Backspace, and Return are mapped into these sub sections. Each key's location in this double ring layout is determined based on two factors: 1) its position relative to other keys in the traditional QWERTY layout, and 2) its left or right hand zoning in the traditional QWERTY layout. For example, as shown in Fig. 5, letter "Q" is to the right of "W" and on top of "A" in both the traditional QWERTY and CTDR layouts. Letter "F" is located on the left ring, while letter "J" is on the right ring.

The rationale behind the key locations is to leverage users' familiarity with the traditional QWERTY layout to optimize their learning curves of this new text entry method. The reason why we did not directly adopt the traditional QWERTY layout is to avoid the possibility of a mis-touch resulting from swiping on the QWERTY layout. When a user swipes from one key to another, they will likely swipe through several other keys. The ring or circle layout, on the other hand, would allow the user to swipe in a way that touches only one relevant character key. This was demonstrated by Mankoff et al. [12] in a design using a single circle layout for pen swiping operations.

As as example of the RIO mechanism, when a user needs to input a letter "O", she first moves the touch point onto the "O" key through the inner boundary of the ring. As shown in Fig. 5, the touch point is moved from point 1 inside the right ring to point 2 on the "O" key. At this instance, the "O" key is in a pre-selection state. Moving the touch point into the "O" key area through other boundaries (i.e., outside the ring, between "I" and "O", or between "P" and "O"), will not trigger the pre-selection state.

Next, the user moves the touch point out of the "O" key through the inner boundary of the ring (from point 2 to point 3 in Fig. 5) to confirm the selection of "O" for input. During the pre-selection state, moving the touch point out of the "O" key through the boundaries other than the inner circle or lifting finger off the touchscreen will cancel the pre-selection state.

The RIO is "Refined" because our design only allows swiping through inner circle to trigger pre-selection states. The benefits include: 1) allowing a cancel operation, 2) reducing user confusion by limiting their options, and most importantly 3) supporting additional layers of buttons/keys outside of the rings to enable functions such as predictive text.

3.3   Apparatus

Theoretically, our text entry interfaces can work with any AR/VR HMDs that are connected to a smartphone either via a cable or wireless connection. However, to avoid the latency that may interfere with our studies, we implement the CTT9 and CTDR using OPPO AR Glass 2021 designed by smartphone manufacturer OPPO. It employs optical see-through design and tethers to a smartphone via a USB 3.1 cable. The theoretical latency of USB 3.1 is less than 1 ms compared with 34 ms for Bluetooth connections. The smartphone provides power, computing, graphics rendering, and serves as an input device for the glasses. Both eyes of the glasses have 1080p resolution, and diagonal field of view of about 45°.

4   Study 1 and System Optimizations

We conducted an informal preliminary study to collect information about user interaction with the original designs, so that we could find some clues to optimize

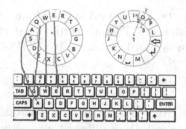

Fig. 5. CTDR and QWERTY layouts

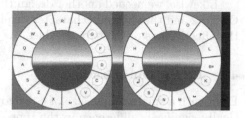

Fig. 6. CTDR-2 layout

Fig. 7. CTDR-3 layout

Fig. 8. CTDR-4 layout

the two layouts. The study has 6 participants and the task is to enter 5 short sentences with CTT9 and CTDR. Our intention was not to draw any conclusion from this study, and given the small sample size, the details of the study is not discussed in this paper. This section introduces the possible optimizations of CTT9 and CTDR, and how they are inspired from Study 1 results.

4.1 CTT9 Optimizations

The first optimization was motivated from the post interviews of the Study 1. Several subjects mentioned that they were used to operating the traditional T9 with either both hands or only their right hand. All of the participants were right-handed. We were interested in investigating if the reversed layout would have an influence on the task performances. Therefore, the optimization CTT9-2 is the original CTT9 with left and right panels switched as shown in Fig. 2

Another major concern of CTT9 discovered from Study 1 was that the character location on the key falsely suggests the direction to swipe and confirm that key. For example, as shown in Fig. 1, "S" is located at the rightmost position on the key, but needs to be confirmed by swiping downward. We proposed an optimization as shown in Fig. 3. When the key "PQRS" is selected, the layout of the key will *change* to be consistent with the layout of the confirmation panel. When the key is not touched, the character display remains in alphabetical order to help the users locate the characters. The users will no longer need to observe the confirmation panel to figure out the direction for swipe confirmation. We name this optimization CTT9-3.

Likewise, we needed another design that adopts the reversed layout change in CTT9-2 and the dynamic character display design in CTT9-3 in order to study the effectiveness of the two variables. As shown in Fig. 4, we name it CTT9-4.

4.2   CTDR Optimizations

Even with a small sample size of 6, we found in Study 1 that there was a statistically significant difference in the time spent on inputting different characters. In specific, with CTDR layout, users took longer time inputting "C", "D", and "B". This result was suggested by a homogeneous-group classification based on the Tukey test. After review of the layouts, we believe the reason is that there are certain keys for which individual users may have typing habits different from what we assumed in the original CTDR design. For example, they can either type "B" with left or right fingers. Similarly, they can type "C" by either extending or bending the left thumb, depending on where they place their thumbs on the phone when they are not typing. Therefore, we adjusted the layout as in Fig. 6. We name it CTDR-2 in this paper. Main changes include: "B" was switched to another ring, "D" was moved to the right side of the left ring so that user can extend the left thumb to reach "D", and "C" was moved to be below "D" to match their relative locations in the traditional QWERTY layout.

In Study 1 several participants motioned that they were prone to swipe into the character key next to the target when moving out of the target character key. CTDR-3 was designed to address this issue. Instead of complete inner circles, we modified them to have jagged edges. As shown in Fig. 7, the actual area of each key is smaller than the first concentric circle design, and there are gaps between each pair of adjacent keys as cushions to prevent swiping into neighboring character keys. A concern with CTDR-3 is the size reduced key, which according to Fitt's Law [9], may reduce the speed. The real effect needs to be tested in a study. Moreover, as shown in Fig. 8, CTDR-4 adopts the layout change in CTDR-2 and the jagged edges design in CTDR-3.

5   User Study 2

We conducted the second user study to learn the task performances, and user experiences of the CTT9 variants and CTDR variants. This research is motivated by enabling the view-device-separated text entry for AR glasses. The purpose of the user study is not to compete the performance with any existing text entry method, but rather to verify and optimize the continuous-touch paradigms which separate the user's view from the smartphone as the input device. Therefore, we did not include any baseline method for comparison.

5.1   Study Procedure

We randomly recruited 30 participants for this second user study, aged from 20 to 60, and half of them were female. A small portion of the participants had experience with VR/AR HMDs, while the majority of them did not have any experience. None of them used HMDs daily. Five of them used T9 and QWERTY virtual keyboard equally when they type on smartphones. Seven of them were more used to T9, and the remaining 18 were more used to QWERTY. The study was conducted in an indoor lab. Only the experimenters and the participant were allowed to be present. Social distancing and masks were required to mitigate the risks of COVID-19. The total duration of the study was about 100 min for each subject, including training, performing the task, and a post-task interview.

There were 8 different versions of input interfaces designed. Testing all of them may lead to boredom and exhaustion. Therefore, we randomly divided the participants into two groups of 15 participants each. One group tested within four CTT9 variants. The other group tested within four CTDR variants. The study is within-subjects counterbalanced design. All of the input interfaces were presented to the users in a randomized order.

During the study, the participants went through a training session and a test session for each text entry method. They were required to type 1 sentence in the training session, and 5 in the test session. All the sentences were randomly selected from [11]. They were told that accuracy and speed were equally important. All tasks were not case sensitive. To investigate perceived usability, the participants were asked to respond to SUS questionnaires in between each input method session.

5.2   Measurements

We are interested in investigating the performance in terms of typing speed and error rate, as well as the user experiences in the user study. The independent variable for the metrics below is the type of text entry method.

Words per Minute (WpM): This is a metric that is derived from the number of characters with the following equation, as suggested by MacKenzie [8] and Jiang et al. [6]:

$$WpM = \frac{|S| - 1}{t} \times 60 \times \frac{1}{5} \tag{1}$$

where S is the input string, t is the time spent on the task in seconds, and $(|S| - 1)/t$ is the number of characters entered per second without considering the first input character as suggested by [8]. Then, we multiple this number by 60 s and divide the result by 5 to compute WpM. The number 5 is an estimation of the average length of each word [10].

Corrected Error Rate: This is calculated with the number of errors corrected during the input tasks. In specific, we use Keystrokes per Character (KSPC) as defined in [15]: the number of keystrokes of the input stream divided by the number of characters in the final transcribed text.

Not-Corrected Error Rate: The number of errors remaining after the task divided by the number of keystrokes of the input stream. Levenshtein Distance algorithm is used to calculate the number of errors remaining.

Table 1. Mean values and standard deviations of WpM and KSPC

	CTT9	CTT9-2	CTT9-3	CTT9-4	CTDR	CTDR-2	CTDR-3	CTDR-4
Mean (WpM)	5.516	5.733	5.998	6.434	7.501	7.648	7.732	7.711
SD (WpM)	1.544	1.424	1.576	1.582	1.741	2.063	2.405	1.815
Mean (KSPC)	1.129	1.125	1.104	1.107	1.152	1.093	1.191	1.143
SD (KSPC)	0.07	0.24	0.078	0.063	0.125	0.039	0.132	0.085

5.3 Hypotheses

We wanted to learn if the optimization decisions would improve or worsen the task performances and error rates. We would love to test both tails, therefore we made the following null hypotheses:

Hypothesis 1 (H1): There is no performance and error rate difference among all the variants of CTT9.

Hypothesis 2 (H2): There is no performance and error rate difference among all the variants of CTDR.

5.4 Results

We performed paired t-tests on normally distributed data (numerical data, such as the WpM), Wilcoxon signed rank tests on data that did not have a normal distribution (ordinal data, such as the questionnaires), and Two-Way ANOVA test to find out how the optimization factors affected the measurements, using Bonferroni correction where appropriate. All significant differences found are reported in this section.

CTT9 Results - Overall, we found the novice users performance within CTT9 family achieved a mean value of 6.43 WpM with CTT9-4 and 1.10 KSPC (i.e. Corrected Error Rate) with CTT9-3. In the test of H1, with the paired-T tests we found: 1) subjects reached significantly higher WpM with CTT9-4 compared with the original CTT9 ($t = 2.575$, $p = 0.023$), 2) subjects reached significantly higher WpM with CTT9-4 compared with the original CTT9-3 ($t = 2.203$, $p = 0.046$). No significant differences were found in the KSPC and Not-Corrected Error Rates. Table 1 shows the mean WpMs and KSPC of the CTT9 family and standard deviations.

CTDR Results - Overall, we found the novice users performance within CTDR family achieved a mean value of 7.64 WpM with CTDR-2 and 1.09 KSPC with CTDR-2. In the significance test of H2, we did not find any evidence to suggest the WpMs were statistically different among the variants of CTDR. However, the Two-Way ANOVA test showed a trend at the significant level of 0.1, that the layout adjustments would affect the KSPC ($F = 3.791$, $p = 0.057$). In the paired-t tests we found: 1) the KSPC of CTDR-2 is significantly lower than the KSPC of CTDR-3 ($t = -3.109$, $p = 0.008$), 2) the KSPC of CTDR-2 is significantly lower than the KSPC of CTDR-4 ($t = -2.484$, $p = 0.027$), and 3) although the significance level did not reach 0.05, at the level of 0.1, there was a trend that the KSPC of CTDR-4 is lower than the KSPC of CTDR-3 (t = −1.808, p = 0.093). Table 1 shows the mean WpMs and KSPC of the CTDR family and standard deviations.

Across the Input Interfaces - Moreover, we were also interested in seeing how the designs influenced the task performance and usability across the CTT9 family and CTDR family. Therefore, we conducted a between subjects analysis with unpaired t-tests for the WpM, error rates, and Rank Sum tests for usability questionnaires, with Bonferroni correction where appropriate.

We found: 1) within the 16 comparisons among the CTT9 family and CTDR family (4 CTT9 variants × 4 CTDR variants), we found 14 significant differences. The CTDR family is consistently significantly faster than the CTT9 family in these 14 comparisons at a significance level of 0.05, but 2) surprisingly, with the performance increased, subjects consistently reported better usability with the CTT9 family with a significance level of 0.05.

6 Discussion

Within the CTT9 family, the performance analysis shows that we can reject H1. CTT9-4, which has the dynamic character display and reversed key panel and confirmation panel (i.e., the key panel on the right side), outperformed the original CTT9 design in terms of WpM. Moreover, CTT9-4 outperformed CTT9-3. The difference between CTT9-4 and CTT9-3 is the reversed panels. It is clear that combining the reversed panels and the dynamic character display has improved the WpM of the subjects who use this layout. The effectiveness of solely reversing the panels has been further confirmed by CTT9-4's higher WpM compared with CTT9-3, but the effectiveness of solely applying the dynamic character display has not yet been proved by this study. The questionnaire results were consistent with the objective performance. Subjects said CTT9-4 was less difficult than the original CTT9 and CTT9-3. CTT9-4 was also described as being easier to learn and required less preparation than CTT9-2. We can tell that both optimization decisions of reversing the panels and dynamically displaying the characters on the key may improve the efficiency of CTT9. We believe it is possible that the effects of reversed panels may be associated with the handedness of the study subjects. After reviewing the study participants sample, we found that 28 out of the 30 subjects were right-handed. Whether the effects of the reversed panel were associated with the user's handedness or not is a question to be answered in a future work.

Within the CTDR family, the performance analysis shows that we can reject H2. Although we could not find any significant difference with the metric WpM, we found that CTDR-2, which adjusted the order of the keys of the original CTDR, resulted in lower Corrected Error Rates compared with CTDR-3 and CTDR-4. This strongly suggests that the jagged shape optimization did not work as expected. Between CTDR-3 and CTDR-4, the trend shows the adjusted key layout outperformed the original layout with the jagged shape keys. We found the jagged shape increased the KSPC. The adjusted key order may help to decrease the KSPC, but the evidence is not strong enough. Since no significance is found comparing with the original design, it is difficult to confirm the effectiveness of the optimizations. More studies are needed to verify the optimizations.

Across the CTT9 family and CTDR family, the results were surprising. We found that the CTDR family resulted in significantly higher WpM but was rated significantly lower in the SUS usability questionnaire. We think the CTT9's two-step mechanism may have greatly increased the finger movement length to input a character. According to Fitt's Law [9], the movement distance between key pairs will have an influence on key selection time which in turn will affect the estimated efficiency. The better usability ratings, such as "easier to learn" and "less preparation", probably came from users' familiarity with the original T9 layout. Due to this familiarity, even when the subjects achieved a faster speed with CTDR, they still subjectively thought CTT9's usability was better.

7   Conclusion

We proposed two smartphone touchscreen continuous-touch paradigms to facilitate view-device-separated text entry method for AR glasses, and implemented them as CTT9 and CTDR. CTT9 uses one finger for key selection and the other finger for input confirmation. CTDR uses the same finger for selection and a Refined In-and-Out operation as confirmation. We conducted two user studies to optimize the designs. The results showed that with a population that was majorly right-handed, using the left thumb for confirmation and right thumb for key selection and dynamically changing the characters displayed on a key were effective optimizations for the CTT9 paradigm in terms of typing speed. The jagged shape design of CTDR resulted in more error corrections during the input.

In this paragraph, we provide some design guidelines for future touchscreen-enabled text entry interfaces. First, we believe that with the two-stage confirmation paradigm like CTT9, left and right hand fingers would perform differently on selection and confirmation tasks. Although the handedness association remains to be studied in the future, we think it is optimal to provide users with the option of customizing the side location of the selection and confirmation panels. Second, for the ring-like layout with the in-and-out confirmation paradigm, increasing the size of the keys will reduce the errors made during the text entry tasks. Third, when introducing a new input method, matching users' existing habits will help improve the usability perceived by the users. It is possible the perceived usability may conflict with the objective performances.

In the future, we plan to study more about the research questions raised from this work. First, we want to study the handedness association with the CTT9 panel location. Then, with improved field of view, we want to study how peripheral views impact these text entry methods for AR glasses. The answers to these questions will help us better understand how to build efficient and usable text input methods for AR glasses.

Acknowledgement. The authors would like to thank Chris Vick for proofreading and Baosong Xu and Chao Ren for helping with user studies. The first author was partially supported by a gift grant from OPPO.

References

1. Budhiraja, R., Lee, G.A., Billinghurst, M.: Using a HHD with a HMD for mobile AR interaction. In: 2013 IEEE International Symposium on Mixed and Augmented Reality (ISMAR), pp. 1–6 (2013)
2. Doronichev, A.: Daydream Labs: exploring and sharing VR's possibilities. https://blog.google/products/google-ar-vr/daydream-labs-exploring-and-sharing-vrs/. Accessed 26 July 2021
3. Fashimpaur, J., Kin, K., Longest, M.: Pinchtype: text entry for virtual and augmented reality using comfortable thumb to fingertip pinches. In: Extended Abstracts of the 2020 CHI Conference on Human Factors in Computing Systems (CHI EA 2020), pp. 1–7. Association for Computing Machinery, New York (2020). https://doi.org/10.1145/3334480.3382888
4. Grubert, J., Witzani, L., Ofek, E., Pahud, M., Kranz, M., Kristensson, P.: Text entry in immersive head-mounted display-based virtual reality using standard keyboards. In: 2018 IEEE Conference on Virtual Reality and 3D User Interfaces (VR), pp. 159–166 (2018)
5. Gugenheimer, J., Dobbelstein, D., Winkler, C., Haas, G., Rukzio, E.: FaceTouch: enabling touch interaction in display fixed UIs for mobile virtual reality. In: Proceedings of the 29th Annual Symposium on User Interface Software and Technology (UIST 2016), pp. 49–60 (2016)
6. Jiang, H., Weng, D.: HiPad: text entry for head-mounted displays using circular touchpad. In: 2020 IEEE Conference on Virtual Reality and 3D User Interfaces (VR), pp. 692–703 (2020)
7. Lee, Y., Kim, G.J.: Vitty: virtual touch typing interface with added finger buttons. In: Virtual, Augmented and Mixed Reality, pp. 111–119 (2017)
8. MacKenzie, I.S.: A note on calculating text entry speed. https://www.yorku.ca/mack/RN-TextEntrySpeed.html. Accessed 26 July 2021
9. MacKenzie, I.S.: Fitts' law as a research and design tool in human-computer interaction. Hum.-Comput. Interac. **7**, 91–139 (1992)
10. MacKenzie, I.S., Soukoreff, R.W.: Text entry for mobile computing: models and methods, theory and practice. Hum.-Comput. Interac. **17**(2–3), 147–198 (2002)
11. MacKenzie, I.S., Soukoreff, R.W.: Phrase sets for evaluating text entry techniques. In: Extended Abstracts on Human Factors in Computing Systems (CHI 2003), pp. 754–755. CHI EA 2003 (2003)
12. Mankoff, J., Abowd, G.D.: Cirrin: a word-level unistroke keyboard for pen input. In: Proceedings of the 11th Annual ACM Symposium on User Interface Software and Technology (1998)
13. Millette, A., McGuffin, M.J.: Dualcad: integrating augmented reality with a desktop GUI and smartphone interaction. In: 2016 IEEE International Symposium on Mixed and Augmented Reality (ISMAR-Adjunct), pp. 21–26 (2016)
14. Misra, S., Singha, J., Laskar, R.H.: Vision-based hand gesture recognition of alphabets, numbers, arithmetic operators and ascii characters in order to develop a virtual text-entry interface system. Neural Comput. Appl. **29**(8), 117–135 (2018)

15. Soukoreff, R.W., MacKenzie, I.S.: Metrics for text entry research: An evaluation of MSD and KSPC, and a new unified error metric. In: Proceedings of the ACM Conference on Human Factors in Computing Systems (CHI 2003) (2003)
16. Surale, H.B., Gupta, A., Hancock, M., Vogel, D.: TabletInVR: exploring the design space for using a multi-touch tablet in virtual reality. In: Proceedings of the 2019 CHI Conference on Human Factors in Computing Systems, pp. 1–13 (2019)
17. Walker, J., Li, B., Vertanen, K., Kuhl, S.: Efficient typing on a visually occluded physical keyboard. In: Proceedings of the 2017 CHI Conference on Human Factors in Computing Systems, pp. 5457–5461 (2017)
18. Whitmire, E., et al.: DigiTouch: reconfigurable thumb-to-finger input and text entry on head-mounted displays. Proc. ACM Interact. Mob. Wearable Ubiquitous Technol. **1**(3) (2017)
19. Xu, W., Liang, H.N., Zhao, Y., Zhang, T., Yu, D., Monteiro, D.: RingText: dwell-free and hands-free text entry for mobile head-mounted displays using head motions. IEEE Trans. Visual. Comput. Graph. **25**(5), 1991–2001 (2019)
20. Yu, C., Gu, Y., Yang, Z., Yi, X., Luo, H., Shi, Y.: Tap, dwell or gesture? exploring head-based text entry techniques for hmds. In: Proceedings of the 2017 CHI Conference on Human Factors in Computing Systems, pp. 4479–4488 (2017)
21. Yu, D., Fan, K., Zhang, H., Monteiro, D., Xu, W., Liang, H.N.: PizzaText: text entry for virtual reality systems using dual thumbsticks. IEEE Trans. Visual. Comput. Graph. **24**(11), 2927–2935 (2018)
22. Zhu, F., Grossman, T.: BISHARE: exploring bidirectional interactions between smartphones and head-mounted augmented reality. In: Proceedings of the 2020 CHI Conference on Human Factors in Computing Systems (CHI 2020), pp. 1–14 (2020)

Tracking and Rendering (Scientific Session 3)

A Simulation System for Scene Synthesis in Virtual Reality

Jingyu Liu[1]([envelope]) [iD], Claire Mantel[1] [iD], Florian Schweiger[2] [iD],
and Søren Forchhammer[1] [iD]

[1] Technical University of Denmark, Kgs. Lyngby 2800, Denmark
{jing,clma,sofo}@fotonik.dtu.dk
[2] BBC Research and Development, London W12 7TQ, UK
florian.schweiger@bbc.co.uk

Abstract. Real-world scene synthesis can be realized through view synthesis or 3D reconstruction methods. While industrial and commercial demands emerge for real-world scene synthesis in virtual reality (VR) using head-mounted displays (HMDs), the methods in the literature generally do not target specific display devices. To meet the rising demands, we propose a simulation system to evaluate scene synthesis methods in VR. Our system aims at providing the full pipeline of scene capturing, processing, rendering, and evaluation. The capturing module provides various input dataset formulations . The processing and rendering module integrates three representative scene synthesis methods with a voluntary performance-aid option. Finally, the evaluation module supports traditional metrics as well as perception-based metrics. An experiment demonstrates the use of our system for identifying the best capturing strategy among the three degrees of foveation tested. As can be expected, the FovVideoVDP metric (based on a model of the human visual system) finds the highest degree of foveation giving best results. The three other quality metrics from the evaluation module (which use features to measure similarity) confirm that result. The synthetic scenes in the experiment can run in VR with an average latency of 5.9 ms for the two selected scenarios across the tested methods on Nvidia GTX 2080 ti.

Keywords: View synthesis · 3D reconstruction · Virtual reality

1 Introduction

In recent years, virtual reality (VR) as a novel display and interactive platform has made many experimental manifestations possible in the field of media. Synthesis of real-world scenes in VR with high-fidelity, for example, is an active

This project has received funding from the European Union's Horizon 2020 research and innovation programme under Marie Skłodowska-Curie Grant Agreement No. 765911 (RealVision). Special thanks to BBC Research & Development for providing the dataset and the consultancy of scene synthetic methods.

P. Bourdot et al. (Eds.): EuroXR 2021, LNCS 13105, pp. 67–84, 2021.
https://doi.org/10.1007/978-3-030-90739-6_5

research topic. A complete scene synthesis pipeline for VR includes steps of data capturing of the real-world scene, data processing, and synthetic scene rendering in VR. The literature on 3D reconstruction or view synthesis usually covers only a part of the pipeline, furthermore the methods are relatively general-purpose and lack adaptation and/or optimization for VR. In addition, it is complex to a priori identify the best scene synthesis method for a specific application scenario, due to the lack of VR-tailored evaluation mechanisms. Thus in practice, to have a VR-tailored integrated solution for scene synthesis is an open question.

To access this question, in this paper, we present a scene synthesis system for VR through a simulation test-bed built upon a game engine (Unreal). The system aims to provide a solution for users to screen various scene synthesis methods on the dataset to be tested. A virtual capturer in our system can help the users with dataset simulation (which will generate computer graphics images), users can also capture dataset as real-world photographs using cameras and input into our system. A VR-tailored evaluation module in our system can score the methods to provide users with perception-based objective assessments.

The structure of this paper is as follows: Sect. 2 summarizes scene synthesis methods in the literature. Section 3 designs the system with the following four aspects in mind: 1. Input dataset with different features, 2. Geometric proxies and their pros and cons, 3. Texturing and rendering methods with an adaptation and/or optimization for VR, and 4. Objective metrics and their feasibility across various geometric proxies. Section 4 details the implementation of the system for the four major modules: capturing, processing, rendering, and evaluation. Section 5 describes an experiment that demonstrates an application of our system: evaluating the quality for different scene synthesis methods in regard to the capturing strategy for the input dataset. (The simulated input datasets for the experiment are computer graphic images). Finally, Sect. 6 discusses the system with a future work. An illustration of the pipeline is depicted in Fig. 1.

The main contributions of the paper are:

– A VR-tailored simulation system integrates a whole pipeline of scene synthesis of capturing, processing, rendering and evaluation, with adaptations and/or optimizations to the selected representative scene synthesis methods.
– An experiment that gives objective scores to compare different capturing strategies for the input dataset for the scene synthesis methods with four quality evaluation metrics, including a HVM-based metric FovVideoVDP.

2   Related Work

2.1   Scene Synthesis Methods

In this paper we choose to categorize the scene synthesis methods according to the way of processing the geometry of the scene. Since the subsequent rendering method for the view synthesis will be affected by the geometric proxy. Thus the methods are subdivided into three categories: without, explicit and implicit geometric proxy restoration. Richardt et al. [22] updated a similar categorization

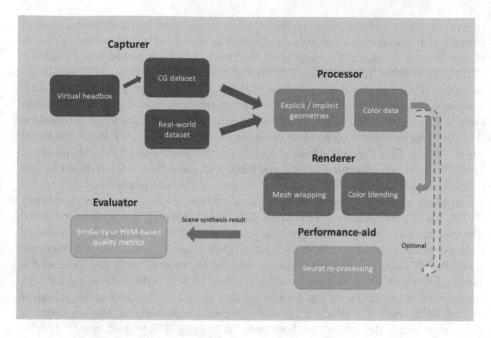

Fig. 1. Pipeline illustration of our simulation system.

in the form of continuum which was proposed by [25]. The synthesis approach without geometric proxy represents a collection of pure image-based rendering (IBR) methods. Explicit geometric proxy reconstruction means that the geometric information is presented in the form of a 3D mesh, i.e. a collection of point cloud or triangles, while implicit geometric proxy restoration means that the geometric information is stored in an intermediate data structure. While different geometric proxies can sometimes be convertible, the purpose of this categorization is mainly to guide the design and optimization of different processing and rendering pipelines in Sect. 3.

A typical scene synthesis method without geometric proxy is through *light field* [11] or *lumigraph* [7] rendering. This IBR method realizes purely through view synthesis. Another improved version of light field rendering is proposed in [2] as unstructured light field rendering (ULR). In general IBR-based methods suffer from artifacts that they can not align objects with different depths. Panorama or omni-directional stereo (ODS) is another solution without geometric proxy widely applied in VR scene synthesis. However, it only has three degree of freedom (DoF) without parallax. Luo et al. [14] and Bertel et al. [1] brought parallax into ODS, however the enhanced motion parallax is limited.

Photogrammetry [5] refers to the solutions with explicit geometric proxy. The advantage of the photogrammetry is that once the geometry of the scene is reconstructed, users truly have 6 DoF to observe novel views in the reconstructed synthetic scene. However, to output a high-definition synthetic scene, photogrammetry needs to create models with dense meshes, which is challenging in practice. For instance, Quixel [9] builds a single asset with around 1 million polygons. It means that the polygon budget of a reconstructed scene will be of the order of billions, i.e. far more than the overhead of VR rendering. *COLMAP* [23,24] is another photogrammetry method that draws upon structure-from-motion (SfM) and multi-view stereo (MVS). Compared to Quixel, COLMAP sacrifices the accuracy of the geometric reconstruction in exchange for time efficiency. Artifacts can be seen as holes and seams in the reconstructed 3D meshes. Another representative method to reconstruct explicit geometry is unstructured point clouds. This data structure is an intermediate state of COLMAP pipeline. However, in other implementations, together with color information, point clouds can also be the final explicit geometry output of 3D reconstructions [27].

Implicit geometric proxy restoration methods, such as per-view geometry [8,19], multi-plane images (MPI) [4,17,31], voxels [13] etc., is worth an extended discussion. The reason is that it is more consistent with the goal we want to achieve: scene synthesis in VR with high-fidelity novel views, but not accurate geometries. Thus the geometric proxy should be treated as a medium, not a target. Overbeck et al. [19] proposed a method that is light-field-based with an implicit local geometric proxy generated and stored. Note that as an inheritor of the light field, [19] made a special-designed camera rig as the capturer to retrieve a dense dataset with thousands of images. Mildenhall et al. [4] alleviates the data density by utilizing machine learning: with a learned gradient descent, the implicit geometric proxy is represented as MPI. The method even supports photo-realistic reconstruction for volumetric effects like fire with only a sparse light field dataset. In addition to still scenes, dynamic scenes reconstruction is also supported with an upgraded multi-sphere images (MSI) geometric proxy. However, novel views can only be synthesized over a limited baseline, i.e. an inside-out experience will be hard to achieve. Mildenhall et al. [18] utilizes volume as an alternative to voxel as its geometric proxy. It defines 5D neural radiance fields (NeRF) (3D for location and 2D for direction), which can handle complex materials, detailed geometries, and multiple depths. Wizadwongsa et al. [29] (NeX) supports view-dependent effects that are derived by reflectance coefficients adapted in its model, while the method can realize view synthesis in real-time. Note that while neural network-based geometric proxies can provide better synthesis quality, they are not necessarily the best choice for VR. Since the information of the trained geometry is stored in a checkpoint structure. On the one hand, reading the information from the checkpoint and then generating a synthetic view may not be in a real-time manner (such as NeRF). On the other hand, even if the method can generate synthetic view in real-time from the original network (such as NeX). There is no reliable solution to directly process the result to VR displays.

2.2   System Integration and Methods Evaluation

In addition to the discussion of scene reconstruction methods, Dupont et al. [3] provides a toolkit from the perspective of system design, which is a good reference for our work. However, the design of the evaluation module of the system is relatively simple and can be further improved.

Pixel-based image quality metrics such as PSNR is still applied in the latest scene synthesis methods such as [29]. However, for scene synthesis applications, perceptual image similarity metrics are required - as suggested by [12] - which analyze more the high-level similarity (or structural similarity) between images, rather than pixel-to-pixel differences.

In addition, there is no preference for specific display devices when comes to evaluation of the scene synthesis methods in general. However, whether a direct application of traditional metrics can really reflect the perceptual quality for scene synthesis in VR is worth questioning. VR devices are very different from desktop displays regarding to parameters such as lens distortion, resolution, field of view (FoV), distance from the screen, and shielding of ambient light sources. Especially, due to the large FoV, the visual acuity feature in the human visual model (HVM) is worthy of attention in perceptual quality. As it is focused on visualization on HMDs through both display modeling and inclusion of differentiated center/periphery aspects in the HVM, the recent FovvideoVDP metric from [15] is very relevant.

3 Design

To design a good simulation system, various factors should be considered: 1. What scene capturing patterns should be included? 2. How different geometry proxies can adapt to the platform? 3. What rendering methods should be implemented? 4. What metrics are geometric proxy independent and can be VR-tailored? etc. In this section, the questions above will be addressed.

3.1 Data Capturing

Realizing a virtual capturer is the main focus for our capturing module design, which simulates a real-world camera set up. Considering the real-life application scenarios, limited data types can be obtained from commercial cameras, of which a vast majority produce RGB images. Additionally, as a test-bed, we can also generate a ground truth depth map for users' reference and calibration.

When designing the set up of the virtual capturer, on the one hand, it should meet the needs of an immersive VR experience (i.e. an inside-out experience for the major cases). On the other hand, users should be able to toggle the configuration of the capturer (i.e. camera parameters, capturing density, capturing pattern, etc.). In our design, we use a *datapoint* to represent a piece of capturing, and we call the region in a scene that datapoints distribute and cover as *headbox*. To support various scene synthesis methods, a datapoint can be either a cube-map or an image, with or with out a corresponding depth map. The configuration of the virtual capturer will reflect the complexity of the setup in real-life. For example, a uniformly distributed sampling implies high calibration requirements while a random distributed sampling represents a more casual setup. Besides, to simulate the photograph as much as possible, we need to make full use of a high-definition rendering pipeline in the synthetic test-bed. Features such as ray-traced ambiance occlusion, reflection, and refraction should be enabled for capturing to restore geometry, lighting, and material information of the scene.

3.2 Geometric Proxies

Different geometric proxies have each their advantages and disadvantages, and we must especially consider their applicability in VR. While an explicit geometric proxy stored in a data type such as .obj is natively supported by most game engines, usually implicit geometric proxies need to be further converted into application-friendly data structures to utilize game engines' VR-ready rendering pipeline, and corresponding rendering strategies are required.

We first consider improving a photogrammetry method and adapted it to our system. COLMAP is a good baseline that has been widely applied due to its open-source and continuous maintenance. Note that we only use partial of the functions, which are the camera poses restoration from SfM and depth estimation and mesh reconstruction from MVS. The explicit global 3D mesh and implicit per-view meshes can be branches from the utilization of the COLMAP modules (i.e. the explicit global 3D mesh is reconstructed from MVS, with the fusion to generate point cloud that eventually turns to a 3D mesh from triangulation; The per-view meshes are reconstructed from the per-view depth maps from local depth estimation with triangulation). Note that we only use COLMAP for the reconstruction of geometric proxies, for texturing we will bring up an optimized solution (in Sect. 3.3). In addition, we can make a calibration based on the features of our simulation system (we have the ground truth of camera poses and scene depth) on top of COLMAP's solution.

A state-of-the-art neural-network-based view synthesis method that supports view-dependent effect pretty well is NeX [29], which we choose to implement in our design. However, as mentioned the neural network model cannot be directly streamed into VR. Therefore, in order to represent the implicit geometric proxy that is trained from neural network and stored in the form of checkpoints, we need to do some conversion. The detailed implementation is introduced in Sect. 4.3.

3.3 Rendering Methods

First we can discuss the texturing method for explicit 3D meshes. A direct texture mapping applied on top of a global mesh can be unsatisfactory since view-dependent effects such as reflections are not supported because they will be averaged out in the textures, in other words, all pixels in the textures are default to be diffuse. Here we consider using a classic multi-view-based blending method ULR to restore the view-dependent effects. However, a straightforward ULR method can be performance intensive for VR as [3] suggests, thus an optimization should be applied.

Disk-based texturing (DBT), originally proposed by [19], is the texturing method we choose for implicit pre-view proxies. As the textures are sampled to the viewing direction, DBT also supports view-dependent reflection and highlight. An extra benefit is that DBT was brought up for VR experience in its original purpose. The disk-shaped texturing window can reduce the per-view texture sampling overhead, which is performance friendly.

In NeX, the MPI geometry and the reflectance coefficients it adopts bring in unique advantages in reconstructing transparent surfaces with refraction compared with the methods discussed above. To render the mesh converted from the checkpoints, we need to figure out the color of vertices in the runtime. The detailed implementation is introduced in Sect. 4.4.

3.4 Evaluation

Identifying the relevant objective quality metrics is the focus while designing the evaluation module. The following requirements are considered: 1. Appropriate metrics should be independent from the geometric proxy. 2. Ideally, quality metrics should be VR-tailored to reflect the real experience.

The first requirement has already screened out many scene synthesis evaluation metrics since they focus on evaluating the reconstructed explicit geometries proxies itself. Metrics applied for images and rephotography are found to be better fits. Besides, for VR-tailored evaluation, perceptual image similarity metrics are required, as suggested by [12]. We found that FovVideoVDP [15] is a good fit since it is not only perception-based, but also take features in HVM into consideration. If the conditions are relaxed and not to consider HVM features, MS-SSIM [28] and LPIPS [30] can also be taken into our model. All these metrics were designed to evaluate more the high-level similarity between images, rather than pixel-to-pixel differences such as PSNR, and therefore they are more consistent with our system. Metrics such as 1-NCC discussed in [26] is a good supplement. All those metrics require the registration of the synthetic views with a reference. With the camera poses restored by SfM, the selected ground truth input can be compared with the synthetic view setting to the corresponding camera pose in the evaluation.

4 Implementation

In this section, we explain the details of implementing our design into a simulation system. First, we introduce the platform for our implementation. Then we break down the system into four modules: 1. A capturing module that generates a user-defined dataset from synthetic scenes. 2. A processing module that inputs the user-defined data and outputs user-selected geometric proxies. 3. A rendering module that inputs geometric proxies from the processor and outputs synthetic views in VR with the corresponding rendering methods. 4. An evaluation module that takes a random or user-selected reference view, and outputs the score of the corresponding synthetic view. The overview of the pipeline is illustrated in Fig. 1.

4.1   Platform Introduction

The system has been implemented on top of the Unreal engine. Our implementation utilizes the engine's libraries for shaders. The reason why we chose Unreal is because it has good built-in support for VR, furthermore, game engines support various 3D model types, which endorse our implementations for geometric proxies. Note that choosing to implement a system on game engines means we rely on the platform's resource management, which may not always provide the best performance.

4.2   Capturer

Our virtual capturer realized with blueprints in Unreal. We utilized the built-in command-line "High Resolution Screenshot". Note that in our implementation, we have enabled the ray-tracing-related functions in the engine to get the photo-realistic capturing results. We also accessed to depth buffer for ground truth depth map acquisition.

According to the parameters input by the users, the virtual capturer generates a datapoint distribution. Corresponding datapoints will be dumped into the hard disk. The specific parameters that can be set by users are shown in Table 1. The options define the configuration of virtual capturer from different dimensions. Most options function as the name suggests. For datapoints density ρ, we define a term *cone density*, which means the average angle difference (υ) between the adjacent two datapoints in either θ or ϕ axis in the polar coordinate. The smaller the υ is, the denser the datapoints is. For *pattern*, uniform distribution for a sphere follows a cosine-based hemisphere sampling [20] which applies an inversion method that generates uniformly sampled random values ξ_1 and ξ_2 that fall in the range of the FoV trigonometric (if FoV is set, otherwise the value ranges $[0, 1)$). Then apply the inverse cumulative distribution functions (CDF) to obtain θ and ϕ. Finally convert from polar space to Cartesian space. The pattern for the uniform cuboid sampling follows a similar logic, but instead of using inverse CDFs to get θ and ϕ, u and v values are obtained, and there is no extra need for coordinate transformation. If the pattern is set to "foveated", we implement a method that introduced in [16] which is kernel based foveation: The random values ξ_1 and ξ_2 stand for the samplings for the two axis in polar space. From ξ_1 and ξ_2 we have Eq. 1.

$$
\begin{aligned}
y &= \exp(\frac{\log(\sqrt{2})\xi_1^{\omega}}{2}) \cdot \cos(\pi\xi_2) \\
z &= \exp(\frac{\log(\sqrt{2})\xi_1^{\omega}}{2}) \cdot \sin(\pi\xi_2) \\
x &= \sqrt{1 - (y^2 + z^2)}
\end{aligned}
\tag{1}
$$

Where ω is the kernel parameter indicate how the datapoints spread across correlated to foveation. xyz are the normalized datapoint location taking $(0, 0)$ as the origin. When sampling, skip the yz pairs fall out of the unit circle when it is "sphere" type.

Note the datapoints distribute on the surface of the headbox. For sphere, the datapoints' direction is the outward normal of the spherical surface; For cuboid, the datapoints' direction is the outward normal of the faces.

In principle, by using this capturing module, users can generate datasets as they were camera-captured photographs.

Table 1. Parameters for the main modules

(a) Capturing module		(b) Processing & rendering module	
Parameters	Description	Parameters	Description
$shape$	cuboid / sphere	$cali_c$	calibrate SfM camera poses
$type$	panorama/ forward-facing	$cali_d$	calibrate MVS depth map
$depth$	capture depth	th_c	NeX cube marching threshold
$pattern$	uniform / foveated		
res	datapoint resolution	Parameters	Description
o	headbox center	n	# of textures / meshes for blending
ρ	datapoints density by υ	$disk$	DBT blending disk radius
r	diameter / side length	th_o	NeX occlusion check threshold
FoV	optional for forward-facing	α, d	pruning parameters

4.3   Processor

In our processing module, we first implemented an SfM interface, linked to the SfM command lines of COLMAP. After running SfM, camera poses are recovered. All the three geometric proxies our system supports require this step. As we have the ground truth of the virtual camera poses, user can optionally use the ground truth camera poses as the known poses in the COLMAP function for a calibration. We have provided a function for a conversion from left-hand z-up coordinates used by Unreal to right-hand y-up coordinates that is required by COLMAP. From our observations, the camera poses restored from the native COLMAP SfM on our synthetic dataset is worse than a restore from the real-world photographs, so a calibration is recommended. One possible reason is that even if we enabled physical-based rendering functions in Unreal, the rendering results are still quite different from real-world photographs, which may cause errors in feature detection and matching in SfM.

From here, the processor branches to get different geometric proxies. For generating explicit global 3D meshes, we use COLMAP's MVS module for stereo patch matching, dense points fusion and eventually using Delaunay triangulation to generate a 3D mesh in a .ply format. For generating implicit per-view meshes, we utilized the depth maps estimated from each camera pose in MVS. Our implementation is straightforward: instead of using COLMAP to fusion an integrated global mesh, we do a fusion for every depth map to get local meshes. After the reconstruction, per-view meshes are stored as a set of .ply files. Besides, if the user chose to store depth maps from capturing, there is an option to opti-mize the depth map reconstruction in the MVS: We subtract the reconstructed depth map from the ground truth (i.e. use the ground truth value to replace the value that exceeds the error threshold). Note that we cannot directly use the ground truth depth map to do the fusion, since the depth information of translucent objects is eliminated in the game engine's depth buffer.

For neural network models, geometry information from the checkpoints needs to be re-translated into mesh, i.e. from the 3D space occupancy probability provided in the model to a collection of vertices. NeX does not have a native support for this type of conversion. But we can find references from [18] and [21]: divide the whole 3D space into cubes, and do a cube marching that compares the occupancy probability (σ) with a threshold to determine if there is a vertex at the location within the cube. After traversing the cubes in the scene, we finally get a collection of vertices as the converted mesh.

The parameters for users to experiment for the processing module are listed in Table 1.

4.4   Renderer

For our rendering module, since it is running upon game engines, the imple-mentation is based-on shaders. We have implemented three rendering shaders: ULR on explicit global mesh, DBT for per-view meshes and NeX renderer for the vertices collection. We have made VR adaptations and/or optimizations for the three methods based on their original design and implementation.

For the original ULR method, all the source images (i.e. textures) can be candidates to contribute in texturing vertices. A brute force implementation is with computation complexity of $O(n^2)$, which can be performance intense for complex scenes with large number of triangles. In our implementation, we design a checklist to pre-filter the vertices versus textures:

- check the boundary: check if vertices' projection fall out of the uv boundary of the texture.
- check the occlusion: an occlusion is likely to happen when the vertices pro-jected depth and the data from the depth map differ a lot (i.e. 20 engine units).
- check the normal: check if the vertices and texture are backward-facing.

If any of the case happens, the texture will never contribute to the vertices in the runtime rendering. The record of the pre-filtering is stored by an offline processing. With our optimization, the runtime rendering for ULR achieve better performance since traverse got canceled for unpaired vertices and textures.

At runtime, given the novel view's transform, assign the weights to the n most relevant textures. Textures closer to the novel view's transform will be assigned a higher weight, since textures closer to the camera have higher resolution, and the color trace back from the ray looking at a similar direction is also similar in the common cases. (It is not necessarily applicable to complex BRDF and occlusion, which brings in a drawback for the blend-based texturing method.) The color for the vertices are the blended color from the selected textures. Note only the textures passed the above checklist contribute in blending for some vertices.

Disk-based blending is applied upon per-view meshes. The method is adapted from [19]. At runtime, per-view meshes are wrapped when overlap (transform of the vertices blend). The wrapping weight for the meshes is based on their original camera poses' relative transform to the novel view, which is logically similar to the texture weighting mechanism applied in ULR. While the per-view meshes participating in the mesh wrapping for the novel view have their corresponding textures, a disk is set for masking the textures. Only the vertices whose uv map within the disk are rendered out to save the rendering budget. All the disks add together to complete the novel view. When the radius of the disk is too small, there will be holes and seams; When the radius is too large, there will be blurry artifacts as more disks overlap.

The logic to render NeX vertices is similar to the process we applied for ULR, except for how to check an occlusion, as there is no depth map reconstructed from NeX for cameras. However, we still can find a way to check if an occlusion happens in between a pair of camera and vertex: check the σ function on the ray from the camera to the vertex. For all the steps along the ray, if all the steps' σ are lower than the threshold, we think there's no occlusion in between, on the contrary, if any of the step's σ is higher than the threshold, the vertex is occluded from the camera.

We adapt a pruning method to approach the target fps. The pruning works when fps drops with 2 mechanisms:

- Partial of the vertices that projected to the outer most α degree of the novel view skip rendering for the current frame.
- Partial of the vertices that are far away than the threshold d from the novel view skip rendering for the current frame.

Both α and d are adjustable. Using the pruning, we can handle the occasional fps drops.

As the previous modules, parameters that can be tweaked for rendering are listed in Table 1.

4.5 Performance Aid

However, if the synthetic scene is too complex with a large number of triangles, the pruning method can help a little. Rendering the synthetic scene directly in VR will still be disturbed by low fps. Here, we introduce another option to further boost VR performance. We adopt a method to re-process and simplify the synthetic scene while maintaining fidelity, which is called *Seurat* [6,10]. The pipeline of Seurat goes through a headbox re-define, data re-capturing, re-processing, and rendering. Seurat uses cubemap as the datapoint. In addition to RGB, Seurat also requires the depth map, thus it is only applicable when an explicit geometric proxy (i.e. a global 3D mesh) is selected for the scene synthetic method. After the RGB-D cubemaps re-capturing, Seurat generates a layer of quad tiles that roughly represent the 3D mesh from a combination of depth maps. Along with the quad tiles, Seurat generates a corresponding texture atlas. Eventually, quad tiles and texture atlas are combined to reconstruct an simplified scene.

In the process of integrating Seurat, we re-write its out-dated capturing module with the same "High Resolution Screenshot" function that we applied in our pipeline. In this way, the adapted Seurat can provide the correct result. A comparison is illustrated in Fig. 2.

(a) Reference   (b) Adapted Seurat re-   (c) Native Seurat recon-
                            construction   struction

Fig. 2. Comparison of the reference test scene and the scene reconstructed by Seurat.

5   Experiment

After implementing all the modules, our system is ready to be tested. Here we provide an experiment towards a research question: what is the relationship of input datapoints' pattern and the perceptual quality of the synthetic views when considering the eccentricity in visual acuity in the HVM?

5.1   Synthetic Datapoints Setup

The synthetic scene we prepared as a test-bed completely replicates a bar in the real-world. For the purpose of investigating the raised question, we have a headbox set up in the scene, which is called "Gallery". The headbox contains diffuse surfaces with some glossy objects. As for the capturing parameters, the headbox is forward-facing sphere type, with a radius of 100 engine unit, a resolution of 1024×1024, and a FoV of $120° \times 180°$ (H × W). (This FoV is the approximate inadvertent visual range when the head moves at will.) First we use a preliminary test to figure out a balanced datapoints density that can maintain a good perceptual quality level while saving the processing time with the target FoV. We set different level of v of the density parameter ρ in the headbox and run COLMAP to generate corresponding explicit 3D meshes, and observe if there are major seams or holes in the mesh. Then to investigate the research question, with an adequate v set for cone density, we set the pattern of datapoints on different level of ω. We have a top-view illustration of the datapoints as shows in Fig. 3:

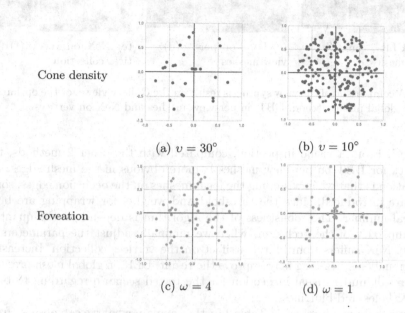

(a) $v = 30°$ (b) $v = 10°$

(c) $\omega = 4$ (d) $\omega = 1$

Fig. 3. Sampling density and pattern illustration. v stands for the angular cone density, and ω stands for the level of foveation: the larger the level, the more even the distribution is.

5.2 Objective Metrics

For the objective metrics implemented in the system, FovVideoVDP can fit the experiment's well best, because it is the only metric that takes into account the gaze point on the view and the HVM features such as eccentricity in visual acuity in its model. Therefore, for the evaluation of this experiment, FovVideoVDP metric is the target metric while other metrics are for the reference.

5.3 Results

For the preliminary test for finding an adequate ρ for a FoV of $120° \times 180°$. An visual inspection shows that at a level of $v = 20°$, the seams and holes become minor in the reconstructed explicit 3D mesh which indicate the turning point of an adequate density.

Figure 4 illustrates the scene synthesis result from the three methods we implemented in the system (i.e. ULR on global mesh, DBT on per-view meshes, and NeX on vertices collection) for the research question in selected views from

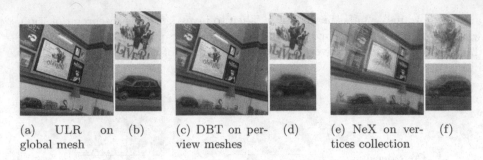

(a)   ULR   on   (b)   (c) DBT on per-   (d)   (e) NeX on ver-   (f)
global mesh   view meshes   tices collection

Fig. 4. A comparison of the view synthesis result on the Gallery views for the optimized ULR on global mesh method, DBT on per-view meshes and NeX on vertices.

"Gallery". From a visual inspection, compared with the other 2 methods, the drawback for DBT on per-view meshes is more obvious in the mesh edges. An explanation is that when wrapping the local meshes on the occlusion edges, some errors are introduced, since the threshold and weights for wrapping are both empirical number. The robustness of the algorithm is depend on the quantity and complexity of the occlusions when we manually adjust the parameters in practice. NeX suffers from blurry artifact on the vertices collection. Increasing epochs number in training may improve the result. ULR on global mesh presents a best result under visual inspection for the tested scenario regarding to both seams & holes and blurriness.

The metrics results show in Table 2 further explain what we can observe from a visual inspection. The colors map a scale of blue-white-red for each metric, with blue meaning better quality and red worse quality. MS-SSIM shows high scores (i.e. above 0.87) for all the dataset patterns among the tested methods, which indicates a good structural similarity in general for the scene synthesis methods implemented in our system. Lower LPIPS scores indicate that the ULR on global mesh has a better perceptual quality which is important for VR applications. FoVVideoVDP and 1-NCC both give a better score for ULR on global mesh. Since these two metrics are good indicators for rephotography methods. All the metrics provide a consistent evaluation, in general, we can say ULR on global mesh provides a better reconstruction in our system for the tested scenario.

For the evaluation towards the capturing pattern, we focus on the scores from FoVVideoVDP since that is the most relevant score for HVM-based features such as eccentricity in the visual acuity. FovVideoVDP uses Q_{JOD} (just-objectionable-difference score) to quantify the quality. We asked FovVideoVDP to take the center pixel in the view as the gaze point across the evaluation. As we can see from Table 2, when the ω is lower, the datapoints are more concentrated in the importance sampling for foveation. The corresponding score is equivalent or better then the higher ω patterns for the method ULR on global mesh and DBT on per-view meshes. As for the exception value for $\omega = 2$ in NeX on vertices collection, it may be related to specular datapoints' contribution, repeated experiments may average the singular value out. However, the score difference

Table 2. Quality scores for the selected novel view in gallery

	FovVideoVDP	LPIPS	MS-SSIM	1-NCC	
$\omega = 1$	8.722	0.102	0.98	0.811	ULR
	7.18	0.257	0.901	0.798	DBT
	7.01	0.243	0.877	0.736	NeX
$\omega = 2$	8.618	0.148	0.974	0.801	ULR
	7.161	0.265	0.905	0.784	DBT
	7.1	0.259	0.883	0.747	NeX
$\omega = 4$	8.609	0.104	0.973	0.805	ULR
	7.064	0.263	0.899	0.776	DBT
	6.885	0.278	0.874	0.705	NeX

is minor, suggesting that the pattern for capturing may not contribute to the perceptual quality as much as other parameters such as density.

Frame Timing with Performance Aid. We also performed a frame timing test with performance aid module enabled. Result shows the re-processing can maintain a good fidelity within the headbox (Fig. 2). The original scene has 1.3 m triangles in total. With the ray-tracing refraction enabled for high-definition rendering, the average rendering latency on a high-end computer (with Nvidia GTX 2080 Ti) is around 43 ms. In the reconstructed scene from Seurat, the total triangle number downsized to 72k, and we got an average latency of 5.9 ms in VR on the same PC.

6   Discussion

At present, modules in our system are applied in the form of actor blueprints in Unreal. We have realized that the system needs further integration - better to be in the form of a integrated plug-in for the game engine. As Dupont et al. [3] did for Unity.

We have obtained more robust geometric proxies through the calibration in our capturing and processing modules. A manual calibration in the dataset capturing to filter out the datapoints with features less than 200 from entering into the following pipeline is suggested. By experiments we found images with less than 200 feature points sometimes cause an error in the following mesh reconstruction with wrong mapping among other features.

For NeX modelling, in its original implementation, the training time for a 17 images dataset with a 4000 high epoch runs for 18 h [29]. For the practical reason, we had to decrease the training epoches. Coupled with the information loss in the adaptive conversion to integrate the model to Unreal, the quality scores in our system for NeX are lower than the scores they reported.

As for the evaluation module, it can be further tailored for VR. Since fps can determine a comfortable VR experience, integrate a temporal metric has the potential to support spatial-temporal quality evaluation for VR.

If we push our system to dynamic scenes, much interesting content is coming along. However, it requires geometric proxies to be temporal consistency. Also there will be a much stricter requirement for the accuracy as human sensitivity to perceptual effects over time is high, e.g., any flickering at the edges of objects on a geometry reconstruction is particularly noticeable.

7   Conclusion

In this paper we presented a system that used four modules to integrate a whole pipeline of scene synthesis for VR. The capturing module was calibrated for better pose restoration, which supported both real-world photographs and synthetic images. The processing and rendering module adapted and/or optimized three representative scene synthesis methods with various geometric proxies, in which the neural-network-based method NeX became available for VR with our adaptation. The evaluation module was VR-tailored, based on HVM, perceptual quality, structural similarity, and rephotography. In addition, we provided an optional performance-aid module for performance-intense use cases. The proposed system can be widely applied in scene synthesis for VR and support further research.

We have proved the practicability of the system by demonstrating the pipeline through an experiment studying which of the tested capturing strategies performs best. Experimental metrics evaluations indicate that the foveation capturing pattern performs best when applied on the tested scenario.

References

1. Bertel, T., Campbell, N.D.F., Richardt, C.: MegaParallax: casual 360° panoramas with motion parallax. IEEE Trans. Visual. Comput. Graph. **25**(5), 1828–1835. https://doi.org/10.1109/TVCG.2019.2898799
2. Buehler, C., Bosse, M., McMillan, L., Gortler, S., Cohen, M.: Unstructured Lumigraph Rendering. In: Proceedings of the 28th Annual Conference on Computer Graphics and Interactive Techniques (SIGGRAPH 2001), pp. 425–432. ACM, New York, NY, USA (2001). https://doi.org/10.1145/383259.383309, http://doi.acm.org/10.1145/383259.383309
3. Dupont De Dinechin, G., Paljic, A.: From real to virtual: an image-based rendering toolkit to help bring the world around us into virtual reality. In: 2020 IEEE 6th Workshop on Everyday Virtual Reality (WEVR). Atlanta, March 2020. https://hal.archives-ouvertes.fr/hal-02492896

4. Flynn, J., et al.: DeepView: View Synthesis With Learned Gradient Descent, pp. 2367–2376 (2019)
5. Foster, S., Halbstein, D.: Integrating 3D Modeling, Photogrammetry and Design. Springer, London (2014). https://doi.org/10.1007/978-1-4471-6329-9
6. googlevr: Seurat (2019). https://github.com/googlevr/seurat
7. Gortler, S.J., Grzeszczuk, R., Szeliski, R., Cohen, M.F.: The lumigraph. In: Proceedings of the 23rd Annual Conference on Computer Graphics and Interactive Techniques (SIGGRAPH 1996), pp. 43–54. Association for Computing Machinery (1996). https://doi.org/10.1145/237170.237200
8. Hedman, P., Ritschel, T., Drettakis, G., Brostow, G.: Scalable inside-out image-based rendering. ACM Trans. Graph. Assoc. Comput. Mach. **35**(6), 231:1–231 (2011). https://doi.org/10.1145/2980179.2982420
9. Jonathan: Are there high-poly source meshes? (2018). https://help.quixel.com/hc/en-us/articles/115000604189-Are-there-high-poly-source-meshes-
10. Lall, P., Borac, S., Richardson, D., Pharr, M., Ernst, M.: View-region optimized image-based scene simplification. Proc. ACM Comput. Graph. Interact. Tech. **1**(2), 26:1–26:22 (2018). https://doi.org/10.1145/3233311, https://doi.acm.org/10.1145/3233311
11. Levoy, M., Hanrahan, P.: Light field rendering. In: Proceedings of the 23rd Annual Conference on Computer Graphics and Interactive Techniques (SIGGRAPH 1996), pp. 31–42. ACM. https://doi.org/10.1145/237170.237199, https://doi.acm.org/10.1145/237170.237199
12. Lin, W., Jay Kuo, C.C.: Perceptual visual quality metrics: a survey. J. Vis. Commun. Image Represent. **22**(4), 297–312. https://doi.org/10.1016/j.jvcir.2011.01.005, http://www.sciencedirect.com/science/article/pii/S1047320311000204
13. Liu, L., Gu, J., Zaw Lin, K., Chua, T.S., Theobalt, C.: Neural sparse voxel fields. In: Larochelle, H., Ranzato, M., Hadsell, R., Balcan, M.F., Lin, H. (eds.) Advances in Neural Information Processing Systems. vol. 33, pp. 15651–15663. Curran Associates, Inc. (2020). https://proceedings.neurips.cc/paper/2020/file/b4b758962f17808746e9bb832a6fa4b8-Paper.pdf
14. Luo, B., Xu, F., Richardt, C., Yong, J.: Parallax360: Stereoscopic 360° scene representation for head-motion parallax. IEEE Trans. Visual. Comput. Graph. **24**(4), 1545–1553. https://doi.org/10.1109/TVCG.2018.2794071
15. Mantiuk, R.K., et al.: Fovvideovdp: a visible difference predictor for wide field-of-view video-supplementary material. ACM Trans. Graph. **40**, 1–19 (2021)
16. Meng, X., Du, R., Zwicker, M., Varshney, A.: Kernel foveated rendering. Proc. ACM Comput. Graph. Interact. Tech. **1**(1), 1–20 (2018)
17. Mildenhall, B., et al.: Local light field fusion: practical view synthesis with prescriptive sampling guidelines. In: ACM Transactions on Graphics (TOG) (2019)
18. Mildenhall, B., Srinivasan, P.P., Tancik, M., Barron, J.T., Ramamoorthi, R., Ng, R.: Nerf: Representing scenes as neural radiance fields for view synthesis. In: ECCV (2020)
19. Overbeck, R.S., Erickson, D., Evangelakos, D., Pharr, M., Debevec, P.: A system for acquiring, processing, and rendering panoramic light field stills for virtual reality. ACM Trans. Graph. **37**(6), 197:1–197:15 (2018). https://doi.org/10.1145/3272127.3275031, https://doi.acm.org/10.1145/3272127.3275031
20. Pharr, M., Jakob, W., Humphreys, G.: Physically Based Rendering: From Theory to Implementation. Morgan Kaufmann, San Francisco (2016)
21. Quei-An, C.: Nerf_pl: a pytorch-lightning implementation of nerf (2020). https://github.com/kwea123/nerf_pl/

22. Richardt, C., Tompkin, J., Wetzstein, G.: Capture, reconstruction, and representation of the visual real world for virtual reality. In: Magnor, M., Sorkine-Hornung, A. (eds.) Real VR - Immersive Digital Reality: How to Import the Real World into Head-Mounted Immersive Displays, pp. 3–32, LNCS, Springer International Publishing (2020). https://doi.org/10.1007/978-3-030-41816-8_1
23. Schönberger, J.L., Frahm, J.M.: Structure-from-motion revisited. In: Conference on Computer Vision and Pattern Recognition (CVPR) (2016)
24. Schönberger, J.L., Zheng, E., Pollefeys, M., Frahm, J.M.: Pixelwise view selection for unstructured multi-view stereo. In: European Conference on Computer Vision (ECCV) (2016)
25. Shum, H.Y., Chan, S.C., Kang, S.B.: Image-Based Rendering. Springer Science & Business Media, google-Books-ID: 93J3Z96ZVwoC
26. Waechter, M., Beljan, M., Fuhrmann, S., Moehrle, N., Kopf, J., Goesele, M.: Virtual rephotography: novel view prediction error for 3D reconstruction. ACM Trans. Graph. **36**(1), 8:1–8:11 (2016). https://doi.org/10.1145/2999533
27. Waechter, M., Moehrle, N., Goesele, M.: Let there be color! large-scale texturing of 3D reconstructions. In: Fleet, D., Pajdla, T., Schiele, B., Tuytelaars, T. (eds.) ECCV 2014. LNCS, vol. 8693, pp. 836–850. Springer, Cham (2014). https://doi.org/10.1007/978-3-319-10602-1_54
28. Wang, Z., Li, Q.: Information content weighting for perceptual image quality assessment. IEEE Trans. Image Proces. **20**(5), 1185–1198 (2011). https://doi.org/10.1109/TIP.2010.2092435
29. Wizadwongsa, S., Phongthawee, P., Yenphraphai, J., Suwajanakorn, S.: Nex: real-time view synthesis with neural basis expansion. In: IEEE Conference on Computer Vision and Pattern Recognition (CVPR) (2021)
30. Zhang, R., Isola, P., Efros, A.A., Shechtman, E., Wang, O.: The unreasonable effectiveness of deep features as a perceptual metric, pp. 586–595 (2018)
31. Zhou, T., Tucker, R., Flynn, J., Fyffe, G., Snavely, N.: Stereo magnification: learning view synthesis using multiplane images. Comput. Vis. Patt. Recogn. **37**(4), 65:1–65:12 (2018). https://doi.org/10.1145/3197517.3201323

Pose Tracking vs. Pose Estimation of AR Glasses with Convolutional, Recurrent, and Non-local Neural Networks: A Comparison

Ahmet Firintepe[1,2](✉), Sarfaraz Habib[1], Alain Pagani[3], and Didier Stricker[2,3]

[1] BMW Group Research, New Technologies, Innovations,
Garching (Munich), Germany
{Ahmet.Firintepe,Sarfaraz.Habib}@bmwgroup.com
[2] TU Kaiserslautern, Kaiserslautern, Germany
[3] German Research Center for Artificial Intelligence (DFKI),
Kaiserslautern, Germany
{Alain.Pagani,Didier.Stricker}@dfki.de

Abstract. In this paper, we analyze various outside-in approaches for pose tracking and pose estimation of AR glasses. We first provide two frame-by-frame pose estimation approaches. The first one is a VGG-based CNN, while the second method is the state-of-the-art, ResNet-based AR glasses pose estimation method named GlassPoseRN. We then introduce LSTMs in the mentioned approaches to achieve AR glasses pose tracking. We compare methods with and without non-local blocks, which are theoretically promising for Pose Tracking as they consider non-local neighbor features in one image and among multiple images. We further include separable convolutions in some networks for comparison, which focus on maintaining the individual channels and therefore the triple images. We train and evaluate seven different algorithms on the HMDPose dataset. We observe a significant boost on the dataset from pose estimation to tracking approaches. Non-local blocks do not improve our performance further. The introduction of separable convolutions in our recurrent networks results in the best performance with an estimation error of 0.81° in orientation and 4.46 mm in position. We reduce the error compared to the state-of-the-art by 76%. Our results suggest a promising approach for more immersive AR content for AR glasses in the car context, as high a 6-DoF pose accuracy improves the superimposition of the real world with virtual elements.

Keywords: Augmented Reality · Pose tracking · Deep learning

1 Introduction

In recent years, Augmented Reality (AR) applications started to flourish in many new scenarios, and the simple laboratory or indoor experiments have extended

© Springer Nature Switzerland AG 2021
P. Bourdot et al. (Eds.): EuroXR 2021, LNCS 13105, pp. 85–106, 2021.
https://doi.org/10.1007/978-3-030-90739-6_6

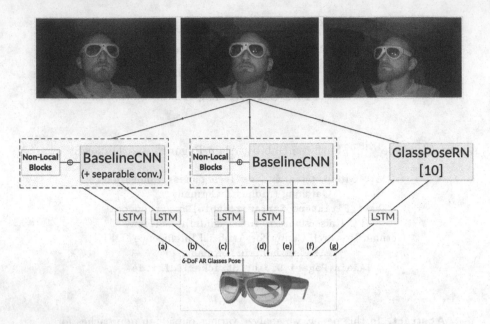

Fig. 1. An overview of our evaluation. We compare seven different pose estimation and tracking approaches on triple images of the HMDPose dataset: (e) and (f) show the baseline, frame-by-frame pose estimation methods, (f) being the state-of-the-art Glass-PoseRN [13] approach. In (d) and (g), we introduce LSTMs to the baseline approaches. (c) depicts the standard CNN with non-local blocks and an LSTM. (b) shows a CNN variant with separable convolutions and an LSTM, while (a) extends the approach with non-local blocks.

to much more challenging use cases. In general, in order to ensure a convincing experience, it is paramount to localize the used smartphone or AR glasses with a high precision in its environment. Usually, this is required in a highly accurate and latency-free way. Smartphones are more error-tolerant regarding tracking, as they are equipped with video-see-through displays. They have the advantage of frequency and speed adjustment of the real world shown through the display. AR glasses steadily matured over the years and are currently being used in the industry. In the future, consumer adaptation of AR glasses is highly likely. In contrast to smartphones, AR glasses mostly consist of optical-see-through displays, where the real world is perceived directly by the wearer. This elevates the latency and accuracy requirements for a realistic experience (Fig. 1).

As larger AR glasses usually come with RGB or depth sensors and IMUs to enable inside-out tracking, it is the standard for pose estimation in static environments. In dynamic environments like airplanes or cars, IMUs register both head and vehicle movement. Thus, it is relatively challenging to utilize them in a standalone manner. In the case of a car driver, the optical sensors register mostly parts of the outside world, which delivers a limited set of features of the car interior for tracking.

In this scenario, outside-in tracking becomes a valuable option for tracking. Outside-in tracking is done frequently in case of head pose estimation. Similar algorithms can be deployed for pose estimation of Head-Mounted Displays as done for head pose estimation. The head pose is different from the AR glasses, as the relation between head and glasses differs from user to user. This relation can change with slight glasses movement on the wearer's head. Thus, it is necessary to estimate the AR glasses directly. Algorithms adjusted to handle different types of glasses models can enable scalability to new types of models. Thus, tracking AR glasses through external sensors placed inside a car can lead to a wider adoption of AR glasses in cars.

Even though depth information improved pose estimation quality in recent works on pose estimation [2, 4, 39], they are still more costly than RGB or infrared (IR) cameras. Due to the changing lighting conditions in a driving scenario, RGB cameras can output significantly varying images. However, IR cameras come in handy due to their property of being less sensitive to change by lighting conditions compared to RGB images.

Recent works on AR glasses pose estimation [13, 14] on the HMDPose dataset [12] have shown accurate results for the pose estimation from a single and multi-view images, but did not attempt to use temporal coherence in the pose estimation. Our idea is to exploit the temporal continuity of the video sequences given in the dataset by proposing new learning-based pose tracking algorithms. We introduce five different alternatives taking advantage of the present continuous data. We first present Recurrent Neural Networks (RNNs) based on VGG- and ResNet backbones. We then introduce non-local blocks into our methods, a novel type of Neural Network maintaining object properties over time [37]. To the best of our knowledge, we are the first to use them in the pose estimation and tracking context. We furthermore introduce separable convolutions [7] into our networks for comparison. We finally evaluate them on the HMDPose dataset, where we compare them with CNN-only frame-by-frame methods, including the state-of-the-art "GlassPoseRN" method.

In detail, our contributions are:

- We present seven approaches based on combinations of three Neural Network categories for AR glasses pose estimation and tracking: convolutional, recurrent, and non-local Neural Networks.
- We introduce non-local blocks in our methods, being the first to utilize them for pose estimation. Additionally, we evaluate networks with separable convolutions instead of normal convolutions.
- We evaluate our approaches on the HMDPose dataset, where we outperform the state-of-the-art and reduce the error by 76%. Our detailed comparison of various methods enables us to recommend certain network types for AR glasses tracking.

In the remainder of the paper, we discuss the related work on object pose estimation and RNN-based pose estimation in Sect. 2. We present our AR glasses pose estimation and tracking techniques in Sect. 3. In Sect. 4, we discuss our evaluation on the HMDPose dataset, comparing our models against the state-of-the-art approach benchmarked on the dataset.

2   Related Work

In this section, we review recent work on pose estimation from camera images. Some approaches either work with intensity images or depth maps or combine different data modalities.

2.1   Object Pose Estimation

6-DoF pose estimation approaches can primarily be divided into two categories. One category is direct pose regression, where the image is taken to estimate a pose directly by a Neural Network. The second category must first detect 2D targets and 2D-3D Object correspondence and then solve for Perspective-n-Point (PnP) problem for the 6-DoF pose. We shortly summarize methods for both categories.

The approaches that first detect the targeted object in the given image and subsequently solve a PnP problem for their 6-DoF pose, mostly dominate the state-of-the-art work in object pose estimation. In this category, keypoints-based and 2D-3D correspondence methods are popular. The keypoint-based methods either use the keypoints from the object's surface [28,34,35] or directly predict the 2D projections from 3D models of the object using furthest point algorithm [6,26,33]. The dense 2D-3D correspondence methods predict the corresponding 3D model point for each 2D pixel of the object and later use the PnP to get the 6-DoF pose [22,25,40]. Some methods also use additional networks to further refine the pose by using cropped images of an object.

However, adding processes like keypoints or other landmarks extraction involves chances of introducing errors. An alternative for 6-DoF pose estimation of an object is to regress it directly based on the image information only. PoseNet [19] introduces a deep CNN to estimate the 6-DoF camera pose based on a single RGB image as input. The network can predict the pose in an end-to-end manner with real-time performance. They argue that training individual networks to regress position and orientation separately performed poorly compared to when they were trained with full 6-DoF pose labels. PoseCNN [38] decouples the problem of pose estimation into estimating the translation and orientation separately. It uses a pre-trained VGG network [32] as a backbone for feature extraction and splits into three output branches. Two fully convolutional branches estimate center directions and the depth for every pixel of the image. The third branch consists of a ROI pooling and a fully connected architecture that regresses a quaternion describing the rotation for each region of interest. PoseConvCNN [5] further developed a fully convolutional architecture evolved from PoseCNN [38], and rather than ROI-based orientation prediction, they perform pixel-wise quaternion prediction, keeping the translations and ROI exactly the same from PoseCNN [38]. Recently, Peng et al. [26] also removed the ROI pooled orientation prediction branch and used 2D keypoints predicted using Hough-based voting to estimate the pose, creating a hybrid between the two major categories. In this approach, the ground truth 3D keypoints are generated using 3D models of target objects. The direct estimation of 3D rotations information is difficult because of the non-linear rotation space. For this reason, other works avoid introducing pose refinement steps after directly estimating poses from monocular images. Li et al. [21] present a render and compare technique as a pose estimation step that improves the estimation only using the original RGB input. Although this can lead to accurate results, the pose refinement procedure requires additional computing time.

Regarding our specific use case of AR glasses pose estimation based on IR images, Firintepe et al. [13] developed and tested various methods on the HMD-Pose dataset. Their first method named "GlassPose" is a VGG-based CNN. They separate the estimation into two branches, estimating the orientation on cropped images of the head while using the full images for translation prediction. Their second approach "GlassPoseRN" is based on a ResNet-18 backbone, predicting the full 6-DoF pose based on the full images, outperforming GlassPose by a large margin. Another AR glasses pose estimation approach derives point clouds from IR images for further pose estimation [14]. A network was trained on triple IR input images in a semi-supervised fashion to generate a self-centered point cloud and to estimate the 3D position of the cloud. After training, the network can extract the point cloud representation from a single IR input image. Two pose regressors called P2R and P2P were proposed to estimate the rotational and translational poses given the point clouds. In P2R, a backbone extracts features followed by a rotation estimation module consisting of convolutional and dense layers. The predicted output represents the rotation in the 4D quaternion. In P2P, the model is extended with a voting process used to identify keypoints and extract descriptor vectors. The descriptive keypoints are fed to rotation and translation estimation modules to get the final 6-DoF pose.

We choose to compare our methods to the GlassPoseRN algorithm, as it performs better than the benchmarked state-of-the-art Regression via Classification head pose estimator [1] and a point cloud based object pose estimator named CloudPose [15] on the HMDPose dataset [13,14].

2.2   RNN-Based Pose Tracking

An alternative to frame-by-frame pose estimation is 6-DoF pose tracking based on RNNs. Inspired by You Only Look Once (YOLO) [29], Ning et al. [24] propose Rotated Logging (ROLO), in which LSTMs are used to learn sequential information in the high-level visual features with the region information. They use YOLO to learn features from images and detect objects' bounding boxes in the images. These extracted features and detected regions are then fed into the LSTM. ROLO only used the regression capability of RNN in the temporal domain and not its temporal correlation. Considering this, Zhang et al. [41] predict directions first based on RNN and later use the direction of the next frame to reduce the search for ROI. Once the search area is reduced, the object is detected only in that area. They perform this by utilizing a direction prediction model based on RNNs and a detection model later for tracking.

Several works in object pose estimation specifically focus on the head as an object. As our work is closely related to head pose tracking, we further discuss related work in head pose estimation using RNNs. Most of the works used particle filters with face image renderer to track faces [23]. However, these filters require complex, problem-specific design and feature tuning. Work from Gu et al. in [16] presents a comparison between Bayesian filtering and RNNs while proposing an RNN-based approach to solve the tracking problem. They use a VGG network to regress the head pose Euler angles. Instead of improving single frame prediction by modifying the network structure, it focuses on using an RNN to improve pose prediction by leveraging the time dimension. They evaluate their work on a synthetic dataset as well as a real-world dataset. Borghi et al. [3] propose to utilize stream of depth images and perform 3-DoF pose estimation of the head, especially for in-car automotive applications. The principle idea is to utilize time information on the depth-based images and directly estimating the Euler angles. Head detection and localization are not performed in this work, and they assume that the head center is already provided. They utilize this to first crop the head part from the input images and only use it to train the proposed network. They mostly use a shallow architecture with L_2 training loss. The method achieved good results on Biwi dataset [10] and was implemented in a car which shows its real-time feasibility. Similarly, Peng et al. in [27] used spatial-temporal data and RNNs for sequence-based facial tracking without facial landmarks.

Camera pose tracking is an intrinsic part of visual odometry, where several works have focused on CNN and LSTM combinations for pose tracking [8,36,42]. Wang et al. [36] and Constante [8] deploy CNNs with consecutive LSTMs to extract continuous poses based on RGB video input. Zou et al. [42] present a self-supervised learning method for visual odometry with special consideration for consistency over longer sequences. They model the long-term dependency by using a pose network that features a two-layer convolutional LSTM module. All methods use CNNs developed for Optical Flow estimation as their backbone. One typical backbone is FlowNet [9]. The extracted features are then fed into the LSTMs for further pose regression.

In contrast to the state-of-the-art, we propose several novel Neural Network concepts combined with LSTMs for AR glasses pose tracking. For the first time, we introduce separable convolutions, non-local blocks, or a combination of both to achieve improved tracking accuracy. Both concepts are promising for our multi-view, continuous data. Especially non-local blocks have not been used for 6-DoF pose tracking, despite its interesting property of learning the long-range object dependencies in video sequences. Based on this comparison of various novel concepts on AR glasses pose tracking, we can make recommendations for our use case.

3 AR Glasses Pose Estimation and Tracking Architectures

3.1 AR Glasses Dataset and Preprocessing

To conduct our analysis, we use the HMDPose dataset [12]. HMDPose is a large-scale data glasses dataset, consisting of around 3 million 1280 × 752 pixel images. It contains IR images from three different perspectives of four different AR glasses, worn by 14 different subjects.

We first downscale the images 320×188 and normalize them. Next, the images from different views from the same timestep are stacked together channel-wise. This increases the information space for the neural network to learn from. We present different neural network architectures based on CNNs and RNNs trained on IR images to perform AR glasses pose estimation. We create sequences from these multi-view images using the individual frames' timestamp as required by RNN-based networks. The data split acquired while sequence generation is used for all the networks, CNNs or RNNs. Figure 2 gives an overview of the pipeline of pre-processing such sequences. We train and evaluate various networks based on single frames and sequences to regress the 6-DoF pose of AR glasses.

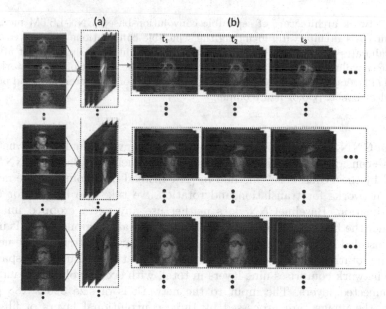

Fig. 2. Our pipeline to conduct sequence generation from multi-view IR images for LSTM-based methods. (a) We first stack IR images channel-wise and then (b) generate sequences of the stacked images according to their timestamp.

3.2   CNN Baseline Methods

We benchmark two networks that only utilize CNNs to see the effect of learning by using spatial information only. The networks are called "BaselineCNN" and "GlassPoseRN". GlassPoseRN is a deeper model containing a ResNet-18 backbone compared to BaselineCNN. The two networks act as our baseline to compare with our networks based on RNNs.

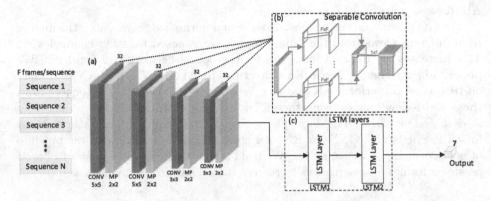

Fig. 3. Network architecture of separable convolution-based CNN-LSTM model. (a) shows our CNN architecture, including the separable convolutions highlighted in (b), which elaborates on their working principle [7]. The light green layers right after the separable convolutions are max pooling layers. In (c), the output of the network is fed into LSTM layers, performing estimation of the orientation in quaternions and position in Euclidean space. (Color figure online)

BaselineCNN. Our first approach is a basic convolutional neural network, which we consider as our baseline. We name this method "BaselineCNN". It is inspired by the "GlassPose" method in [11]. Instead of decoupling the network into subnetworks for translation and rotation, we take one branch for 6-DoF pose estimation. BaselineCNN does neither use any extra cropped images of glasses nor the bounding box of glasses in the translation subnetwork. It utilizes full downscaled images to regress the 6-DoF pose per frame triple. The network learns the rotations in quaternion space and translation in Euclidean space.

The network comprises nine layers in total, with six convolutional and three fully connected layers. The input to the network is of size 320×188 pixels. Initially, the images are processed by three convolutional layers of filter size 5×5, each having 32 neurons followed by a max pooling layer of 2×2. The remaining three convolutional layers have a filter size of 3×3. The fourth and fifth convolution layers have a hidden size of 32, while the sixth convolution layer has 128 neurons. Only the fourth layer has a consecutive max pooling layer. In the end, the fully connected layers of sizes 128, 80, and 7 neurons are used to regress the 6-DoF pose.

GlassPoseRN. We benchmark the state-of-the-art pose estimation "Glass-PoseRN" [11] approach of the HMDPose dataset. We compare our methods to the GlassPoseRN method, as it performs better than the benchmarked Regression via Classification head pose estimator [1] and a point cloud based object pose estimator called CloudPose [15] on the HMDPose dataset [13,14]. It also shows better results than the point cloud-based P2P method [14]. We retrain this network on our 80/10/10 data split. We give more details on our data split in Subsect. 3.5. The model consists of a ResNet-18 [17] backbone. GlassPoseRN maintains information and feature within the building blocks of ResNet with skip connection as described in [17]. The ResNet-18 block of the network is followed by two dense layers of size 256 and 64 with a final output layer which regresses the translation and orientation together.

3.3 LSTM-Based Approaches

As an alternative to the models mentioned above, we introduce RNN-based networks to compare the convolution and recurrent operations. The idea is to exploit the temporal information in the data by introducing RNNs in the network. Our custom-built hybrid CNN-RNN model utilizes this enhanced spatio-temporal feature space to learn the glass pose in an improved way. CNNs can learn the spatial information avoiding feature engineering, while RNNs avoid manual engineering of object tracking logic, which can be prone to errors. They learn the temporal information directly from the data. Hence, a hybrid model could achieve enhanced AR glasses pose estimation.

We use LSTMs as our RNN variant due to their ability to avoid vanishing gradient problem and the poses time-dependent property. The LSTMs map the pose estimation per frame in a sequence to the sequence of known ground truth poses.

CNN-LSTM. The first hybrid model is referred to as "CNN-LSTM". The CNN part of the network extracts optimal features from the IR images, and LSTM tracks the extracted features as sequences. Therefore, the features from a single triple image in a sequence act as one time step for LSTM. The designed model takes a sequence of IR images as input and outputs continuous 6-DoF pose of AR glasses, tracking the pose in all the frames of a sequence.

The architecture consists of only six layers in total. The CNN part is kept identical to BaselineCNN to enable a fair comparison. The CNN consists of four layers where each is followed by max pooling layer of 2×2. Two convolutional layers have a filter size of 5×5, and the remaining two layers have a filter size of 3×3. The hidden size of each layer is 32 neurons. The features from the CNN are flattened before using it as an input to the LSTMs. The LSTM network comprises two layers, each having 128 neurons. The dense layers are used as the output layers to regress the continuous 6-DoF pose of AR glasses.

SepConv-LSTM. This method introduces a more efficient network by utilizing depthwise separable convolutions instead of normal convolutions. Depthwise separable convolutions [7] are a special type of convolutions in which convolution operations are separately applied to channels. The information from multiple channels in the input is not mixed together, which are the different views of the triple images in our case. Pointwise convolutions increase the depth of the output to be further processed. Separable convolutions increase efficiency by decreasing the number of computations. They are also used in standard architectures like MobileNet [18].

Figure 3 shows an overview of the architecture, referred as "SepConv-LSTM". The network architecture remains the same as CNN-LSTM. Only normal 2D convolution layers are replaced with separable convolutions. Table 1 highlights the difference in parameters, showing the reduction of approximately 40,000 parameters using separable convolutions.

Table 1. Size and parameter comparison of CNN-LSTM and SepConv-LSTM.

Network	Total parameters
CNN-LSTM	3,849,575
SepConv-LSTM	3,808,274

GlassPoseRN-LSTM. The next LSTM-based model is the GlassPoseRN method coupled with LSTMs. This model is designed for spatio-temporal data. The LSTM at the end of the network learns from the temporal information and is used in a regression manner to predict continuous 6-DoF AR glasses pose. We call this model "GlassPoseRN-LSTM". The model is built over the ResNet-18 architecture as in GlassPoseRN. The reason for using the same backbone is to compare the effect of RNNs and CNN-based methods.

The GlassPoseRN model is modified by removing the three dense layers from the end and adding the LSTM layers. It is done by first adding a global average pooling layer right after the ResNet blocks to reshape the feature maps. This pooling layer is followed by the two LSTM layers with 128 neurons each. In the end, a dense layer is used to regress the translation and rotations, making it a layer of 7 neurons.

3.4 RNN with Non-local Blocks

In previous sections, convolutional and recurrent operations were used to build networks due to our data modality's nature. This subsection describes a novel neural network architecture based on non-local operations. Non-local operations help in learning long-range dependencies in the video sequence. Wang et al. [37] introduced non-local filtering as general operations in a neural network as a building block to learn the non-local neighbourhood information and long-range

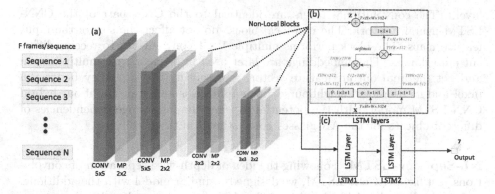

Fig. 4. Network architecture of non-local block-based CNN-LSTM model. (a) shows our CNN architecture, including the non-local layers highlighted in (b), which elaborates on their working principle [37]. In this block, $\otimes$ denotes matrix multiplication and $\oplus$ represents element wise addition. The light blue box within non-local block represents the $1 \times 1 \times 1$ convolutions. In (c), the output of the network is fed into LSTM layers, performing estimation of the orientation in quaternions and position in Euclidean space. (Color figure online)

dependencies. Before introducing this variant, learning the long-range dependencies was done by either repeatedly deep stacking convolutional operations with large receptive fields or deep stacking of recurrent operations consecutively. This multi-hop dependency with deep stacked networks, however, is hard to model and difficult to optimize making it an inefficient and computationally expensive solution.

NL-CNN-LSTM. We alter our hybrid CNN-LSTM model by adapting non-local blocks in the CNN part of the network. The convolution and recurrent layers only consider the local neighbourhood of a given pixel position while learning features from the input and the fully connected layers lose the positional correspondence. Hence, the long-range dependencies between the sequenced IR frames and even the non-local neighbor pixels within one frame are missed. Therefore, non-local blocks add the capability to learn this non-local information within a single frame and between multiple frames of a sequence to the network.

The network is designed by modifying the CNN-LSTM architecture. The change includes the addition of non-local blocks in a conventional convolutional network part to experiment with their performance in an LSTM-based network. The architecture is visualized in Fig. 4. The light blue blocks in the figure represent the location of where the non-local blocks are inserted. Due to limited computation resources and a large image resolution size, the non-local block is not inserted after the first convolutional layer, despite it potential benefit to the overall network. The architecture is kept similar to the CNN-LSTM architecture to keep a fair comparison between the two models. This network consists of six layers with four convolutional layers, three non-local blocks, and two LSTM layers. The convolutional layers are identical to the CNN part of the CNN-LSTM neural network. The non-local blocks do not affect the size of the input feature maps. The block performs multiple 1×1 convolutions to receive different embeddings. The embeddings are later used in element-wise multiplication and get the final output feature vector, representing the similarity between a pixel and its non-local neighbours. This approach is an extension of our hybrid CNN-LSTM model, with the potential to learn the long-range dependencies of different objects for the AR glasses pose estimation task.

NL-SepConv-LSTM. Following the idea of depth-wise separation of convolutions just like SepConv-LSTM, we designed a similar model with the additional inclusion of non-local blocks. As non-local blocks are introduced to learn non-local neighbor features [37], by their inclusion in our network, we aim to learn the non-local neighbor features from separate views.

The architecture of the network remains the same as NL-CNN-LSTM, which we described in the previous subsection. The only change is the replacement of normal convolution layers by separable convolutions. We call this network "NL-SepConv-LSTM".

Fig. 5. Example triple images of the four AR glasses models included in the HMD-Pose [12] dataset. It includes the four glasses models a) Mini Augmented Vision, b) Everysight Raptor, c) Microsoft Hololens 1, and d) North Focal Generation 1.

3.5   Network Training

Our training, validation, and test split is 80% for training and 10% for validation and test set. In contrast to the 94/3/3 split used in [13], more extensive test and validation sets are required, as sequencing data comes with the loss of frames. For this reason, we train the GlassPoseRN method again on our data split to enable comparability with our LSTM-based models. We split the dataset for all individual glasses types as well as for individual subjects. For the CNN baseline methods, the dataset is being shuffled.

We train our models with an Adam optimizer with the initial learning rate $\alpha = 0.01$. The learning rate is scheduled to decrease if the validation loss has not improved for more than ten epochs. For our RNN-based neural networks, sequences are generated by stacking the frames, sorted according to the times-tamp. Our activation function for all layers besides the output layer is the ReLU activation. We deploy a linear activation for the output layers.

We use the weighted L_2 Euclidean distance for translation and orientation. The loss function is based on Kedall et al. [20] and is defined as follows:

$$Loss = \beta||t - \tilde{t}||_2 + ||q - \frac{\tilde{q}}{||\tilde{q}||}||_2 + \gamma||q|| \tag{1}$$

q and t describe the ground truth quaternion and translation, whereas $\tilde{q}$ and $\tilde{t}$ represent the estimated quaternion and translation. We normalize the predicted quaternion and compute the Euclidean distance to the ground truth quaternion. It is important to note that regularization parameter γ and the norm of the predicted quaternion are added in the loss to cater to any large predictions. In addition, the Euclidean distance is being computed for the translation. The translation is weighted accordingly through the scaling factor β to have similar scaling to the orientation before adding the orientation loss, which we set empir-ically. We train all networks on two NVIDIA GeForce 2080Ti GPUs for 200 epochs for all glasses combined and individually. All the networks are trained on full images down-scaled to 320×188 pixels. The initial learning rate is set to 0.001 and scheduled to 50% decrease after every 10 epochs if the validation loss has not improved from previous best loss. The batch size used for CNN base-line methods is 128, while, for RNN-based methods, a sequence length of 8 and batch size of 32 was utilized while training. The trained networks can predict an absolute 6-DoF pose per frame, up to a pose per sequence of 8 frames.

4   Evaluation

4.1   Dataset and Evaluation Metrics

We conduct the training and evaluation of our approaches on the HMDPose dataset [12]. The large-scale multi-view IR dataset HMDPose contains around 3 million images with AR glasses pose annotations, resulting in 1 million image triples. The dataset has been recorded with 14 different subjects, wearing four different AR glasses models each. It includes the four glasses models Everysight Raptor, Microsoft Hololens 1, North Focal Generation 1, and Mini Augmented Vision (Fig. 5). In our paper's evaluation, we refer to the Everysight Raptor as EVS, Hololens 1 as HOLO, North Focal Generation 1 as NORTH, the Mini Aug-mented Vision glasses as MAV, and all glasses combined as ALL for readability. There are around 250,000 image triples per glasses model available.

We benchmark our results on the same metrics as Firintepe et al. [13], with one exception. We consider the Mean Absolute Error (MAE) and the Root Mean Squared Error (RMSE) for orientation. An additional metric is the Bal-anced Mean Angular Error (BMAE), which takes the unbalanced amount of the full range of head orientations by introducing sections [11,30,31] into account. Despite its interesting insight into a networks' performance over the complete range, we exclude this metric, as the section definition is invalid for sequenced data. This would implicate the definition of ranges per sequence, where the sample size is too small to represent the test set. We use the L_2 loss for the position error on all axes separately and together for the position estimation.

4.2 Results

Frame-by-Frame Pose Estimation Approaches. We benchmark two frame-by-frame pose estimation methods for comparison. The first network is our GlassPose-inspired BaselineCNN, the second network being the state-of-the-art "GlassPoseRN" approach. They are the only networks formed on convolutional operations only, so they cannot work on sequential data. Table 2 and 4 lists all orientation results of all methods on our data split. We trained and tested both approaches on all individual glasses as well as combined. BaselineCNN achieves

Table 2. Rotation results of the Frame-by-Frame Pose Estimators BaselineCNN and GlassPoseRN [13] as well as our LSTM-based Pose Trackers CNN-LSTM, SepConv-LSTM, NL-CNN-LSTM, NL-SepConv-LSTM, and GlassPoseRN-LSTM on the given error metrics in degrees. The Everysight Raptor is referenced as EVS, Hololens 1 as HOLO, North Focal Generation 1 as NORTH and the Mini Augmented Vision glasses as MAV. ALL stands for all glasses combined. The average value of all three axes is given on the defined metrics in this table. The full results including the errors regarding roll, pitch, and yaw can be seen in the end of the document in Table 4.

Glasses-type	Metric	Frame-by-frame pose estimation		LSTM-based pose tracking				
		Baseline-CNN	GlassPose-RN [13]	CNN-LSTM	SepConv-LSTM	NL-CNN-LSTM	NL-SepConv-LSTM	GlassPoseRN-LSTM
EVS	MAE	2.62	1.79	**0.74**	0.76	0.76	1.27	1.34
	RMSE	3.95	2.71	**0.77**	0.79	0.80	1.34	1.43
MAV	MAE	2.71	2.25	0.81	0.79	0.82	**0.78**	1.22
	RMSE	3.94	3.26	0.84	**0.82**	0.85	**0.82**	1.37
HOLO	MAE	2.75	3.31	0.94	**0.86**	0.97	2.57	1.67
	RMSE	4.63	4.82	0.97	**0.90**	1.01	2.68	1.77
NORTH	MAE	2.47	1.40	**0.89**	0.91	0.89	2.33	1.37
	RMSE	4.29	2.98	**0.94**	0.97	**0.94**	2.44	1.47
ALL	MAE	2.98	3.86	0.88	**0.81**	0.94	0.92	1.90
	RMSE	4.33	5.26	0.92	**0.86**	1.00	0.98	1.98

Table 3. Results for the positional, Euclidean error in millimeters of the Frame-by-Frame Pose Estimators BaselineCNN and GlassPoseRN [13] as well as our LSTM-based Pose Trackers CNN-LSTM, SepConv-LSTM, NL-CNN-LSTM, NL-SepConv-LSTM, and GlassPoseRN-LSTM on all three axes combined. The Everysight Raptor is referenced as EVS, Hololens 1 as HOLO, North Focal Generation 1 as NORTH and the Mini Augmented Vision glasses as MAV. ALL stands for all glasses combined. The full results including the errors regarding the x-, y-, and z-axes can be seen in the end of the document in Table 5.

Glasses-type	Frame-by-frame pose estimation		LSTM-based pose tracking				
	Baseline-CNN	GlassPose-RN [13]	CNN-LSTM	SepConv-LSTM	NL-CNN-LSTM	NL-SepConv-LSTM	GlassPoseRN-LSTM
EVS	12.06	8.41	4.18	**3.96**	4.55	7.18	8.89
MAV	15.07	5.97	4.23	**3.22**	3.59	3.56	5.65
HOLO	13.10	8.75	5.31	**4.57**	5.93	11.67	9.39
NORTH	13.49	4.88	5.18	**5.09**	5.19	12.79	11.83
ALL	14.82	11.95	5.22	**4.46**	5.44	5.43	15.86

comparable results among all glasses models as well as the glasses combined. The average MAE ranges from 2.47° on NORTH to 2.98° on ALL, showing slightly higher errors on the combination of the glasses compared to them individually. On the RMSE, the largest glasses model HOLO and the smallest glasses NORTH result in the highest errors. GlassPoseRN shows more significant differences among the individual glasses and combined. It can be observed that the smaller glasses types like NORTH and EVS perform better than the larger models. Considering all glasses at once increases the error.

We additionally evaluate the positional error of the methods on our data split (Table 3 and 5). We trained and tested both approaches on all individual glasses as well as combined. BaselineCNN again performs similarly for all glasses types. The GlassPoseRN errors differ more between the glasses models. When comparing the two pose estimation approaches, we observe GlassPoseRN to achieve mostly better results on the metrics for orientation and translation.

LSTM-Based Pose Tracking Methods. Based on the two pose estimation methods, we introduced and benchmarked five AR glasses tracking approaches.

Table 2 and 4 show the orientation results. Our extension of the GlassPoseRN method with LSTM performs better than GlassPoseRN. GlassPoseRN-LSTM estimates the orientation with less than 1.98° error. Regarding the individual glasses, we observe a similar pattern as for GlassPoseRN. ALL has a lower performance than the glasses individually. On NL-SepConv-LSTM, the error is high for NORTH and HOLO, being the smallest and the largest glasses models. The average error of all other glasses models and their combination is below 1.50°. The performance of CNN-LSTM, SepConv-LSTM, and NL CNN LSTM is comparable when differences on individual glasses are considered. The averages of all three methods for MAE on the various glasses models range from 0.74° to 0.94°. On the RMSE, the average values range from 0.77° to 1.01°. Regarding all five methods, SepConv-LSTM performs consistently best overall. The method achieves the best results on ALL and HOLO on both metrics.

The position benchmark results in a comparable pattern (Table 3 and 5). In the case of GlassPoseRN-LSTM, the errors are the highest, with an L_2 error of 15.86 mm on ALL and values between 5.65 mm to 11.83 mm on the individual glasses. NL-SepConv-LSTM has higher errors on HOLO and NORTH, as already seen on the orientation error. NL-CNN-LSTM, Sep-Conv-LSTM, and CNN-LSTM attain errors in a similar range for the individual glasses and combined. Overall, SepConv-LSTM performs best among all methods. This is the case for all objects. Although close error ranges between the three aforementioned approaches are observable, SepCon-LSTM performs consistently best. Similar to our orientation comparison, NL-SepConv-LSTM and GlassPoseRN-LSTM achieve higher errors than the rest.

AR Glasses Pose Estimation and Tracking Comparison. One of our fundamental goals in this work is comparing pose estimation and pose tracking methods for AR glasses. For this purpose, we benchmarked two frame-by-frame pose estimation and five pose tracking approaches. The results of the approaches show significant improvements in favor of pose tracking methods.

Pose Accuracy. Regarding pose accuracy, the best frame-by-frame method Glass-PoseRN achieves orientation errors on the MAE between 1.40° and 3.86°, which is reduced to an error of 0.76° to 0.91° with the SepConv-LSTM method. Thus, we observe a reduction of estimation errors of up to 76%. A similar tendency is visible on the position estimation. Furthermore, the estimation differences between various glasses models decrease significantly with the introduction of LSTMs, especially with separable convolutions without non-local blocks.

Inference Time. Comparing their performance regarding inference time is possible by measuring the estimation time between feeding images into a network and the time a network makes a prediction. Our measurements were made on a single NVIDIA GeForce 2080Ti. The Baseline-CNN achieves 100 fps, compared to 42 fps of GlassPoseRN. The pose tracking methods all achieve similar inference times due to their similarity in depth. Thus, each method achieves 74 fps. All methods fulfill the real-time requirement. Only the GlassPoseRN architecture estimates poses slower than 60 fps, which is the acquisition speed of the used HMDPose dataset. Subsequently, both the pose tracking and frame-by-frame pose estimation can perform similarly in real-world conditions.

Discussion. We chose our methods with a mostly identical CNN-backbone to ensure a network as similar as possible. This had the aim to deduce if the LSTM, the additional non-local blocks, or separable convolution deployment contributes to the changes in the accuracy. Between the various LSTM-based methods, the combination of non-local blocks and separable convolutions decreased estimation accuracy compared to approaches with the individual components separately. An explanation for this might be the concurring properties of separable convolutions and non-local blocks. Separable convolutions separately handle various channels of the images by applying the convolutions individually, which are the individual IR images in our case. Non-local blocks aim to learn non-local dependencies in the images. The layers containing non-local blocks might enjoy the information of three images mixed, which collides with the separable convolution concept. Individually applied, they output similar errors.

Finally, the introduction of LSTMs to the ResNet-18-based GlassPoseRN brings improvement but underperforms compared to the methods based on a simple CNN. This underlines once more the enhancement of the pose estimation accuracy with the introduction of LSTMs. The advanced feature extraction properties of ResNet seem redundant in the case of IR image-based AR glasses pose estimation when LSTMs are deployed. In addition, our combined methods work more efficiently compared to the GlassPoseRN approach. We achieve around 74 fps inference time for the BaselineCNN-LSTM combinations, whereas the inference time for GlassPoseRN is 42 fps.

The LSTM-based methods were trained with image sequence lengths of 8. The images of the HMDPose dataset were recorded with 60 fps, thus, the networks would potentially profit from longer sequence lengths. However, a longer sequence implicates dropping more images in the process of training, validation, and test split generation. This would endanger a proper training of the Deep Neural Networks, especially for individual AR glasses models. A networks with an even lower sequence lengths than 8 frames would most likely not register temporal information, as the movement is hardly visible.

Regarding deploying the algorithms in a real world setting where AR content is shown to a driver of a vehicle through AR glasses, we suggest the efficient CNN with separable convolutions named SepConv-LSTM to track the pose. They save computation time and, compared to CNN-LSTM and NL-CNN-LSTM, achieves better results at the same time. Thus, our LSTM-based methods improve the pose tracking of AR glasses. As a highly accurate pose is required when AR glasses are deployed into the car, our methods can improve the stability in which the AR content is shown while driving, leading to an improved AR experience.

5 Conclusion

In this paper, we analyzed outside-in approaches on pose tracking and pose estimation of AR glasses. We first introduced and benchmarked two frame-by-frame pose estimation approaches. One method is the state-of-the-art Glass-PoseRN model, developed for AR glasses pose estimation. Based on the baseline variants, we extended them with LSTMs to achieve AR glasses pose tracking. We presented methods with and without non-local blocks and further added separable convolutions in some networks for comparison. Non-local blocks consider non-local neighbor features in one image and among multiple images, while separable convolutions focus on maintaining the individual channels, and therefore the triple images. We observe a significant boost on the HMDPose dataset from pose estimation to tracking approaches. Separable convolutions improve our recurrent networks' results, where our SepConv-LSTM algorithm shows the best performance with an estimation error of 0.81° in orientation and 4.46 mm in position. In contrast to GlassPoseRN, we decrease the estimation error by 76%. The results are promising to improve the in-car AR experience in the case of AR glasses deployment, as a high 6-DoF pose estimation accuracy positively affects the superimposition of the real world with virtual elements, which we further improve in this work.

On the one hand, future work will consist of potential fusion and Neural Network ensemble methods to evaluate combinations of frame-by-frame pose estimation and tracking approaches. On the other hand, the variance of the performance across individuals will be analyzed.

Table 4. Rotation results of the Frame-by-Frame Pose Estimators BaselineCNN and GlassPoseRN [13] as well as our LSTM-based Pose Trackers CNN-LSTM, SepConv-LSTM, NL-CNN-LSTM, NL-SepConv-LSTM, and GlassPoseRN-LSTM on the given error metrics in degrees. The Everysight Raptor is referenced as EVS, Hololens 1 as HOLO, North Focal Generation 1 as NORTH and the Mini Augmented Vision glasses as MAV. ALL stands for all glasses combined. The roll, pitch, yaw and the average of all three axes are given on the defined metrics.

Method type		Frame-by-frame pose estimation								LSTM-based pose tracking																			
		BaselineCNN				GlassPoseRN [13]				CNN-LSTM				SepConv-LSTM				NL-CNN-LSTM				NL-SepConv-LSTM				GlassPoseRN-LSTM			
Glasses-type	Metric	Roll	Pitch	Yaw	Avg	Roll	Pitch	Yaw	Avg	Roll	Pitch	Yaw	Avg	Roll	Pitch	Yaw	Avg	Roll	Pitch	Yaw	Avg	Roll	Pitch	Yaw	Avg	Roll	Pitch	Yaw	Avg
EVS	MAE	2.44	2.55	2.86	2.62	1.65	1.89	1.83	1.79	0.65	**0.63**	**0.94**	**0.74**	0.64	**0.63**	1.01	0.76	**0.62**	0.66	1.01	0.76	0.99	1.01	1.81	1.27	0.99	1.74	1.31	1.34
	RMSE	3.54	3.43	4.89	3.95	2.56	2.40	3.16	2.71	0.67	**0.65**	**1.00**	**0.77**	0.66	**0.65**	1.07	0.79	**0.65**	0.68	1.06	0.80	1.04	1.05	1.93	1.34	1.06	1.79	1.43	1.43
MAV	MAE	2.52	2.90	2.73	2.71	2.56	2.33	1.87	2.25	0.84	0.83	0.77	0.81	0.86	0.73	0.76	0.79	**0.82**	0.88	0.76	0.82	0.88	**0.72**	**0.74**	**0.78**	1.30	1.10	1.25	1.22
	RMSE	3.53	3.93	4.35	3.94	3.52	3.30	2.97	3.26	0.86	0.85	0.82	0.84	0.89	0.75	0.81	0.81	**0.84**	0.90	0.81	0.85	0.91	**0.75**	**0.80**	**0.82**	1.42	1.22	1.47	1.37
HOLO	MAE	2.38	2.56	3.32	2.75	2.70	4.78	2.44	3.31	0.85	0.76	1.21	0.94	**0.84**	**0.74**	**1.00**	**0.86**	0.96	0.83	1.16	0.97	2.68	1.62	3.41	2.57	1.4	2.14	1.47	1.67
	RMSE	3.18	3.61	7.09	4.63	3.65	6.07	4.74	4.82	0.87	0.78	1.26	0.97	**0.87**	**0.76**	**1.06**	**0.90**	0.98	0.83	1.23	1.01	2.70	1.81	3.53	2.68	1.47	2.20	1.65	1.77
NORTH	MAE	2.43	2.47	2.51	2.47	1.48	1.25	1.48	1.40	**0.76**	**0.67**	1.22	**0.89**	0.90	0.75	1.09	0.91	0.84	0.74	1.10	0.89	1.63	2.19	3.15	2.33	0.91	1.67	1.52	1.37
	RMSE	3.54	3.83	5.50	4.29	2.68	2.06	4.19	2.98	**0.79**	**0.72**	1.30	**0.94**	0.93	0.80	1.18	0.97	0.86	0.80	1.17	**0.94**	1.69	2.28	3.35	2.44	0.97	1.77	1.67	1.47
ALL	MAE	2.82	2.88	3.24	2.95	2.95	6.01	2.61	3.86	0.81	0.84	0.98	0.88	**0.74**	**0.72**	0.98	**0.81**	0.91	0.87	1.06	0.94	0.84	0.83	1.11	0.92	1.30	3.13	1.25	1.90
	RMSE	3.94	4.06	4.98	4.33	4.08	7.21	4.48	5.26	0.83	0.87	1.05	0.92	**0.77**	**0.77**	1.05	**0.86**	0.95	0.91	1.14	1.00	0.87	0.88	1.18	0.98	1.36	3.19	1.39	1.98

Table 5. Results for the positional, Euclidean error in millimeters of the Frame-by-Frame Pose Estimators BaselineCNN and GlassPoseRN [13] as well as our LSTM-based Pose Trackers CNN-LSTM, SepConv-LSTM, NL-CNN-LSTM, NL-SepConv-LSTM, and GlassPoseRN-LSTM on the individual axes and combined. The Everysight Raptor is referenced as EVS, Hololens 1 as HOLO, North Focal Generation 1 as NORTH and the Mini Augmented Vision glasses as MAV. ALL stands for all glasses combined.

Method type	Frame-by-frame pose estimation								LSTM-based pose tracking																				
	BaselineCNN				GlassPoseRN [13]				CNN-LSTM				SepConv-LSTM				NL-CNN-LSTM				NL-SepConv-LSTM				GlassPoseRN-LSTM			
Glasses-type	x	y	z	L_2	x	y	z	L_2	x	y	z	L_2	x	y	z	L_2	x	y	z	L_2	x	y	z	L_2	x	y	z	L_2
EVS	6.31	7.04	4.60	12.06	5.06	3.87	3.70	8.41	2.86	1.74	1.44	4.18	2.84	1.83	1.06	**3.96**	2.90	2.19	1.64	4.55	4.73	3.70	2.11	7.18	6.43	2.74	3.52	8.89
MAV	6.53	10.15	5.40	15.07	3.34	2.50	2.64	5.97	2.85	1.66	1.62	4.23	2.19	**1.37**	1.21	**3.22**	2.29	1.59	1.37	3.59	2.55	1.40	**1.18**	3.56	4.11	2.02	1.99	5.65
HOLO	7.33	7.73	4.20	13.10	5.74	3.78	3.22	8.75	3.38	2.51	1.89	5.31	3.15	2.02	1.42	**4.57**	3.52	2.94	2.36	5.93	6.80	3.20	5.65	11.67	5.39	3.41	4.79	9.39
NORTH	7.28	7.66	5.14	13.49	3.26	2.40	**1.63**	4.88	3.13	2.70	1.73	5.18	**3.02**	2.52	1.70	**5.09**	3.24	2.70	1.77	5.19	7.45	6.50	5.27	12.79	6.38	3.89	6.55	11.83
ALL	7.23	9.53	5.05	14.82	6.47	5.36	6.04	11.95	3.01	2.70	1.97	5.22	**2.67**	2.43	1.53	**4.46**	3.48	2.67	1.85	5.44	3.40	2.69	1.91	5.43	8.55	7.67	7.52	15.86

References

1. Berg, A., Oskarsson, M., O'Connor, M.: Deep ordinal regression with label diversity. In: 2020 25th International Conference on Pattern Recognition (ICPR), pp. 2740–2747 (2021)
2. Borghi, G., Fabbri, M., Vezzani, R., Calderara, S., Cucchiara, R.: Face-from-depth for head pose estimation on depth images. IEEE Trans. Pattern Anal. Mach. Intell. **42**(3), 596–609 (2018)
3. Borghi, G., Gasparini, R., Vezzani, R., Cucchiara, R.: Embedded recurrent network for head pose estimation in car. In: 2017 IEEE Intelligent Vehicles Symposium (IV), pp. 1503–1508. IEEE (2017)
4. Borghi, G., Venturelli, M., Vezzani, R., Cucchiara, R.: Poseidon: face-from-depth for driver pose estimation. In: The IEEE Conference on Computer Vision and Pattern Recognition (CVPR), July 2017
5. Capellen, C., Schwarz, M., Behnke, S.: ConvPoseCNN: dense convolutional 6D object pose estimation, pp. 162–172 (2020)
6. Chen, B., Parra, A., Cao, J., Li, N., Chin, T.J.: End-to-end learnable geometric vision by backpropagating PnP optimization. In: Proceedings of the IEEE/CVF Conference on Computer Vision and Pattern Recognition, pp. 8100–8109 (2020)
7. Chollet, F.: Xception: deep learning with depthwise separable convolutions. In: 2017 IEEE Conference on Computer Vision and Pattern Recognition (CVPR), pp. 1800–1807 (2017)
8. Costante, G., Mancini, M.: Uncertainty estimation for data-driven visual odometry. IEEE Trans. Rob. **36**(6), 1738–1757 (2020)
9. Dosovitskiy, A., et al.: FlowNet: learning optical flow with convolutional networks. In: 2015 IEEE International Conference on Computer Vision (ICCV), pp. 2758–2766 (2015)
10. Fanelli, G., Dantone, M., Gall, J., Fossati, A., Gool, L.: Random forests for real time 3D face analysis. Int. J. Comput. Vision **101**(3), 437–458 (2013)
11. Firintepe, A., Mohamed, S., Pagani, A., Stricker, D.: The more, the merrier? A study on in-car IR-based head pose estimation. In: 2020 IEEE Intelligent Vehicles Symposium (IV). IEEE (2020)
12. Firintepe, A., Pagani, A., Stricker, D.: HMDPose: a large-scale trinocular IR augmented reality glasses pose dataset. In: 26th ACM Symposium on Virtual Reality Software and Technology. ACM (2020)
13. Firintepe, A., Pagani, A., Stricker, D.: A comparison of single and multi-view IR image-based AR glasses pose estimation approaches. In: 2021 IEEE Conference on Virtual Reality and 3D User Interfaces Abstracts and Workshops (VRW), pp. 571–572 (2021)
14. Firintepe, A., Vey, C., Asteriadis, S., Pagani, A., Stricker, D.: From IR images to point clouds to pose: point cloud-based AR glasses pose estimation. J. Imag. **7**(5) (2021). https://www.mdpi.com/2313-433X/7/5/80
15. Gao, G., Lauri, M., Wang, Y., Hu, X., Zhang, J., Frintrop, S.: 6D object pose regression via supervised learning on point clouds. In: 2020 IEEE International Conference on Robotics and Automation (ICRA), pp. 3643–3649 (2020)
16. Gu, J., Yang, X., De Mello, S., Kautz, J.: Dynamic facial analysis: from Bayesian filtering to recurrent neural network. In: 2017 IEEE Conference on Computer Vision and Pattern Recognition (CVPR), pp. 1531–1540 (2017)
17. He, K., Zhang, X., Ren, S., Sun, J.: Deep residual learning for image recognition. In: Proceedings of the IEEE Conference on Computer Vision and Pattern Recognition, pp. 770–778, June 2016

18. Howard, A.G., et al.: MobileNets: efficient convolutional neural networks for mobile vision applications. arXiv preprint arXiv:1704.04861 (2017)
19. Kendall, A., Grimes, M., Cipolla, R.: PoseNet: a convolutional network for real-time 6-DOF camera relocalization. In: Proceedings of the IEEE International Conference on Computer Vision, pp. 2938–2946 (2015)
20. Kendall, A., Grimes, M., Cipolla, R.: PoseNet: a convolutional network for real-time 6-DOF camera relocalization, pp. 2938–2946, December 2015
21. Li, Y., Wang, G., Ji, X., Xiang, Yu., Fox, D.: DeepIM: deep iterative matching for 6D pose estimation. In: Ferrari, V., Hebert, M., Sminchisescu, C., Weiss, Y. (eds.) ECCV 2018. LNCS, vol. 11210, pp. 695–711. Springer, Cham (2018). https://doi.org/10.1007/978-3-030-01231-1_42
22. Li, Z., Wang, G., Ji, X.: CDPN: coordinates-based disentangled pose network for real-time RGB-Based 6-DoF object pose estimation. In: 2019 IEEE/CVF International Conference on Computer Vision (ICCV), pp. 7677–7686 (2019)
23. Murphy-Chutorian, E., Trivedi, M.M.: Head pose estimation and augmented reality tracking: an integrated system and evaluation for monitoring driver awareness. IEEE Trans. Intell. Transp. Syst. 11(2), 300–311 (2010)
24. Ning, G., et al.: Spatially supervised recurrent convolutional neural networks for visual object tracking, pp. 1–4 (2017)
25. Park, K., Patten, T., Vincze, M.: Pix2Pose: pixel-wise coordinate regression of objects for 6d pose estimation. In: Proceedings of the IEEE/CVF International Conference on Computer Vision, pp. 7668–7677 (2019)
26. Peng, S., Liu, Y., Huang, Q., Zhou, X., Bao, H.: PVNet: pixel-wise voting network for 6DoF pose estimation. In: The IEEE Conference on Computer Vision and Pattern Recognition (CVPR), June 2019
27. Peng, X., Feris, R.S., Wang, X., Metaxas, D.N.: A recurrent encoder-decoder network for sequential face alignment. In: Leibe, B., Matas, J., Sebe, N., Welling, M. (eds.) ECCV 2016. LNCS, vol. 9905, pp. 38–56. Springer, Cham (2016). https://doi.org/10.1007/978-3-319-46448-0_3
28. Rad, M., Lepetit, V.: BB8: a scalable, accurate, robust to partial occlusion method for predicting the 3D poses of challenging objects without using depth. In: 2017 IEEE International Conference on Computer Vision (ICCV), pp. 3848–3856, October 2017
29. Redmon, J., Divvala, S., Girshick, R., Farhadi, A.: You only look once: unified, real-time object detection. In: Proceedings of the IEEE Conference on Computer Vision and Pattern Recognition (CVPR), June 2016
30. Schwarz, A., Haurilet, M., Martinez, M., Stiefelhagen, R.: DriveAHead-a large-scale driver head pose dataset. In: Proceedings of the IEEE Conference on Computer Vision and Pattern Recognition Workshops, pp. 1–10, July 2017
31. Selim, M., Firintepe, A., Pagani, A., Stricker, D.: AutoPOSE: large-scale automotive driver head pose and gaze dataset with deep head pose baseline. In: International Conference on Computer Vision Theory and Applications (VISAPP). SCITEPRESS Digital Library (2020)
32. Simonyan, K., Zisserman, A.: Very deep convolutional networks for large-scale image recognition (2015)
33. Song, C., Song, J., Huang, Q.: HybridPose: 6D object pose estimation under hybrid representations. In: 2020 IEEE/CVF Conference on Computer Vision and Pattern Recognition (CVPR), pp. 428–437 (2020)
34. Tekin, B., Sinha, S.N., Fua, P.: Real-time seamless single shot 6D object pose prediction. In: The IEEE Conference on Computer Vision and Pattern Recognition (CVPR), pp. 292–301, June 2018

35. Tremblay, J., To, T., Sundaralingam, B., Xiang, Y., Fox, D., Birchfield, S.: Deep object pose estimation for semantic robotic grasping of household objects. In: Proceedings of the 2nd Conference on Robot Learning. Proceedings of Machine Learning Research, vol. 87, pp. 306–316. PMLR, 29–31 October 2018

36. Wang, S., Clark, R., Wen, H., Trigoni, N.: DeepVO: towards end-to-end visual odometry with deep Recurrent Convolutional Neural Networks. In: 2017 IEEE International Conference on Robotics and Automation (ICRA), pp. 2043–2050 (2017)

37. Wang, X., Girshick, R., Gupta, A., He, K.: Non-local neural networks. In: 2018 IEEE/CVF Conference on Computer Vision and Pattern Recognition, pp. 7794–7803 (2018)

38. Xiang, Y., Schmidt, T., Narayanan, V., Fox, D.: PoseCNN: a convolutional neural network for 6d object pose estimation in cluttered scenes. In: Kress-Gazit, H., Srinivasa, S.S., Howard, T., Atanasov, N. (eds.) Robotics: Science and Systems XIV, Carnegie Mellon University, Pittsburgh, Pennsylvania, USA, 26–30 June 2018 (2018)

39. Xu, Z., Chen, K., Jia, K.: W-PoseNet: dense correspondence regularized pixel pair pose regression. arXiv preprint arXiv:1912.11888 (2019)

40. Zakharov, S., Shugurov, I., Ilic, S.: DPOD: 6D pose object detector and refiner. In: 2019 IEEE/CVF International Conference on Computer Vision (ICCV), pp. 1941–1950 (2019)

41. Zhang, Y., Ming, Y., Zhang, R.: Object detection and tracking based on recurrent neural networks. In: 2018 14th IEEE International Conference on Signal Processing (ICSP), pp. 338–343. IEEE (2018)

42. Zou, Y., Ji, P., Tran, Q.-H., Huang, J.-B., Chandraker, M.: Learning monocular visual odometry via self-supervised long-term modeling. In: Vedaldi, A., Bischof, H., Brox, T., Frahm, J.-M. (eds.) ECCV 2020. LNCS, vol. 12359, pp. 710–727. Springer, Cham (2020). https://doi.org/10.1007/978-3-030-58568-6_42

Use Case and User Study (Scientific Session 4)

Building a Mobile AR Engagement Tool: Evaluation of Citizens Attitude Towards a Sustainable Future

Tina Katika(✉) (iD), Spyridon Nektarios Bolierakis, Nikolaos Tousert,
Ioannis Karaseitanidis, and Angelos Amditis

Institute of Communication and Computer Systems, Athens, Greece
tina.katika@iccs.gr

Abstract. Adopting a sustainable way of living in today's cities requires a high level of citizen empowerment, motivation, and engagement. The mobile Augmented Reality (AR) technology offers an accessible, inexpensive, and rich user experience that has the potential to lead towards this adoption. The widespread smartphones and tablets with unique features (e.g., embedded sensors, cameras, high-speed Internet, accessibility, and portability) provide powerful and ubiquitous platforms for supporting such applications. Mobile technology, and the easiness of immersing a mobile user in AR, impact the interaction of citizens with their environment. We leverage the deep penetration of mobile phones in urban environments and their advanced features to design and develop an AR citizen engagement tool. The tool is employed in a municipality and studied as means to foster citizen engagement in sustainable practices. The Technology Acceptance Model is used to study the acceptance of this application and the factors that may affect its adoption. In total, 127 end users were exposed to the prototype system that allowed 3D, audio, and 2D visualizations as well as interactions with them. Through a web-based survey, we assessed the factors and measures influencing the acceptance of technology and how they can be aligned with the characteristics of the contemporary urban settings and utilize the potentials offered by mobile AR technologies. Providing detailed information regarding the system design we expect that the results of this study will contribute to the discourse on the use of mobile AR as a tool for citizen engagement to guide the development of future efforts.

Keywords: Augmented reality · Citizen engagement · Mobile AR · Content management service · Technology acceptance model

1 Introduction

As the European Commission emphasizes [1], the transition towards a more sustainable future must bring together citizens in all their diversity and be supported by behavioral, social, and cultural changes. The complexity of the challenges that municipalities worldwide are facing, related to population growth and climate change, illustrates that

© Springer Nature Switzerland AG 2021
P. Bourdot et al. (Eds.): EuroXR 2021, LNCS 13105, pp. 109–125, 2021.
https://doi.org/10.1007/978-3-030-90739-6_7

the issues are not localized, and there must be partnership between governments and citizens, private and public sectors [2]. To ensure higher participation, the inclusion of citizens in public matters should be enhanced, and gender, social differences, and other heterogeneities should also be addressed.

New technologies and digital transformation play an essential role in the process to secure more active participation, reconfigure social relations and empower citizens, connect individuals and facilitate knowledge exchange across ever-widening spatialities [3]. Citizens empowered and committed transform from passive audience to interactors, and immersive technologies and interactive media are designed to generate such transformative experiences.

This paper aims to report on the design and development of a content management system (CMS) and a mobile AR app (CirculAR) and to study the factors influencing the acceptance of such a citizen engagement tool. We shed light on the interest and willingness to improve citizen engagement towards sustainable practices regarding the proper consumption of resources, better management of waste and pollution, and reuse of material via this tool. In the next section, we provide further background on engagement tools and the technology acceptance model. The methodology and AR system design is described in detail further ahead. The description of the system design aims to demonstrate the features that affected the acceptance of this technology and also to assist future development efforts. Finally, the evaluation of the application is described and discussed in the last section with recommendations for practice before concluding the article.

1.1 Citizen Engagement

Citizen engagement can be described as a particular type of user engagement and refers to how citizens participate in a community's life to improve conditions for others or help shape the community's future [4]. Direct engagement with relevant individuals or groups in society is the richest, most revealing, and valid source of knowledge about them. The process of citizen engagement involves many elements to be defined as efficient according to Olphert and Damodaran [4], and Information and communication technologies (ICT) have proved essential to foster an environment where the citizens become active participants. The critical success factors for achieving commitment and loyalty via citizen engagement include the perceived relevance of the shared knowledge, accessibility, usability, and value from participating in the process.

An effective engagement process should include the voices and needs of all citizens and increase their knowledge about a public issue, encouraging them to apply that knowledge and finally what they learned to improve their quality of life and the community [4, 5]. Creating opportunities for citizens to engage each other, and ensuring that these opportunities are regular and ongoing, contribute to the long-run success of these initiatives.

Over the past decade, media, technologies, software, and cultural practices have emerged that change how we experience the environment and interact with it. Various ICT tools, including websites, mobile solutions, and platforms, have been proposed to improve the understanding of public matters and engage citizens in a great variety [4]. Nevertheless, despite all efforts, such initiatives often fail since they are not inclusive.

They are designed for a specific target group, such as expert users and stakeholders, and they do not improve the participation of young people or are hard to use for seniors. Their content is often limited and very often not engaging. Finally, they are restrictive in terms of portability, usability, and accessibility; or they do not comply with a specific framework or measures [4, 5].

Olphert and Damodaran [4] presented evidence regarding the link of ICT technologies and citizen engagement to achieving broader citizen participation and increased social inclusion. Church [5], demonstrated the usefulness of methodologies encouraging participation from marginalized groups. An effective ICT solution should emphasize the inclusivity of the citizens, where past experiences, lack of knowledge, and cultural context do not limit involvement. Sections of the community that have not participated in the past and might not seem to be fertile ground for recruitment should be reached. An impactful engagement process is built upon diversity and equality. All members of a community need to participate in representing different viewpoints and interests, and it should be clear that everyone respectfully participates on an equal basis. The work of the community group needs to be open, transparent, and consistent. At the same time, the engagement process should create opportunities for learning and use or applying that knowledge further at a non-restrictive timeframe and pace. It is, therefore, apparent that engagement tools should be inclusive, accessible, transparent, support learning and long-run well-being to engage all citizens with their heterogeneities.

1.2 AR for Engagement

Given the immersive nature of AR technology, the extended use of smartphones, and the ability to couple them together with advanced location and camera settings, AR can be part of the citizen participatory process. AR offers experiences that enable the end users to move from observation to immersion which is often associated with the encouragement they experience in the digitally enhanced setting [6]. AR's immersive nature helps the audience see details believe in actions, and make connections between the events in the story and their own lives. Consequently, they are able to understand the positive impact of specific policies and changes [7]. Digital media are conveyed interactively, and physical experiences are recreated and enhanced with virtual content that enables participants to move beyond static images and gives them the freedom to choose any viewpoint and explore [8]. Mobile AR offers the advantage of portability and mobility to the end-user and accessibility and availability [9].

Due to the adaptable nature of the technology, mobile AR has the possibility of comforting the limitations that other engagement tools face. Up to our knowledge, a similar solution has not been developed to leverage advanced mobile functionalities and features (e.g., embedded sensors, cameras, 3D object manipulation, educational content, virtual assistant). Small scale projects have been proposed, but they have been examined in a narrow target group or fail to extract concrete results due to the lack of adherence to specific research frameworks or assessment models (e.g., [10]).

Acceptance of mobile AR technology is critical for the success and adoption of such a novel engagement tool. The assessment of the usability of mobile AR, allows researchers and designers to extract valuable information from end-users and improve the user experience [11]. The technology acceptance model (TAM) developed by Davis [12] is one of the most prominent models examining the acceptance of ICT tools with end-users. The model suggests that the actual use of technology is anticipated by behavioral intention, which is determined by the attitude towards using it, both being affected by the perceived ease of use and perceived usefulness. Perceived ease of use describes the extent to which an individual is able to use a technological system without effort, and perceived usefulness suggests an essential construct in swaying the adoption of new technologies as it may promote the confidence that utilizing a particular technological system may enhance performance [12].

Many empirical researchers have tested TAM, and the tools used with the model have proven to be of quality and to yield statistically reliable results [13]. TAM was used to analyze the use and acceptance of ICT by senior citizens and its comparison with the younger population. In their analysis, Guner and Acarturk [14], demonstrated the similarities of these two groups when using ICT services that they both consider helpful. Gefen and Staub, [15], tested the gender differences related to computer-based media and concluded with remarks regarding how females and males have different perceptions of use and usability. Burton-Jones and Hubona [16], studied the effect of age and educational level on the acceptance of ICT systems. The authors revealed that even though seniors had excess trouble navigating the ICT systems, this did not affect the perceived usefulness. Their study also demonstrated that if a task is not over-complicated, then the education level has only a minor impact on the perceived usefulness in favor of the users with higher education. Considering the multiple parameters affecting the acceptance of the engagement tool (such as age, education, gender, and tech-savviness), and the ability of TAM to reflect on such parameters, the TAM model is considered the most appropriate means to assess and explain the measures affecting the acceptance of the proposed mobile AR tool.

2   Research Hypothesis

As Davis [12] described, the perceived usefulness (PU), the perceived ease of use (PEoU), and attitude towards using (AU) affect the behavioral intention (BI) and, after that, the overall user acceptance of the technology. The following hypotheses were formulated and Fig. 1, provides a visualization of the research model.

H1: Perceived ease of use (PEoU) will positively influence users' attitude (AU) towards the AR engagement tool.
H2: Perceived Usefulness (PU) will positively influence users' attitude (AU) towards the AR engagement tool.
H3: Perceived Usefulness (PU) will positively influence users' behavioral intention (BI) to use of the AR engagement tool.
H4: Perceived Ease of Use (PEoU) will positively influence Perceived Usefulness (PU) of the AR engagement tool.
H5: Attitude towards use (AU) will positively influence users' behavioral intention (BI) to the AR engagement tool.

Since a significant role in adopting an engagement tool is inclusivity described by its ability to reach end-users regardless of any heterogeneities and educational background, the following research question was formulated.

Q: Is there any difference in the acceptance of the AR engagement tool depending on the tech-savviness, education level, gender, and age of the end-users?

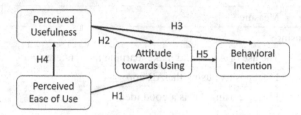

Fig. 1. Research model based on original TAM (Davis et al. [12]).

3 Methodology

3.1 Data Collection

A web survey was prepared and distributed to the citizens of the municipality of Karditsa in Greece, where end-users were exposed to the AR engagement tool via a video demonstrating its content, features, and interactive design, and filled out a questionnaire providing answers regarding their PEoU, PU, AU, and BI. Karditsa is an evolving peripheral town that belongs to the Municipality of Karditsa, Region of Thessaly – Central Greece. The survey was translated to the native language of the citizens (Greek) to avoid any language barriers or bias. All participants revealed information regarding their age, gender, education level, and tech-savviness. Since there were no missing responses and no patterns of incoherent answers observed, no questions were excluded from further analysis and all collected questionnaires were taken into account.

3.2 Measures

The questions in the web survey used the Likert Scale to demonstrate the agreement of the participant with statements ranging from "strongly agree" to "strongly disagree". We chose a unipolar scale to measure the attribute of agreement in each statement that was treated as interval level (with intervals from 1 to 4). We chose four maturity levels in all measures for the Likert Scale to enable the user to form a clear opinion on each statement. As we ensured that all questions apply to our AR application user, we concluded that a specific user opinion is essential.

The questionnaire enclosed 14 items assessing the users' PEoU, PU, AU, and BI, and four items assessing age, gender, education, and tech-savviness. The questions assessing PU, PEoU, AU and BI were adopted from literature [13–16]. Table 1 summarizes all TAM measures used in this study. Age, gender, and education, were assessed via drop-down predefined menus and tech-savviness was determined by the confidence of the user towards the use of smartphones and their features (such as camera and mobile apps), the frequency of playing mobile games, and their exposure to other AR technologies (Table 2).

Table 1. Summary of survey items assessing the TAM measures.

Construct	Measure
Attitude towards using	
AU1	The use of AR would make learning more interesting
AU2	I feel positive using the AR app
AU3	I believe using AR is a good idea
Perceived ease of use	
PEoU1	I believe it will be easy for me to use the AR app
PEoU2	The AR app appears intuitive to use
PEoU3	The AR app is not complex
PEoU4	The use of AR technology does not confuse me
PEoU5	The use of the AR app does not confuse me
Perceived usefulness	
PU1	I am satisfied with this experience as it seems novel
PU2	Using the app will help me learn factual information about CE
PU3	I find the AR app useful
Behavioral intention	
BI1	Spending time on AR seems worthwhile
BI2	I am satisfied with the type of the activity
BI3	I would recommend the AR app to my friends and family

Table 2. Summary of survey items assessing tech-savviness.

Item	Measure
Use of smartphones	Everyday/Sometimes per week/Sometimes per month/Never
Use of smartphone camera	
Playing mobile games	
Using AR	

4 System Design

4.1 System Architecture

The overall system architecture is designed to support two different users, the administrators of CMS, and the mobile application users of CircularAR. The administrators are considered the content owners. Their role is to produce and add content in the platform to create meaningful and educational experiences, so-called AR campaigns, that will be later enhanced with various gamification aspects and visualized by the mobile application end users.

The platform consists of two core components to support both the addition and editing of the content and its visualization and demonstration. The AR Content Management Service (CMS) is a web-based application that allows the administrators to create campaigns and add content to the platform, and the AR mobile application (CircularAR) is designed to provide the generated experiences to the end users. The design of the two AR components is presented in Fig. 2.

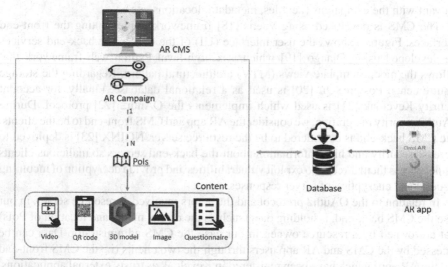

Fig. 2. The system design of the AR components. At the left side the AR CMS allows the administrator of the web-based application to create AR campaigns with Points of Interest (PoIs) on the map. The PoIs contain the content. Through the database that all information is stored, the users of the AR app access the AR content as soon as they reach the location of the PoIs.

The AR Content Management Service (CMS)

The CMS consists of two distinct parts; the back-end which stores the resources in the database and provides the APIs, and the front-end which retrieves resources through the APIs so as to display the CMS interface in the browser [17]. The CMS provides a user-friendly web interface, with a series of functionalities supporting the insertion of data to be displayed in the mobile AR app (Fig. 3).

Each AR campaign that enters the CMS contains all information necessary to create an engaging AR experience. Each campaign has an overall goal and objectives and consists of points of interest (PoIs). These PoIs signify a location or an area on the map containing all the media and educational content provided to the mobile user upon visiting it.

For each PoI, the CMS allows the administrators to perform the following actions:

- Add the location that represents the PoI.
- Add title and description in text format.
- Attach media content (image, video, and audio).
- Attach a 3D model.
- Create and add educational content (questionaries).
- Optionally generate a QR code to be scanned by the mobile app to visualize the previously added content.

The CMS front-end and the mobile app retrieve AR content from the database through REST API services [17]. The database is responsible for storing the content which is relevant with the campaigns (i.e. files, metadata, locations, etc.).

The CMS is developed using Vue.js [18] framework implementing the front-end interfaces. Figure 3 shows the user interface (UI) of the CMS. The back-end services are developed using Django [19] which is a high-level Python web framework that follows the model-template-views (MTV) architectural pattern. Regarding the storage requirements, PostgreSQL [20] is used as a relational database. Finally, for account security Keycloak [21] is used which implements the OAuth2 [22] protocol. During OAuth2 security integration, we consider the AR app and CMS front-end to be the clients. The CMS back-end is considered to be the resource server. NGINX [23] is deployed to increase security and hide information about the back-end servers so malicious clients cannot access them directly to exploit vulnerabilities and provide decryption of incoming requests and encryption of server responses.

In relation to the OAuth2 protocol and the actors involved, a resource server, in our case the CMS back-end, is holding data (such as the digital media and location of PoIs) that are owned by a resource owner, in our case the CMS administrator. Data can be accessed by the CMS and AR app users through the two clients (i.e.the CMS front-end and the AR app) which have been registered in Keycloak as trusty external applications. The resource owners (the CMS administrators) are the only users that can change the resources shown to the CirculAR users through their UIs (e.g. campaigns, content). The Authorization server, used in this study and presented in Fig. 4, keeps two different realms isolated (i.e., sets of users): the administrator handling the CMS front-end and the mobile AR app user of CirculAR. As presended in Fig. 4, the workflow is the following:

The user logs in to interact with the client (AR app or CMS front-end) and the client redirects the user to the token endpoint of the authorization server by providing the arguments redirect_uri, client_id and response_type. The authorization server checks whether the client is a trusty app registered in Keycloak. In this case it presents to the user's browser the login form where the user enters their credentials. If credentials are valid, the authorization server redirects the user back to the given redirect_uri along with the access token. This access token is signed with RS256 algorithm (i.e., an asymmetric

Fig. 3. The user interface (UI) of CMS. Using the functions of the left panel the administrator (user of CMS) can create an AR campaign through the project manager. For each campaign, the administrator decides the number of PoIs through the PoI manager. The Quiz manager allows the addition of educational content (questionaries and feedback). The functions at the right panel allow the customization of the content (including the description, digital media and 3D models, and quizzes) and determination of the location of the PoIs. The location can be added both manually and upon selection on the map.

algorithm that uses public/private key pair). The signature is generated with the private key which is kept secured in the authorization server. After the user is redirected back to a desired page of the client, the client catches the access token. This access token can be passed through the HTTP header in every request the client wants to make so as to retrieve resources. When a client (AR app or CMS front-end) asks for a resource, the CMS back-end which exposes the resources through services, validates the access token based on the public key provided previously by the authorization server).

Upon successful validation, the resource (i.e., PoI metadata, media file, etc.) is provided to the client and the client (AR app or CMS front-end) presents the retrieved resource to the user and updates the user interface accordingly.

The AR Mobile Application (CirculAR)

CirculAR was developed in the Unity game engine [24] using ARCore [25] and Mapbox [26]. The mobile app is compatible with Android smartphones and requires Global Positioning System (GPS) tracking as it supports both marker and location-based applications to overlay the digital data. The markers used in CirculAR to activate the AR experiences are QR codes generated by the CMS during the media attachment. The user of CirculAR should allow the use of the camera and location settings while using the app and be connected to the internet. Figure 5 shows four UIs of the AR app.

4.2 Features, Content and Gamification Mechanisms

Upon creating the AR campaigns from the CMS administrator and adding the respective content, the CirculAR allows the visualization of virtual content at specific locations

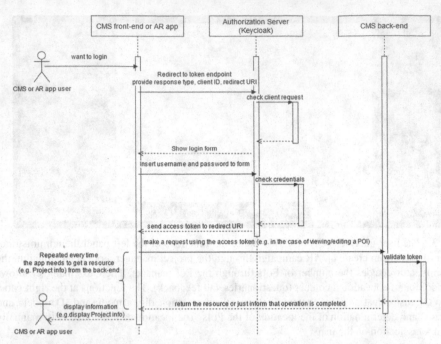

Fig. 4. The Authorization server (Keycloak) integrated in both CirculAR and CMS.

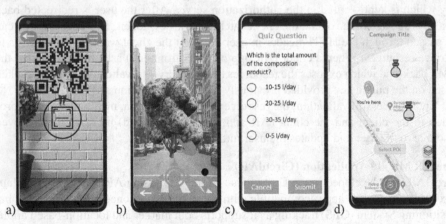

a)   b)   c)   d)

Fig. 5. a) The UI of CirculAR with an open camera setting, showing the virtual assistant. The user is prompted to scan the QR code and view the digital media. b) A UI with an open camera setting, demonstrating 3D content to the user. The media is activated based on the GPS location of the user. The hand indicates that the user is able to rotate the 3D virtual tree that overlays the physical surroundings. The arrows and cursor indicate the ability to move and rescale the virtual object around the physical surroundings. c) A UI with a quiz question that enables the user to test and validate their knowledge and understanding based on the virtual content they were previously exposed. d) The map with instructions navigating the user to the nearest AR experience from the AR campaign of their choice.

through the smartphone's camera. The app user signs up using email or Facebook credentials and can create a personalized profile (i.e., selection of avatar, username). The user then selects an AR campaign (an entity that contains PoIs, virtual experiences at specific locations) with the content of their interest from a list of available campaigns around them. Upon selecting the AR campaign, the mobile app navigates the user to the nearest virtual content, using GPS coordinates, through a map (see Fig. 5d). Upon reaching the location of the AR content, the smartphone's camera is activated, and the virtual content is visible, overlaying the physical world (see Fig. 5b). The virtual content is activated either automatically by reaching the location linked to the POI or by scanning the attached QR code (see Fig. 5a). Depending on the situation, a virtual assistant provides valuable tips and information to guide the user (see Fig. 5a).

The user of CirculAR can utilize finger gestures for object manipulation (both rotation and positioning) on the touch-based display of their smartphone [27]. The 3D object manipulation allows for six degrees of freedom (6DOF) which include 3DOF for object positioning (x, y, and z-axes) and 3DOF for object rotation (x, y, and z-axes). The input is given through arrows and cursors of the UI interface, and finger gestures able to manipulate on-screen objects (see Fig. 5b). The gamification elements include, among others, a scoring system, badges, and a leaderboard. Surveys and quiz questions embedded in the AR content challenge the user's understanding and provide feedback to enhance the learning effectiveness of the process [28] (see Fig. 5c). The quiz questions are embedded to the virtual content and typically link to the knowledge acquired through the visualization process. The gamification and learning elements of the mobile app ensure a captivating and fun yet educative and engaging experience [29].

5 Results

5.1 Participants

In total, 127 valid responses were collected by the web survey distributed to the citizens of Karditsa, Greece. The participants viewed the demo of CirculAR and answered all the questions mentioned in Tables 1 and 2. Additionally, they provided information regarding their demographics. Most of the participants are females (63%), but all share the same distribution in education levels, age, and tech-savviness. In all age groups the percentage of female participants fluctuate from 60 to 70%. Table 3 summarizes the demographics of the participants and tech-savviness.

5.2 Descriptive Statistics

Overall, we used descriptive statistics to summarize the data we collected, and Table 4 shows the mean value and standard deviation for the average values of all measures. According to [30] parametric tests can be used to analyze Likert scale responses and are recommended in cases where fewer concrete concepts are measured such as motivation and satisfaction. Following the next sections, we determine Cronbach alpha to provide evidence that the components of the scale are sufficiently intercorrelated and that the grouped items measure the underlying variable. The mean values closer to 1

Table 3. Summary of survey items.

	N	%
Sex		
Male	44	34,6
Female	80	63
Other	3	2,4
Age		
18–25	12	9,4
26–35	39	30,7
36–45	19	15
46–55	37	29,1
56–65	19	15
Education		
School	11	8,7
Bachelor	86	67,7
Masters	25	19,7
PhD	5	3,9
Other	0	0
Tech-savviness		
Use of smartphone	124	98
Use of camera	127	100
Mobile gaming	84	66.1
Use of AR	73	57,5
Total participants	127	

demonstrate the more robust agreement with the statements provided with the questionnaire and, after that, the higher tendency towards the technology acceptance measures. Participants demonstrate the highest tendency towards using the AR engagement tool, showing the lowest mean value and more minor standard deviation.

5.3 Validation of Measures

For all measures shown in Table 1 we also determined Cronbach's alpha. Cronbach's alpha (α) is a measure of internal consistency and reflects how closely related a set of items are as a group. Values of the parameter from 0.7 to 0.9 were considered "respectable" to "very good," and values above 0.9 were considered "excellent" [31]. Table 5 shows the alpha values (α) for all measures.

Principal component analysis (PCA) was then run with all measures to ensure that a single factor did not emerge. Correlations for the measures used in the study were

Table 4. Descriptive statistics for TAM measures.

Measure	Nr of items	Mean	SD
AU	3	1.609	0.584
PEoU	5	1.676	0.614
PU	3	1.614	0.593
BI	3	1.745	0.618

Table 5. Reliability estimates and intercorrelations for measures.

Measure	α	AU	PEoU	PU	BI
AU	0.83	1			
PEoU	0.94	0.753	1		
PU	0.89	0.842	0.730	1	
BI	0.84	0.854	0.721	0.849	1

calculated and shown in Table 3. They all appeared to be associated with each other, and all correlations were significant at the 0.01 level. The correlation between all measures had associations between 0.6 and 0.9. Overall, there was internal consistency among the four measures.

5.4 Hypotheses Testing

To verify our hypotheses (H1 to H5), we examined the relationships between pairs of the appropriate constructs defined in the research model using regression analysis. IBM SPSS statistics 23 software was used for the analysis. The results are presented in Table 6. The significance was less than the assumed significance level of 0.001 for all calculated regression values. Thus, for each of the hypotheses, we rejected the null hypothesis indicating the lack of dependence. The attitude towards using the AR engagement tool depends to a similar extent on the perceived ease of use (0.753) and perceived usefulness (0.842). The high relevance of PEoU and PU of the AR app with its acceptance might be since the users are willing to adopt a beneficial application that could make their lives convenient and guide them towards a more sustainable society. It has been proposed that to foster individual intention to use technology, a positive perception of the technology's usefulness is crucial [32]. Similarly, we accepted the H3, H4, and H5, as they demonstrated equally high values [33].

PEoU has a substantial influence on PU. To ensure that the bond remains strong, this may imply that proper user training is essential for improving users' perception of the usefulness of new technology to ensure high usage.

Table 6. The regression analysis for all measures in TAM model.

Hypothesis	Specification	Estimate	Significance
H1	PEoU → AT	0.753	p < 0.001
H2	PU → AT	0.842	p < 0.001
H3	PU → BI	0.849	p < 0.001
H4	PEoU → PU	0.730	p < 0.001
H5	AU → BI	0.854	p < 0.001

5.5 External Variables

We proceeded by further studying other factors affecting the TAM measures. The tech-savviness, age, education level, and gender of the users were identified as external variables affecting the acceptance of the technology. These factors were selected based on their effect on adopting similar citizen engagement tools [4, 5]. We analyzed the trends that these factors have on the TAM measures. Since these factors were assessed by either yes/no questions or a never-to-always scale, visual observations were considered more appropriate means of verification. Figure 6 summarizes our findings.

The education level of the participants demonstrated minimal effect on the TAM measures. A slight tendency towards higher behavioral intention appears among participants of higher education. Previous studies have reported that tools that demonstrate a high degree of relevance to their end-users appear to be more accepted, while the simplicity and easiness of navigating an ICT service may favor its acceptance [16]. End users of higher education levels may have been exposed to more information and communication tools.

Tech-savviness as demonstrated by the exposure of the participants to AR technology demonstrated slight variations in most TAM measures but overall, both users and non-AR-users achieved high scores in all measures (above 85%). As expected, participants who were previously exposed to AR technology appear to score higher compared to those who were seeing this type of technology for the first time. These differences should not be discouraging for non-AR users and further research should be contacted to investigate the progression in these values over further exposure. All differences among males and females appear to be less than 5%, proving that the AR engagement tool is positively accepted by both genders equally. This is a positive finding demonstrating that after 24 years, females have filled the gap in the acceptance of computer-based technologies demonstrated by Gefen and Staub [15].

A measure of higher acceptance appears to be among younger participants. While investigating other measures that may affect this tendency, both young and senior age groups demonstrate minor differences, below ~5%, in tech-savviness, education level, and gender variances. The demographics of our research study appear to be following the study performed by Guner and Acarturk [14]. Guner and Acarturk [15] reported that senior citizens prefer more ICT services that enable physical contact. Not only is the AR engagement tool a service to be used by each citizen by themselves, but the way it was presented to the participants (via video demonstration) may have enhanced

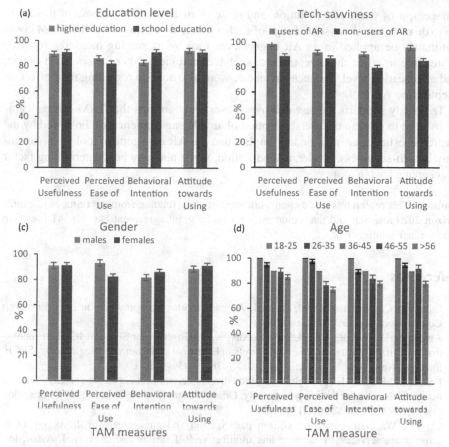

Fig. 6. The effects of (a) education level, (b) tech-savviness via exposure to AR, (c) gender, and (d) age of the participants on the TAM measures (mean agree or disagree statements ± SD, p < 0.001).

the perception that will not empower physical socializing among end-users. As Guner and Acarturk [14], also reported, the usefulness of ICT may positively influence the attitude of senior citizens toward use; however, it may not necessarily imply an intention to use ICT. In Fig. 6, perceived usefulness scored highest among all other measures of acceptance. Overall, answers remain consistent among age groups which agrees with previous research findings that both young and senior adults confirm TAM [14].

6 Conclusions

A mobile AR engagement tool has been designed and developed and its system design is presented to ensure that the features and content of such a tool are better understood and adopted in future efforts. Its use has been demonstrated to engage the citizens of a municipality in sustainable practices that benefit the consumption of resources, management of waste and pollution, and reuse of material. The purpose of this study was to demonstrate the system design of such a tool and determine whether TAM could legitimately be applied in an AR engagement tool by examining measures reported by literature to affect the acceptance of such technologies. Other factors, such as age, gender, education level, and tech-savviness, were also studied regarding their effect on accepting the AR tool.

This study supports the research hypotheses and confirms that TAM can be legitimately used to explain the users' adoption of an AR engagement tool. Followed by the research question, our main finding implies that the AR engagement tool fosters inclusivity in tech-savviness, gender, and education, while age may be a determining factor for accepting such a tool.

Funding. This research is based upon work supported by funding from the European Union's Horizon 2020 research and innovation program under grant agreement No. 776541 (nextGen circular water solutions).

References

1. European Commission. COM, 98 final, A new Circular Economy Action Plan; European Commission: Brussels, Belgium (2020)
2. Anderson, D., Wu, R., Cho, J.S., Schroeder, K.: E-Government Strategy, ICT and Innovation for Citizen Engagement SpringerBriefs in Electrical and Computer Engineering. SECE. Springer, New York. https://doi.org/10.1007/978-1-4939-3350-1
3. Lekan, M., Rogers, H.A.: Digitally enabled diverse economies: exploring socially inclusive access to the circular economy in the city. Urban Geogr. **41**(6), 898–901 (2020). https://doi.org/10.1080/02723638.2020.1796097
4. Olphert, W., Damodaran, L.: Citizen participation and engagement in the design of e-government services: the missing link in effective ICT design and delivery. J. Assoc. Inf. Syst. **8**(9), 27 (2007). https://doi.org/10.17705/1jais.00140
5. Church, S.: Photovoice as a Community Engagement Tool in Place-Based Sustainable Neighborhood Design: A Review of Literature (2020)
6. Dede, C.: Immersive interfaces for engagement and learning. Science **323**(5910), 66–69 (2009). https://doi.org/10.1126/science.1167311
7. Brooks, K.: There is nothing virtual about immersion: narrative immersion for VR and other interfaces. Motorola Labs/Human Interface Labs (2003)
8. Billinghurst, M., Duenser, A.: Augmented reality in the classroom. Computer **45**(7), 56–63 (2012). https://doi.org/10.1109/MC.2012.111
9. Bilge, G., Hehl-Lange, S., Lange, E.: The use of mobile devices in participatory decision-making. JoDLA J. Digit. Landscape Archit. 234–242 (2016)
10. Goudarznia, T., Pietsch, M., Krug, R.: Testing the effectiveness of augmented reality in the public participation process: a case study in the city of bernburg. J. Digit. Landscape Archit. **2**, 244–251 (2017). https://doi.org/10.14627/537629025
11. Santos, M.E.C., Taketomi, T., Sandor, C., Polvi, J., Yamamoto, G., Kato, H.: A usability scale for handheld augmented reality. In: Proceedings of the 20th ACM Symposium on Virtual Reality Software and Technology, pp. 167–176, November 2014
12. Davis, F.: Perceived usefulness, perceived ease of use, and user acceptance of information technology. MIS Q. **13**(3), 319–340 (1989). https://doi.org/10.2307/249008

13. Legris, P., Ingham, J., Collerette, P.: Why do people use information technology? A critical review of the technology acceptance model. Inf. Manage. **40**(3), 191–204 (2003). https://doi.org/10.1016/S0378-7206(01)00143-4
14. Guner, H., Acarturk, C.: The use and acceptance of ICT by senior citizens: a comparison of technology acceptance model (TAM) for elderly and young adults. Univ. Access Inf. Soc. **19**(2), 311–330 (2018). https://doi.org/10.1007/s10209-018-0642-4
15. Gefen, D., Straub, D.W.: Gender differences in the perception and use of e-mail: an extension to the technology acceptance model. MIS Q. 389–400 (1997)
16. Burton-Jones, A., Hubona, G.S.: Individual differences and usage behavior: revisiting a technology acceptance model assumption. ACM SIGMIS Database DATABASE for Adv. Inf. Syst. **36**(2), 58–77 (2005)
17. Masse, M.: REST API Design Rulebook: Designing Consistent RESTful Web Service Interfaces. O'Reilly Media, Inc. (2011)
18. VUE.js: The Progressive Javascript Framework. https://vuejs.org/
19. Django: Python Web framework. https://www.djangoproject.com/
20. PostgreSQL: open source object-relational database. https://www.postgresql.org/
21. Keycloak: Open-Source Identity Access Management. https://www.keycloak.org/
22. OAuth 2.0: industry-standard protocol for authorization. https://oauth.net/2/
23. NGINX Service Mesh. https://www.nginx.com/
24. Unity game engine: cross-platform game engine. https://unity.com/
25. ARCore: a software development kit. https://developers.google.com/ar/
26. MapBox: Precise location data. https://www.mapbox.com/
27. Goh, E.S., Sunar, M.S., Ismail, A.W.: 3D object manipulation techniques in handheld mobile augmented reality interface: a review. IEEE Access **7**, 40581–40601 (2019). https://doi.org/10.1109/ACCESS.2019.2906394
28. Pashler, H., Cepeda, N.J., Wixted, J.T., Rohrer, D.: When does feedback facilitate learning of words? J. Exp. Psychol. Learn. Memory Cognit. **31**, 3–8 (2005)
29. Harvey, P.H., Currie, E., Daryanani, P., Augusto, J.C.: Enhancing student support with a virtual assistant. In: Vincenti, G., Bucciero, A., de Carvalho Vaz, C. (eds.) E-Learning, E-Education, and Online Training. eLEOT. LNICSSITE, vol. 160, pp. 101–109. Springer, Cham (2016). https://doi.org/10.1007/978-3-319-28883-3_13
30. Sullivan, G.M., Artino Jr., A.R.: Analyzing and interpreting data from Likert-type scales. J. Graduate Med. Educ. **5**(4), 541 (2013). https://doi.org/10.4300/JGME-5-4-18.
31. Pallant, J.: SPSS Survival Manual: A Step-by-Step Guide to Data Analysis Using SPSS Version 15. McGraw Hill, Nova Iorque (2007)
32. Masrom, M.: Technology acceptance model and e-learning. Technology **21**(24), 81 (2007)
33. Akman, I., Mishra, A.: Sector diversity in green information technology practices: technology acceptance model perspective. Comput. Hum. Behav. **49**, 477–486 (2015)

VR Simulation of Operating Procedure in Construction Based on BIM and Safety Ontology: A Proof of Concept

Barbara Schiavi[1,2,3(✉)], Vincent Havard[1], Karim Beddiar[4], and David Baudry[1]

[1] LINEACT, CESI, 76800 Saint-Étienne-du-Rouvray, France
{bschiavi,vhavard,dbaudry}@cesi.fr
[2] ENSAM, Université Art et Métiers ParisTech, 75013 Paris, France
[3] VINCI Construction France, 92000 Nanterre, France
[4] LINEACT, CESI, 44000 Nantes, France
kbeddiar@cesi.fr

Abstract. Virtual Reality has shown its relevance to assist in various construction activities. However, its use requires a lot of additional work to be integrated into BIM process. In literature, the usefulness of phasing BIM element for creating training session in AR or VR has been highlighted. Operating site procedures involve different stakeholders such as QHSE experts and Design engineers. This paper introduces an architecture and presents a proof of concept that allows interoperability between a phased BIM operating procedure and a VR simulation associated with QHSE knowledge formalized using ontology. As a result, a VR training and safety simulation based on this architecture is presented and use cases are discussed.

Keywords: Virtual Reality (VR) · Operating procedure · Building Information Modeling (BIM) · Construction · Ontology · Safety · System architecture

1 Introduction

Construction industry is constantly evolving and requires resources and training for project stakeholders [1]. In literature, we can find VR/AR technologies used in all phases of a construction project for: Engagement of stakeholders by effectively collaborating around the project 3D model; design assistance, design review and help in the planning and spatial organization on the site; works and their smooth running [2, 3]. Finally, they allow to train on on-site operation, management, or risk prevention in complete safety [4].

With the Building Information Modelling (BIM) adoption in the construction industry [5], it is necessary to use 3D model, metadata and knowledge available in the BIM for VR/AR applications in this sector. Due to the details and complexity of 3D BIM models, they are not usable as such in VR/AR scene. Indeed, the model must go through geometry optimization, which is not possible today in the native BIM format that is IFC because the modelling/optimization software does not support this format [6]. By transforming

© Springer Nature Switzerland AG 2021
P. Bourdot et al. (Eds.): EuroXR 2021, LNCS 13105, pp. 126–141, 2021.
https://doi.org/10.1007/978-3-030-90739-6_8

the format of the model, it loses the associated metadata. Some commercial solutions lighten the steps for consulting the BIM model and data in AR or VR compared to the architectures found in the literature for a specific use [7–9], but they are generic and not suitable for custom interactions and complex AR/VR scenarios. Even by using the commercial plugin that gives a solution to easily bring the BIM model in its 3D engine editor to develop custom VR/AR application, the 3D and the metadata are separated and not usable as an.ifc format. There is a need of recreating the link between 3D model and metadata.

Semantic web technologies and the emergence on the concept of a semantic construction digital twin are promising trends to tackle interoperability issues between various data and knowledge in this domain [10]. In order to use ontologies applied for Construction, the Building Information Modeling in IFC format could be converted in RDF/XML format [11] or in an OWL/XML format, called ifcOWL [12] but interoperability between BIM and VR is still challenging. Moreover, knowledge about QHSE (Quality, Health, Safety, Environment), is needed for VR training simulation in this domain, but is not always available in the BIM and can evolve over time as it is managed by a different department than the one dealing with the BIM. To address this need, semantic modeling of expert knowledge associated to BIM is studied. In [13], they used an IFC ontology combined with safety knowledge in order to automatically prevent potential hazard.

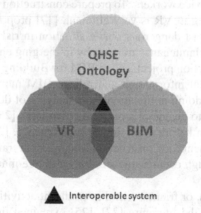

Fig. 1. Study focus scheme for the interoperable system

Therefore, there is a gap to fill between BIM data and VR training scenario considering QHSE rules. The study focusses on working for the interoperability between 3 different fields, represented in the Fig. 1: a phased BIM operating procedure, a VR simulation and QHSE knowledge basis. This paper presents the developed interoperable system following with the proof of concept with use cases studied and discussed.

The contributions of the presented system are multiple, such as:

– the real-time reasoning on QSHE rules regarding the VR simulation event,
– the use of the BIM metadata to populate the ontology with objects in the VR scene,
– the implemented QSHE rules work for different BIM operating procedure uploaded in VR.

The rest of this paper is organized as follows. Section 2 presents an overview of VR training applications in Architecture Engineering and Construction (AEC) sectors and of the association of semantic web and VR applications. Section 3 describes the proposed methodology for interoperability between VR simulation, BIM and domain knowledge. Results and discussion on use cases are presented in Sect. 4. Finally, conclusion and future research directions are presented in Sect. 5.

2 Related Work

2.1 VR Training in AEC

Virtual Reality has proved its usefulness in AEC projects since couple decades. The research trends over the last ten years were conducted due to the release of more and more advanced frameworks and VR devices [14–16]. VR is used more as a headset with a wire connection to PC [17, 18], and for the activities of Design Review or Simulation [19, 20]. But it can also be found for Operation on site training, Safety training, Maintenance training and Construction Management training [21].

To improve the effectiveness of learning methods, [22] proposed to overcome the lack of content diversity by using gamifications elements in VR to teach and train either experienced workers or novice workers. To prepare construction workers to avoid worksite hazards, safety training in VR is very efficient. [17] proposed safety scenarios in VR to train workers to most dangerous onsite situation in risk free simulations. [23] studied the use of VR in Maintenance training by immerging engineering students into the 3D model of a construction project, called BIM for Building Information Modeling, in order to access technical information and related BIM metadata. In another work [24] studied the manager doing notifications and analyses of defects by inspecting the building in virtual reality to decide of a repairing plan later. [25] has shown the viable results of using simulation before a mission of maintenance. [26] proposed to use the Second Life VR environment for Construction Management training purpose. Students experienced to learn through event sequences and resource management on a realistic onsite experience.

Studies, developments, or frameworks that would fit activities and training in AEC industry can be found in the literature [27]. [25] explained that operators trained in augmented reality is a continuum of the simulated activities developed in virtual reality. Onsite activities where operators are confronted with the physical constraints of the worksite can be adapted from existing VR solutions. Indeed, an operator that would follow a step-by-step assistance on given tasks use the same jobsite knowledge than a student learning a material handling task.

The main drawbacks in VR trainings remain the lack of diversity of content and the outdate of the information. Indeed, the creation of content is complex and required a certain amount of development, without update it leads to stiff experiences with non-long-term reusability.

2.2 Semantic Web and VR Applications

Several authors have explored the use of semantic web techniques and ontology associated to VR applications and some of these works are presented in Table 1. The combination of these technologies is used in various fields such as advanced visualization and interactions with complex data like molecular data in immersive environment [28], modeling and configuration in VR of domestic environments for Assisted Living [29], or VR training and simulation.

In order to increase trainee's liberties in term of interactions inside a VR training experience or for the developers of the VR application in term of hard coding scripted scenario, the usage of web semantic techniques can be found in the literature [30–33]. First responders training in VR associated to process knowledge or scenario available

Table 1. Semantic web and VR applications.

Reference	Ontology	Semantic technique and tools	At VR runtime reasoning or query	Domain
[28]	Structural biology and interaction concepts ontology	OWL, SPARQL	X	VR Visualization and Analysis of Molecular Data
[29]	Home Knowledge Base ontology	RDF, OWL, SWRL, Protégé[a]	Not specified	MR/VR configuration of domestic environments for Assisted Living
[30]	Firefighting process	Not specified	X	VR Simulation System for Fire Fighting
[31]	PRESTO ontology for VR scenario and character behaviors	Protégé	Not specified	VR training operations on emergency scenarios
[32]	Industrial ontology for operation in AR or VR	OWL, SPARQL		AR or VR procedures in Manufacturing industry
[33]	Scenario ontology	OWL		VR training in industrial environment
[34, 35]	Virtual interactive environment ontology	Protégé		VR Risk-Hunting training application in AEC

[a]https://protege.stanford.edu/

in the semantic layer is studied in [30, 31]. Ontologies can also be used as the expert knowledge base which helps authoring AR/VR training procedures in manufacturing industry [32]. In [33], authors proposed semantic modeling of VR training in industrial environment. These works show the possibilities offered by the semantic web technologies to model scenarios and expert knowledge and use it in VR. Nevertheless, capability of reasoning and of query new information in relation to events and interactions during the VR training session are very little used and still challenging.

Moreover, only very few studies have been found in the AEC domain despite the emergence of the concept of a semantic construction digital twin [10]. A study developed a VR training application using an IFC ontology in order to prevent risks and hazard recognition by generating random experiences [34, 35]. The limitations of such implementation are that the interactions and scenarios are generic and scripted integrally in the application. Indeed, we can't find any job specific rules such as QHSE in these studies or the opportunity to add any.

3   Methodology

In AEC companies, different departments exist and work all together such as: Design engineering office, Training center and QHSE expert's division, in purpose of providing technical knowledge with safety notions. The objective of our proposal is to gather the knowledge in a VR training considering the different technical constraints and the automatization of updating information.

This section introduces the proposed system that can communicate between the VR simulation and the safety ontology. Through the ontology and the SWRL rules, the system uses reasoning engine to receive warnings information when an endangerment is detected. Moreover, an explanation of the step-by-step workflow of the system at the pre-runtime phase and on runtime phase is detailed.

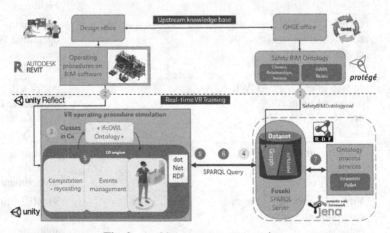

Fig. 2. Architecture system overview

3.1 System Overview

The Fig. 2 is an overview of the system architecture. On the top of the figure, we can find the Upstream Knowledge Base used for the VR simulation of the operating procedure. The information related to the procedure comes from the work collaboration between the Design office and the QHSE office. The Design engineers create each phase of step-by-step instructions of an operating procedure using a BIM software (see Fig. 2–2). Each BIM object's metadata is filled such as: weight, dimensions, here using Autodesk Revit software.

The QHSE experts create ontology axioms based on the Safety BIM Ontology, proposed and detailed later on, which is mainly composed of class Entity, Person and Object (see Fig. 2–1). It is populated based on the ifcOWL ontology [36] associated with our proposed ontology. The ontology is associated with SWRL rules for risks prevention and safety information for the operators, here called QHSE warnings that would be triggered when the operator is in danger or not having a safe behavior.

Virtual Reality simulation of the operating procedure is shown on the bottom-left of the Fig. 2. The VR simulation is created within a 3D engine, here using the Unity engine (see Fig. 2–5). It contains developed scripts for managing the interactions made in VR by the operator, the data connections with the SPARQL Server, here using the dotNetRDF library, to send and receive RDF triple via SPARQL queries (see Fig. 2–6). An automated script developed within the used plugin retrieve BIM data of each BIM object as an ifcOWL ontology in the engine editor. This one will be used for populating the Safety BIM Ontology designed by the QHSE experts (see Fig. 2–3). The SPARQL Server, on the bottom-right of the figure, contains a Dataset containing a Schema graph which is the Safety BIM Ontology. The server is configured to work with reasoners and rule engines such as Pellet, here using the Fuseki server and the Inference API of the Jena Apache framework (see Fig. 2–7).

3.2 The Safety BIM Ontology (SBO)

The Safety BIM Ontology aims to get mid-level information about each entity in the VR scene during the training period. Due to this information, some QHSE rules can be defined. Therefore, at each moment, the SBO can infer risky behavior and detect danger. The detailed SBO ontology is represented in Fig. 3. SBO contains Object and Person classes that inherits from the Entity class, these two classes are disjoint. As shown on Fig. 3, the SBO defines ObjectProperty such as: Person isCarrying Object, Object isCarriedBy Person, Entity isUnder Entity, Entity isAbove Entity. It also defines DataProperty Entity weight float. Finally, SBO defines subclasses of QHSE class. Each instance of a QHSE class represents something that is not respecting the QHSE rules. Therefore, during the training session, rules not following QHSE recommendations can be easily found by requesting all instances of QHSE class with SPARQL queries.

As an example, Person has three subclasses: PersonInDanger, PersonHeavyCarrying and PersonTooExposedToDanger. These classes represent the state of an operator when this one is in a risky behavior.

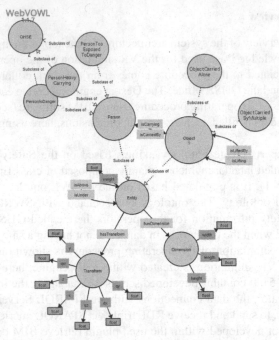

Fig. 3. The safety BIM ontology graph representation

3.3 Detailed Workflow

In this part, the description of how the upstream knowledge base is uploaded and used in the VR simulation is presented. Moreover, data workflow is detailed step-by-step below to explain what is set on pre-runtime of the application and applied on-runtime. Each step is corresponding to a number in Fig. 2.

Pre-runtime Phase. Step 1: The Safety BIM Ontology containing the SWRL rules is uploaded into the server as an.owl file in the Schema graph of the Dataset.

Step 2: From the BIM software, the phased operating procedure and its associated BIM data are exported to the 3D game engine editor using a plugin, here Unity Pro and Unity Reflect. Then the 3D model is placed in the VR scene which will be used for the simulation and which contains VR and Networking frameworks needed to run as a multi-user experience in Virtual Reality, here using Photon Unity Networking.

Step 3: As explain in the introduction, it is difficult to develop a custom VR experience with the 3D BIM model and data as the .ifc format is not supported by the 3D engines. Indeed, the BIM geometry and the BIM data are separated at file export for optimization and then the data are associated back to each BIM object via a script "Metadata" as component once imported in the 3D engine. Therefore, an automatic recreation of the "ifcOWL ontology" of the BIM model is made in C# classes through the 3D engine editor. This will help with managing RDF triples and SPARQL queries to communicate with the server during the VR simulation.

On-runtime Phase. Step 4: This initialization step is done only once at the beginning of the simulation. First, a connection is made with the server to get the Schema graph containing the Safety BIM Ontology. Then the individuals of the operators, the objects in the VR simulation are declared to the Schema graph of the Fuseki Server by sending RDF triples that match our proposed SBO.

Step 5: In the VR simulation, an Events Manager is centralizing any event that could be used by the SBO. An event is triggered when an interaction is made by the operators or if behaviors are detected such as BIM objects being one above others. For example, BIMObject1 is under BIMObject2 because BIMObject2 has been moved by the crane.

Step 6: This information is then sent to the Fuseki server to update the SBO axioms graph by adding or removing the information. Therefore, every property value assignment that would infer with the SWRL rules is made on the VR simulation side. We chose to proceed this way because the engine allows to do computation such as raycast between objects and to easily determine the real-time position of each (see Fig. 2–5), this is more detailed in the use cases.

Step 7: On the server side, the Fuseki server configured to run the Pellet reasoner using the Jena Inference API service is reasoning to infer on the Schema Graph's SWRL rules. The results are written in the Inference Model declared in the config.ttl of the server as InfModel. Technically, the ontology file, SafetyBIMOntology.owl is uploaded to the local Fuseki server, and can exchange triplets with Virtual Reality Simulation of the operating procedure.

Step 8: Back in the VR Simulation, at fixed updated we check for QHSE warnings in the Schema Graph such as QHSE individuals, if so, a message is displayed in the VR simulation.

4   Case Study

This section describes the use cases evaluated, the different QHSE rules tested, and the results obtained by implementing the proposed system.

4.1   General Use Case Description

Before creating the operating procedures in BIM, the Design office and the QHSE office worked together to develop 2D operating procedures. An example can be found in Fig. 4. It is a procedure for an on-site poured concrete wall. Each phase is represented by an illustration and step-by-step instructions. We can also find colored inscriptions coming from the QHSE recommendations: red for safety, blue for quality and green for environment. Therefore, with the creation of the 3D operating procedure in the BIM software and then integrated into the virtual reality simulation the proposed workflow and architecture will be used in order to have the QHSE information, the safety one, for VR training.

In this case study, two phases of a similar procedure have been created on Autodesk Revit software and then imported in Unity Editor using Unity Reflect. Each BIM object would have been assigned with scripts for interaction in the VR scene such as: Grabble by the operator, Connectable with other BIM objects.

To represent the QHSE warnings in the use case, two safety rules have been chosen to be verified while this operating procedure is executed by operators:

– Do not carry weights greater than 25 kg
– Do not stay under the crane's lifting area

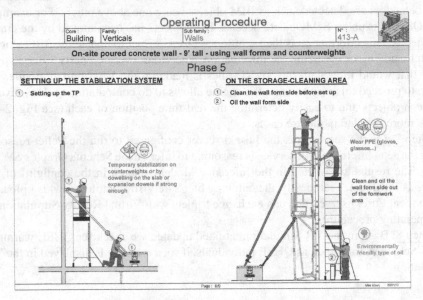

Fig. 4. Page 6 of 9 of the operating procedures

The two safety rules lead to several sub-conditions that need to be verified such as if the object is carried by multiple persons. These are studied in the 3 following use cases.

Regarding the Safety BIM Ontology for the experiment, we chose to create a light version of the SBO since SWRL implementations need computation power and are only usable with small or medium ontologies or using optimized methods [37].

Regarding the VR simulation represented in Fig. 5, two operators are in the scene on runtime phase and initialized as a Person in the SBO stored in Fuseki server through SPARQL request. The same process is applied to the various objects present in the VR scene that are also initialized and sent to the server as Object, such as a crane, a bag of sand of 20 kg, a bag of rocks of 40 kg, a metal tube of 80 kg, and a counterweight of 1750 kg. To identify each of them, the unique BIM element ID is used. The declaration of each entity is done automatically at the upload of BIM model and is represented here in Notation3 as follow:

```
@prefix sbo: <http://www.semanticweb.org/barbara.schiavi/ontologies/2021/3/SafetyBI-
MOntology#>.
@prefix rdfs: <http://www.w3.org/2000/01/rdf-schema#>.
@prefix xsd: <http://www.w3.org/2001/XMLSchema#>.

sbo:257485104 rdfs:is sbo:Object
sbo:w_ xsd:float "40"
sbo:257485104 sbo:weight sbo:w_

sbo:2754481 rdfs:is sbo:Person
```

Finally, SWRL rules have been created and are detailed in the next sections. Once the VR simulation is running and the SBO populated on the server, the 3 following use cases are verified in real-time.

Fig. 5. VR scene in Unity engine

4.2 Results and Discussion

Use Case 1: Do Not Carry Weights Greater Than 25 kg. In this case we are verifying if one of the operators is in danger by carrying an object. We also verify if the operators are carrying the safety rule is also applied if the operators are carrying together an object.

The SWRL rules implemented in the SBO to verify this case are:

```
S1: Person(?op1) ^ ObjectCarriedAlone(?o1) ^ isCarrying(?op1, ?o1) ^ weight(?o1, ?w)
^ swrlb:greaterThan(?w, "25.0"^^xsd:float) -> PersonHeavyCarrying(?op1)

S2: Person(?op1) ^ Person(?op2) ^ ObjectCarriedByMultiple(?o1) ^ weight(?o1, ?w) ^
swrlb:greaterThan(?w, "50.0"^^xsd:float) -> PersonHeavyCarrying(?op1) ^ PersonHeavyCar-
rying(?op2)
```

To proceed, the operator first starts by carrying the bag of sand, then by carrying the bag of rocks. An event is triggered each time an operator grabs an object or drops it off. A new triple is sent to the server to declare that the operator is carrying an object with "isCarrying", and the same triple is removed when the object is dropped off. At fixed update, QHSE warnings are retrieved if exists in the Inference Model and the related QHSE warning message is displayed in the User Interface. The same test is done with two operators starting by carrying together the bag of rocks and then the metal tube.

The results can be found in Fig. 6. We verified that the system works, the Inference API using Pellet reasoner in the server is inferring and storing the results in the Inference Model.

Use Case 2: Do Not Stay Under the Crane's Lifting Area. In this case we verify if the operator is not in danger by being under the counterweight while the crane is lifting it. The SWRL rule implemented in the ontology to verify this case is:

```
S3: Person(?op1) ^ Object(?c1) ^ Object(?o1) ^ isLifting(?c1, ?o1) ^ isAbove(?o1, ?op1)
-> PersonInDanger(?op1)
```

In this experimentation, at the beginning the operator is not under the counterweight and then he moves under the lifted object. This event is triggered by reason of the 3D engine and an implemented code that casts rays, from the top of each object to the up direction. As the hit of the ray collided with the object, a new triple has been sent to the server to declare that the operator was under the counterweight (or the counterweight is above the operator).

The result in this case is a QHSE warning displaying that the operator is in danger such as for the first use case. We chose to give the 3D engine a major role in computing distances, object positions, ray casting, but this would have been possibly done differently. Indeed, a SWRLAPI provides several built-in libraries that can do all the computation needed to verify the rules. However, this must be tested because such implemented rules would take a lot of computation and the system might not maintain a real-time experience.

Another experiment was conducted in this use case to test if the system works with different RDF triples sent to the server from the VR simulation using the same SWRL rule. To proceed we assigned the property "isAbove" instead of "isUnder" and the property "isLiftedBy" instead of "isLifting" with the corresponded property values.

The SBO has been created with inverse properties to simplify the work of QHSE experts while defining their SWRL rules to not try to match what have been implemented in the VR application and vis versa.

Use Case 3. In this use case we want to update the Safety BIM Ontology with new SWRL rules on runtime phase to verify if the system would still be working and the new QHSE warnings be triggered.

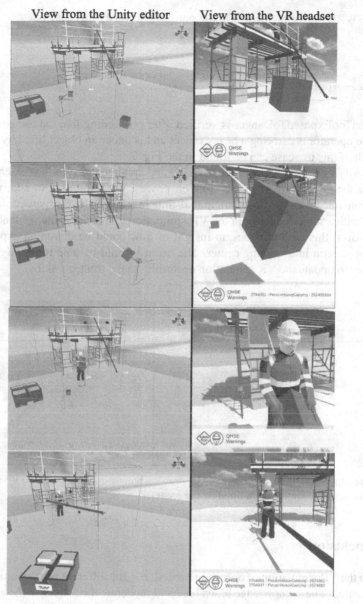

Fig. 6. Results of the first use case [from top to bottom: VR operator carrying a bag of 20 kg (represented by the brown cube), a bag of 40 kg (represented by the grey cube), 2 operators carrying a bag of 40 kg, a metal tube of 80 kg] (Color figure online)

The SWRL rule implemented in the ontology to verify this case is:

```
S4:    PersonHeavyCarrying(?op1)    ^    PersonInDanger(?op1)    ->    PersonTooEx-
posedToDanger(?op1)
```

PersonTooExposedToDanger is verified after proceeding like the use case 1 and 2 where the operator is carrying a heavy object and is under an object lifted by the crane. The result of this use case can be found in the Fig. 7.

By verifying this case, the proposed SBO and architecture system is extending freedoms for the QHSE expert in the creation process by being able to add, remove or adjust some rules while testing them in real-time in VR. A QHSE expert could be easily working with a senior operator in the VR simulation to match on site feedback.

Moreover, this case provides an insight of how could be driven an experience of a training session in a training center. The trainer would be able to modify rules and difficulties to update the VR simulation according to the trainee's skills.

Fig. 7. Results of the third use case [2 operators carrying a metal tube of 80 kg and the VR operator is under a counterweight lifted by the crane]

5   Conclusion

Through the VR simulation of operating procedures, the different professional expertise is represented. These knowledge bases feed and moderate the actions in the application.

This architecture of the system simply allows additions, modifications, deletions of knowledge base as needed. Indeed, the virtual reality simulation could accommodate other ontologies such as for off-site assembly operations from industrial prefabrications, DfMi, etc. [38]. No changes are required on the application side if rules are modified in an ontology. Thus, IT developers are less mobilized as a resource for updating scripts and expert's knowledge in the application. Moreover, this promotes flexibility in the interaction and possibilities in the simulation process with less scripting.

As a result of this system, each ontology author can create, test, and validate these classes, properties, and SWRL rules in VR, in an easily, quickly, and autonomous way.

A dedicated interface is currently in development to facilitate the access of rules edition for users that are not familiar with complex tool such as Protégé or Jena Fuseki. We thus have an efficient design tool that addresses all the stakeholders involved in the realization of a simulation of operating procedure in virtual reality.

The future developments of the system are multiple, first by the addition of new rules of safety related to the physical activity. This would require the addition of sensors or a suit in the VR scene for the preventive measurement of the respect of posture gestures [39]. Then by adding the BIM model of the building in the VR scene to locate the operation and exploit the BIM data for the purpose of constraints and precisions. Indeed, the constraints of the environment where the operation is carried out from one place to another of the building will generate various risks that our system will be able to raise. For example, the position of the operator in relation to obstacles, or the risk of falling if the operation is carried out on a floor above the ground floor.

References

1. Mostafa, K., Leite, F.: Evolution of BIM adoption and implementation by the construction industry over the past decade: a replication study. In: Construction Research Congress 2018: Construction Information Technology - Selected Papers from the Construction Research Congress 2018. pp. 180–189. American Society of Civil Engineers, Reston, VA (2018). https://doi.org/10.1061/9780784481264.018
2. Moraru, A.C., Pozanski, K.: Integrating BIM, virtual reality and serious gaming for effective collaboration and communication between end users and the design team. projekter.aau.dk (2020)
3. Sampaio, A.Z.: Improving BIM with VR in construction. In: 16th International Conference e-Society 2018, pp. 155 162 (2018)
4. Davila Delgado, J.M., Oyedele, L., Demian, P., Beach, T.: A research agenda for augmented and virtual reality in architecture, engineering and construction. Adv. Eng. Informatics. 45 (2020). https://doi.org/10.1016/j.aei.2020.101122
5. Gu, N., London, K.: Understanding and facilitating BIM adoption in the AEC industry. Autom. Constr. 19, 988–999 (2010). https://doi.org/10.1016/j.autcon.2010.09.002
6. Boeykens, S.: <3D_software_game_engine_BIM.pdf>. Des. Together-CAAD. (2011)
7. Xie, H., Shi, W., Issa, R.R.A.: Using RFID and real-time virtual reality simulation for optimization in steel construction. Electron. J. Inf. Technol. Constr. 16, 291–308 (2011)
8. Kwon, O.S., Park, C.S., Lim, C.R.: A defect management system for reinforced concrete work utilizing BIM, image-matching and augmented reality. Autom. Constr. 46, 74–81 (2014). https://doi.org/10.1016/j.autcon.2014.05.005
9. Du, J., Shi, Y., Mei, C., Quarles, J., Yan, W.: Communication by interaction: a multiplayer VR environment for building walkthroughs. In: Construction Research Congress 2016: Old and New Construction Technologies Converge in Historic San Juan - Proceedings of the 2016 Construction Research Congress, CRC 2016. pp. 2281–2290. American Society of Civil Engineers, Reston, VA (2016). https://doi.org/10.1061/9780784479827.227
10. Boje, C., Guerriero, A., Kubicki, S., Rezgui, Y.: Towards a semantic construction digital twin: directions for future research (2020). https://doi.org/10.1016/j.autcon.2020.103179
11. Zhang, L., Issa, R.R.A.: Development of IFC-based construction industry ontology for information retrieval from IFC models. EG-ICE 2011. Eur. Gr. Intell. Comput. Eng. (2014)
12. Pauwels, P., Terkaj, W.: EXPRESS to OWL for construction industry: towards a recommendable and usable ifcOWL ontology. Autom. Constr. 63, 100–133 (2016). https://doi.org/10.1016/j.autcon.2015.12.003

13. Zhang, S., Boukamp, F., Teizer, J.: Ontology-based semantic modeling of construction safety knowledge: towards automated safety planning for job hazard analysis (JHA). Autom. Constr. **52**, 29–41 (2015). https://doi.org/10.1016/j.autcon.2015.02.005
14. Herbers, P., König, M.: Indoor localization for augmented reality devices using BIM, point clouds, and template matching. Appl. Sci. **9**, 4260 (2019). https://doi.org/10.3390/app920 4260
15. Luo, X., Wong, C.-K., Chen, J.: A multi-player virtual reality-based education platform for construction safety. In: 16th International Conference on Computing in Civil and Building Engineering (2016)
16. Abbas, A., Choi, M., Seo, J., Cha, S.H., Li, H.: Effectiveness of immersive virtual reality-based communication for construction projects. KSCE J. Civ. Eng. **23**(12), 4972–4983 (2019). https://doi.org/10.1007/s12205-019-0898-0
17. Sacks, R., Perlman, A., Barak, R.: Construction safety training using immersive virtual reality. Constr. Manag. Econ. **31**, 1005–1017 (2013). https://doi.org/10.1080/01446193.2013.828844
18. Kieferle, J., Woessner, U.: BIM interactive - about combining bim and virtual reality. In: Real Time Proceedings of 33rd eCAADe Conference, Vienna, Austria, vol. 1, pp. 69–75 (2015)
19. Lin, Y.C., Chen, Y.P., Yien, H.W., Huang, C.Y., Su, Y.C.: Integrated BIM, game engine and VR technologies for healthcare design: a case study in cancer hospital. Adv. Eng. Informatics. **36**, 130–145 (2018). https://doi.org/10.1016/j.aei.2018.03.005
20. Natephra, W., Motamedi, A., Fukuda, T., Yabuki, N.: Integrating building information modeling and virtual reality development engines for building indoor lighting design. Vis. Eng. **5**(1), 1–21 (2017). https://doi.org/10.1186/s40327-017-0058-x
21. Behzadi, A.: Using augmented and virtual reality technology in the construction industry. Am. J. Eng. Res. 2320–847 (2016)
22. Wolf, M., Teizer, J., Ruse, J.H.: Case study on mobile virtual reality construction training. In: Proceedings of the 36th International Symposium on Automation and Robotics in Construction, ISARC 2019. pp. 1231–1237. pdfs.semanticscholar.org (2019). https://doi.org/10.22260/isarc2019/0165.
23. Sampaio, A.Z., Ferreira, M.M., Rosário, D.P., Martins, O.P.: 3D and VR models in Civil Engineering education: construction, rehabilitation and maintenance. Autom. Constr. **19**, 819–828 (2010). https://doi.org/10.1016/j.autcon.2010.05.006
24. Sampaio, A.Z., Rosário, D.P., Gomes, A.R., Santos, J.P.: Virtual reality applied on Civil Engineering education: construction activity supported on interactive models. Int. J. Eng. Educ. **29**, 1331–1347 (2013)
25. Sørensen, S.S.: Augmented reality for improved communication of construction and maintenance plans in nuclear power plants. In: Yoshikawa, H., Zhang, Z. (eds.) Progress of Nuclear Safety for Symbiosis and Sustainability, pp. 269–274. Springer, Tokyo (2014). https://doi.org/10.1007/978-4-431-54610-8_27
26. Sulbaran, T., Frederick, L., Iii, J.: AC 2012-5325: utilizing a collaborative virtual reality environment as a training tool for construction students. Int. J. Technol. Knowl. Soc. Int. J. Virtual Real. J. Mark. Educ. Mark. Educ. Rev. J. (2012)
27. Wang, P., Wu, P., Wang, J., Chi, H.L., Wang, X.: A critical review of the use of virtual reality in construction engineering education and training. Int. J. Environ. Res. Public Health. **15** (2018). https://doi.org/10.3390/ijerph15061204
28. Trellet, M., Férey, N., Flotyński, J., Baaden, M., Bourdot, P.: Semantics for an integrative and immersive pipeline combining visualization and analysis of molecular data. J. Integr. Bioinform. **15** (2018). https://doi.org/10.1515/jib-2018-0004
29. Spoladore, D., Arlati, S., Sacco, M.: Semantic and virtual reality-enhanced configuration of domestic environments: the smart home simulator. Mob. Inf. Syst. **2017**, 1–15 (2017). https://doi.org/10.1155/2017/3185481

30. Moreno, A., Zlatanova, S., Bucher, B., Posada, J., Toro, C.: Semantic enhancement of a virtual reality simulation system for fire fighting. 17 (2020)
31. Dragoni, M., Ghidini, C., Busetta, P., Fruet, M., Pedrotti, M.: Using ontologies for modeling virtual reality scenarios. In: Gandon, F., Sabou, M., Sack, H., d'Amato, C., Cudré-Mauroux, P., Zimmermann, A. (eds.) ESWC 2015. LNCS, vol. 9088, pp. 575–590. Springer, Cham (2015). https://doi.org/10.1007/978-3-319-18818-8_35
32. Havard, V., Benoit, J., Xavier, S., David, B.: INOOVAS - industrial ontology for operation in virtual and augmented scene: the architecture. In: 2017 4th International Conference on Control, Decision and Information Technologies, CoDIT 2017, pp. 300–305. IEEE (2017). https://doi.org/10.1109/CoDIT.2017.8102608
33. Flotyński, J., Walczak, K.: Ontology-based representation and modelling of synthetic 3D content: a state-of-the-art review. Comput. Graph. Forum. **36**, 329–353 (2017). https://doi.org/10.1111/cgf.13083
34. Dris, A., Lehericey, F., Gouranton, V., Arnaldi, B., Training, R.: Risk-hunting training in interactive virtual environments to cite this version: HAL Id: hal-01900450 risk-hunting training in interactive virtual (2018)
35. Dris, A.-S., Lehericey, F., Gouranton, V., Arnaldi, B.: OpenBIM based IVE ontology: an ontological approach to improve interoperability for virtual reality applications. In: Mutis, I., Hartmann, T. (eds.) Advances in Informatics and Computing in Civil and Construction Engineering, pp. 129–136. Springer, Cham (2019). https://doi.org/10.1007/978-3-030-00220-6_16
36. González, E., Piñeiro, J.D., Toledo, J., Arnay, R., Acosta, L.: An approach based on the ifcOWL ontology to support indoor navigation. Egypt. Informatics J. (2020). https://doi.org/10.1016/j.eij.2020.02.008
37. de Farias, T.M., Roxin, A., Nicolle, C.: SWRL rule-selection methodology for ontology interoperability. Data Knowl. Eng. **105**, 53–72 (2016). https://doi.org/10.1016/j.datak.2015.09.001
38. Li, H., Lu, M., Chan, G., Skitmore, M.: Proactive training system for safe and efficient precast installation. Autom. Constr. **49**, 163–174 (2015). https://doi.org/10.1016/j.autcon.2014.10.010
39. Havard, V., Jeanne, B., Lacomblez, M., Baudry, D.: Digital twin and virtual reality: a co-simulation environment for design and assessment of industrial workstations. Prod. Manuf. Res. **7**, 472–489 (2019). https://doi.org/10.1080/21693277.2019.1660283

Short Papers (Scientific Poster Session)

Automating Generation of Kinematic Keypoints for Disassembly Process Toward Virtual Reality

Sébastien Pascault[1,2]([⊠]), Frédéric Noël[1] [iD], Jérémie Le Garrec[2], Claude Andriot[2], and Adrien Girard[2]

[1] Université Grenoble Alpes, 621 Avenue Centrale, 38400 Saint-Martin-d'Hères, France
[2] CEA Paris-Saclay, 91191 Gif-sur-Yvette, France

Abstract. This paper describes a novel approach to generate and model assembly semantic meaning enclosed in product assembly features in order to optimize the preparation time of Virtual Reality simulations. The proposed approach is based on a set of heuristic rules to generate semantic KeyPoints (characterisation of a kinematic link or a mates) used to idealize an assembly model. This study identifies through a disassembly process a number of semantic rules in order to extract and translate assembly semantic features from CAD models. The proposed approach is based on two steps: features extraction and semantic recognition of the assembly features. In the first step, internal boundary representation (B-Rep) and mate extraction methods are used to retrieve the engineering meaning from assembly models using SolidWorks' API functions. In the second step, a multi-level semantic rules model is used. The approach is demonstrated and validated on a use-case with a disassembly process scenario and adapted to Virtual Reality.

Keywords: CAD model processing · Virtual reality · Feature extraction · Keypoint generation · Disassembly semantics · Rules engine

1 Introduction

Assembly processes in industrial environments are complex tasks with high total manufacturing and labour costs [1]. In addition, the market shift towards increasingly customised and durable products requires the development of increasingly flexible and robust manufacturing and assembly processes [2]. The traditional approach of manually adapting production cells and configurations to predefined products and product families cannot keep pace with the rapidly changing market requirements and product technologies. To shorten product life cycles (PLCs) and improve process planning, manufacturers are relying on virtual reality (VR) simulation [3].

The scene's behaviour in VR simulations is mainly leaded by user interaction and dynamics of solids including collision and kinematics, which are based on 3D products usually designed with a Computer-Aided Design (CAD) software. However, CAD modellers and VR environment do not use the same internal models even for rendering. The preparation of VR scenes remains time consuming due to the translation of models and the creation of additional information or information lost during translation. Even for

© Springer Nature Switzerland AG 2021
P. Bourdot et al. (Eds.): EuroXR 2021, LNCS 13105, pp. 145–151, 2021.
https://doi.org/10.1007/978-3-030-90739-6_9

basic systems, this requires a significant amount of engineering time, which reach one to several weeks for complex systems. In general, all preparation steps first implement a CAD model processing phase, where the features interesting for the specific process and their relations should be identified. The problem is that in most cases the data extracted from CAD systems rely on geometric information, while the intrinsic engineering meaning of the assembly's components are neglected. Indeed, the details associated with part functionality and technical meanings are usually implied. This kind of data may be in fact included as annotations in the CAD model, but these attributes are not rigorous nor standard since it depends on CAD software on the designer practise; thus it may result difficult to explicitly interpret them.

Here, the vision is to propose a CAD recognition approach for the semantic interpretation of 3D assembly models in order to solve current problems in terms of data preparation for mixed reality simulations in non-homogeneous software environments. The objective is to generate structured model in order to reduce the overall preparation time and minimize the manual intervention of a human operator.

This paper considers an approach to generate a disassembly semantic model based on information extracted from a 3D model to generate automating keypoint and features able to describe VR behaviours during a disassembly process.

2   Virtual Reality Disassembly Concepts

The automated generation of CAD assembly semantic is a subject highly addressed in the last decades. Techniques used in the literature are different, especially according to the format of the analysed 3D objects, which are represented by their surfaces (B-Rep) or by their volumes (CSG) [4]. In general, three main categories of methods are distinguished, namely: geometry based methods, graph based methods and feature based methods [5]. Our approach will focus on this latter.

2.1   Feature Based Approaches

To generate assembly joint from 3D models, assembly features representation are necessary. Assembly features describe the relation of components in an assembly group. A feature is defined here as *"a partial form or a product characteristic that is considered as a unit and that has an engineering semantic meaning for assembly design, process planning or manufacture"* [6]. To extract or recognize semantic features in CAD models many approaches exist. Hasan and Wikander [7] differentiate between three approaches: internal approaches, external approaches and ontology-based approaches. In internal methods, the Application Programming Interface (API) of the CAD software is used in order to extract topological, geometrical and assembly information related to a part or an assembly. While in external methods, a CAD model file is exported in a neutral data format (e.g. STEP-AP 214). C.M. Costat [8] focuses on internal approach to generate assembly sequence planning. A. Neb [2] combined external approaches with internal approaches to get the features directly from the 3D assembly model. Other authors use ontology base approaches to exploit geometric and shape information but those methods will not be covered here.

2.2 Keypoints: Main Specification for Physics Engines

To provide disassembly process in a virtual world, physics engines are used. Those engines provide an approximate simulation of certain physical systems such as rigid body dynamics, soft body dynamics or fluid dynamics. There are many available physics engine on the market such as Bullet, PhysX, ODE or XDE. Knowing our study focuses on VR we decided to use both PhysX and XDE which are direct kinematics engine well suitable for it. XDE Physics on the first hand is an interactive physics engine featuring precise collision detection, multibody and beam dynamics, at rate compatible with haptic rendering [9]. PhysX on the other hand is a scalable multi-platform physics engine providing the same features and already integrated into some of the most popular game engines, including Unreal Engine and Unity3D. Both XDE and PhysX offer a simple programming interface where assembly features (described in Sect. 2.1) can be used and easily implemented. To compute dynamics, most of the previously named physics engine have the ability to rely on specific "point features" in the assembly model allowing them to reason on kinematic links rather than collisions. Those "point features" are referred to as "key points" [10]. A KeyPoint (KP) can be defined as a reference point in the space associated with a part of an assembly that characterize a kinematic link or a mate (Fig. 2). KPs are specified by recognition algorithms according to certain mathematical base or specific rules (described in Sect. 4).

2.3 Extra Issues for Disassembly Process

Regarding assembly/disassembly process, lot of approaches have been proposed over the years. A. Neb [2] proposed an approach to generate automatically an Assembly Graphs just by using feature detection internal approach trough a SolidWorks (SW) API, but with the method of external approaches to generate assembly features out of low-level features. With a similar approach C.M.C. Costa [8] focuses on disassembly sequence from SW Symbolic Geometric Relationships and describes a recursive branch-and-bound algorithm to find the optimal disassembly plan. While the approaches presented above mainly focus on Robotic, our goal is to use all these features recognition methods for VR. Works with a similar objective has been carried out. For example, Z. Liu [11] presents a constrained behaviour management approach that realizes assembly relationship recognition, constraint solution and constrained motion to facilitate assembly interaction in VR. P. Bourdot [12] goes even further and proposes an approach based on a VR-CAD framework making possible intuitive and direct 3D edition on CAD objects within Virtual Environments.

3 Feature Recognition and Semantic Rules Approach

3.1 Feature Extraction from CAD Models

To solve data exchange between CAD design and other software two extraction framework were developed, following the approach of internal B-rep CAD analysis. A first framework has been developed to extract the features from the B-Rep topology. Open CASCADE technology (OCCT) was used to extract these features from a step file

(AP 242). The resulting dataset describes the different B-Rep shells of the model and all the associated data namely: transformation matrix, nature of the surfaces (plane, cone, cylinder, b-spline, etc.) and basic geometry characteristics (normal, radius, axis, orientation, bounding-box, center of mass and inertia). In order to describe VR behaviour of a product and identify the symbolic relationships between parts a second framework was created to extract the different primitive mates from a SW CAD assembly (all assembled). Those mates were extracted trough a SW API. The resulting mates dataset combined with the previous B-Rep dataset was finally imported in Unity3D to be exploited with a physics engine.

3.2 Semantic Rules Engine

Based on input from CAD dataset recognition stage above an assembly design Semantic Rules Engine (SRE) is proposed. This SRE describes a novel approach based on features recognition and detection rules to model assembly semantic meaning. The proposed SRE, is a decomposition into three semantic levels (or layers) inspired by Hasan work [13], namely: Geometric Level, Kinematic Level and Behaviour Level.

- On the Geometric Level regroups two type of features: Shell Feature and Form Features. Shell Feature are related to B-Rep entities extracted from the CAD modeller in order to detect specific surface shape for each assembly part. These shell features are then analysed according to simple heuristic rules based on the analysis of conventional naming or conventional geometric configuration (nearest neighbours, shell dimension or symmetry axis). This set of rules results in a form classification thus called Form Features (e.g., hole form, cylinder form, thread form, etc.).
- On the Kinematic Level, mating features are further analysed in order to determine joining features. Each imported mates is linked to two entities that corresponds to part in the assembly. The first entities represents the origin part where the mates is attached and the second entities represents another targeted part giving a first assembly knowledge for potential Joining Feature between them.
- Lastly, Behaviour Level regroups all the behaviour rules aimed to detect application-specific features whose semantics are carried by KeyPoints. Those KPs are classified into three different types. Handling KP firstly represents position on parts' surface where object can be grabbed by user hands or tools. Interest KP then defines specific positions inside parts where a kinematic joint exists. Lastly, Transition KP describes specific coordinates in parts where mates state and related degrees of freedom (DOF) can change according the part position in assembly at a given time.

The objectives of this SRE is to reproduce with the machine the recognition mechanism of a human engineer. Our approach differs from other methods in the scientific literature by its effectiveness to be applicable in real time. Its interest for the application in VR is that it makes possible to set up aids for the immersed user such as position ghosts, movement indicator or even part snapping close to their final position.

4 Use Case

To experiment the SRE, the use-case of a complex Honda engine CFR250X modeled in SW was chosen. The objective was to redo the complete disassembly process of a 3D model to compare our automatic approach with manual VR preparation methods. To identify the necessary semantic links inside the engine model, a unique disassembly sequence scenario has been defined following the Honda's official manual (Fig. 1).

Fig. 1. Complete range assembly of the Honda engine CRF250X and its Unity 3D preview

Based on this scenario, a "control sample" was prepared in a "standard" manual way where each kinematic link and each KP have been configured manually through the physic engine interface in Unity3D. We then tried to achieve a similar preparation process using the automatically generated feature and KPs from our SRE.

To describe in a more details the behaviour of our SRE on this specific use case, we will focus on the screws and their disassembly sub-process. The SRE starts by analysing each B-Rep data previously extracted and loads the Shell Features. Then the potential class (belong percentage) of the current part is deducted according to its geometry (nature of shell, positions and bounding boxes) as well as its specific naming rules in this case the term "bolt" used multiple time for each screw of the model. While the object class is identified, the SRE uses the mates data to deduce the type of joint between the screw and the part in contact with this latter. Then the SRE generate the KP according to the nature of the joints, the position of the mates in the part and lastly the nature of the surrounding shells. For every screw three KP are generated. A first Transition KP is instantiated at the extremity of the thread, which will determine the screw DOF according to its position. Then an Interest KP is generated at the position of the coincident mates and on the concentric mate's axis to describe the helical joint. Lastly, a Handling KP is generated to specify where the ratchet wrench tool should be position on the screw to be disassembled (Fig. 2).

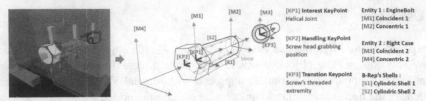

Fig. 2. Operation principle of the semantic rule engine and the automatic generation of keypoints in Unity 3D. Visual illustration of the analyzed features: Color code for the types of shell (cones in blue, planes in green, cylinders in red) - 3D spatial reference points for the mates. https://youtu.be/9az_zTtVwQc (Color figure online)

5 Results

The process time to prepare a VR scene in a manual way was estimated at five days, approximately 40 h of preparation time (human time). The results obtained using our SRE were in accordance with the control sample and the positions and natures of about 60% of the generated KPs appeared to be exact (71 well generated KPs on 117 for an assembly containing 45 parts: 81% Interest KPs, 75% Handling KPs and 33% Transition KPs). Using the SRE allowed us to prepare the scene in about 8 h and reduced the engineering time by 80%.

6 Conclusion and Future Prospect

In this paper, an attempt to create a recognition system based on a semantic keypoints and heuristic rules was presented. Differently from existing methods, our heuristic approach provided reasonable results for complex products with a high number of parts and providing much shorter preparation time. Those heuristic rules may look very basic and not rigorous but further works could use machine learning or specific company rules to adapt the model to local practices. Other works will be carried out in the future in order to consider the assembly reversed-sequence. Those works could raise to more complex behaviour rules and the potential identification of common behavioural class for sub-objects (e.g. using the same class of screws in several locations not previously defined in the assembly sequence). After this initial research work, a question remains unanswered, namely what strategies to adopt in presence of incomplete CAD data that could be solved in the future by exploring data enrichment approaches such has ontological methods or model update methods through VR scene.

References

1. Hasan, B., Wikander, J.: Features extraction from CAD as a basis for assembly process planning, In: DoCEIS, pp. 144–153 (2017)
2. Neb, A.: From 3D product data to hybrid assembly workplace generation using the Automation ML exchange file format (2019). https://doi.org/10.1016/j.procir.2019.03.011
3. Saniuk, S.: Personalization of products in the Industry 4.0 concept and Its impact on achieving a higher level of sustainable consumption. Energies **13**(22), 5895 (2020). https://doi.org/10.3390/en13225895.

4. Piegl, L., Tiller, W.: The NURBS Book, Springer Science & Business Media, Berlin (1997). https://doi.org/10.1007/978-3-642-97385-7
5. Tangelder, A.: Survey of content based 3D shape retrieval methods. Multimedia Tools Appl. **39**(3), 441–471 (2008). https://doi.org/10.1007/s11042-007-0181-0
6. Hasan, B.: Product Feature Modelling for Integrating Product Design and Assembly Process Planning, In: IJENS, vol.4 (10), (2017).
7. Hasan, B., Wikander, J.: A review on utilizing ontological approaches in integrating assembly design and assembly process planning (APP). Int. J. Mech. Eng. **4**(11), 5–16 (2017)
8. Costa, C.M.C.: Automatic generation of disassembly sequences and exploded views from solidworks symbolic geometric relationships. In: 2018 IEEE International Conference on Autonomous Robot Systems and Competitions (ICARSC) (2018)
9. Merlhiot, X.: XDE Physics: https://www.researchgate.net/project/XDE-Physics-multibody-dynamics-with-intermittent-contacts-and-flexible-bodies. Accessed 24 July 2021
10. Spezialetti, R., Salti, S.: Performance evaluation of 3D descriptors paired with learned keypoint detectors. AI **2**, 229–243 (2021). https://doi.org/10.3390/ai2020014
11. Liu, Z., Tan, J.: Constrained behavior manipulation for interactive assembly in a virtual environment. Adv. Manuf. Technol. **32**, 797–810 (2007)
12. Bourdot, P.: VR–CAD integration: multimodal immersive interaction and advanced haptic paradigms for implicit edition of CAD models (2008)
13. Hasan, B., Wikander, J.: Assembly design semantic recognition using solidworks-API. Int. J. Mech. Eng. Robot. Res. 5(4), 280–287 (2016)

Social Virtual Reality: Implementing Non-verbal Cues in Remote Synchronous Communication

Vlasios Kasapakis[1]([✉]), Elena Dzardanova[2], Vasiliki Nikolakopoulou[2], Spyros Vosinakis[2], Ioannis Xenakis[2], and Damianos Gavalas[2]

[1] Department of Cultural Technology and Communication, University of the Aegean, Lesvos, Greece
v.kasapakis@aegean.gr

[2] Department of Product and Systems Design Engineering, University of the Aegean, Syros, Greece
{lena,v.nikolakopoulou,spyrosv,ixen,dgavalas}@aegean.gr

Abstract. Social Virtual Reality (SVR) platforms allow remote, synchronous interaction and communication between individuals immersed in shared virtual worlds. Such platforms commonly implement full-body motion and real-time voice communication, but often lack complete non-verbal cues support. This work presents the development process and preliminary usability evaluation results of an SVR platform, incorporating non-verbal cues such as finger motion, gaze direction, and facial expressions, while allowing inter-communication between remotely located interlocutors.

Keywords: Virtual reality · Social platforms · Non-verbal cues · Remote communication

1 Introduction

The emergence of Social Virtual Reality (SVR) has allowed the simultaneous immersion, interaction, and communication between multiple users in a variety of Virtual Environments (VEs). SVR platforms integrate several tools such as full-body motion and real-time voice communication, which increase overall realism of social interactions and interlocutors' communication performance [1].

Ongoing research regarding intercommunication in VR settings makes use of off-the-shelf technologies to examine the transferability of non-verbal cues into SVR platforms, highlighting their importance for communication efficiency [2, 3]. Aspects of remote interaction and communication are under continuous examination in both commercial SVR platforms and testbeds developed for research purposes [4]. The majority of those shared settings do not provide solutions for gaze, finger/hand gestures, and facial expressions, or, in some cases, when some non-verbal cues are incorporated the implementation is performed locally, meaning that interlocutors are collocated in the same physical space [5].

© Springer Nature Switzerland AG 2021
P. Bourdot et al. (Eds.): EuroXR 2021, LNCS 13105, pp. 152–157, 2021.
https://doi.org/10.1007/978-3-030-90739-6_10

This study presents the in-laboratory development process of an SVR platform and results of its preliminary evaluation. Aside from interaction and communication between remotely located interlocutors, the platform also supports full-body motion tracking, finger-tracking, motion capture of facial expressions, and eye-tracking.

2 System Architecture

2.1 Local Setup

The architecture of the SVR platform presented here is based on the HTC Vive Pro VR system[1], Unity[2], and an avatar created using Reallusion Character Studio[3]. More specifically, the HTC Vive Pro HMD, accompanied by two (2) HTC Vive Base Stations, is used to track the user's head motion. HTC Vive Trackers are used to track the motion of the user's hands, feet, and pelvis. The motion data captured by both the HMD and trackers is transferred into Unity through the SteamVR SDK and integrated into the inverse kinematics solution Final IK[4], which then calculates the posture of the user's body and transfers it to the avatar.

The user's finger motion is captured using Manus VR gloves[5]. Manus VR gloves wirelessly communicate each finger bone rotation data, calculated using flex sensors, to the Manus Apollo finger motion capture software, which then transfers it to Unity, through the Manus Apollo Unity Core SDK, and finally applies it to the corresponding finger bones of a virtual set of hands. However, the prefabs provided by Manus Apollo Unity Core SDK were not compatible with our setup, resulting in inverted and incorrect finger motion. Therefore, a custom script was written, matching the finger bones rotation data as provided by Manus VR gloves with the corresponding finger bones of the avatar user. Prior to applying rotation to each finger bone, we multiplied each rotation axis data with a corresponding float coefficient to fix any motion inconsistencies (Fig. 1).

Fig. 1. Full body motion, including finger motion tracking.

[1] https://www.vive.com/eu/product/vive-pro/.
[2] https://unity.com/.
[3] https://www.reallusion.com/.
[4] http://root-motion.com/.
[5] https://www.manus-vr.com/.

For the integration of direction of gaze into the system, and subsequently, the SVR platform, the Pupil Labs Eye Tracking[6] setup was used compatible with the HTC Vive Pro HMD as an add-on. Using the Unity's SDK for the Pupil Labs Eye-Tracking system, followed by minor customization adjustments, the user's direction of gaze was matched to the eyes of the avatar in real-time. Another script had to be added, using the Transform.LookAt[7] function of Unity which correlated the user's gaze, as tracked by Pupil Labs, with the gaze of the avatar's eyes (Fig. 2).

Fig. 2. Gaze direction tracking using the pupil labs eye-tracking add-on.

Finally, to integrate facial cues into our system we used BinaryVR[8]. BinaryVR is a small infrared camera placed in front of the HMD, which captures facial movements of the lower face of a user. The BinaryVR Unity's SDK includes an example for transferring facial expressions data onto the face of an avatar through blendshapes. However, the model provided by Binary is a custom-made talking head and therefore unsuitable for solving tracked facial expressions onto other human 3D models. To address this issue, the correspondence between blendshape data provided by the BinaryVR SDK and those of the avatar used in our evaluation, had to be first investigated and adjusted accordingly to match differences in model structure. Then, a custom script was utilized which created a float coefficient for each blendshape. By manipulating each coefficient using a slider, while multiplying it with the corresponding blendshape data provided by BinaryVR, we were able to fix any facial expressions offsets. This way we appropriately calibrated BinaryVR for each user, so that her facial expressions in the real-world match the ones of the avatar in the virtual setting (Fig. 3).

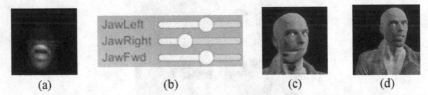

| (a) | (b) | (c) | (d) |

Fig. 3. (a) User facial expression; (b) Jaw right blend shape coefficient manipulated using a slider to fix the facial expression offset of the avatar; (c) Avatar facial expression before float coefficient application; (d) Avatar facial expression after float coefficient application.

---

[6] https://pupil-labs.com/.

[7] https://docs.unity3d.com/ScriptReference/Transform.LookAt.html.

[8] BinaryVR production company, later renamed to Hypersence, is now owned by Epic Games (https://www.epicgames.com/).

2.2 Remote Communication

Following finalization of the local setup, further system development was necessary to support remote interaction of at least two (2) individuals in a shared virtual space (see Fig. 4)[9]. To this end the Mirror[10] networking framework was utilized and a TCP Client-Server connection between two remote VR-ready PCs (Intel Core i7, Nvidia RTX 20280 8 GB, 16 GB RAM) was set up. Transferring the whole skeletal data of the avatars through the network would severely impact system performance and cause latencies. Therefore, only the data required for remote avatar reconstruction were transferred. More specifically, between Client and Server, each locally collected tracking data were first transferred to the respective remote location and only then reconstructed as the corresponding avatar's body motion, direction of gaze, and facial expressions. This limited the reconstruction process of the avatars in a single location each time.

This method helped maintain a small TCP packet size (628 bytes, about half of the packet size safe limit of Mirror), and therefore latencies were kept below 40 ms ensuring high-speed synchronization. Finally, real-time voice inter-communication was supported using the integrated microphone of the HTC Vive HMD along with the Unity Photon Voice Service[11].

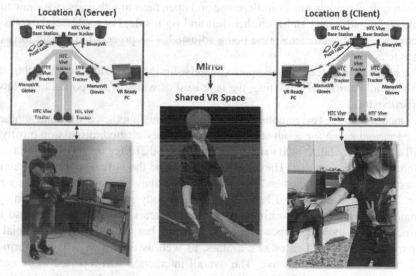

Fig. 4. SVR system architecture incorporating non-verbal cues.

3 Usability Evaluation

A preliminary usability evaluation of the system was conducted by laboratory associates. The equipment was calibrated for two individuals (1 M, 1 F) who went through its

---

[9] The full operation of the proposed SVR platform can be found at: https://tinyurl.com/487wpz9p.

[10] https://mirror-networking.com/.

[11] https://doc.photonengine.com.

calibration process, and participated in a ten (10) minute session where they freely interacted and communicated with one another. The shared virtual space was of simple design and included a mirror through which participants could observe their avatars' appearance and movements.

The calibration process of the equipment included the manual adjustment of the scale of each participant's avatar, along with minor offset adjustments to the Vive trackers position, to ensure correct body motion transference through inverse kinematics. This process required participants to stand in a T-Pose for thirty (30) seconds. Moreover, participants also had to perform specific hand gestures, again, for about thirty (30) seconds, to calibrate the Manus VR gloves. For the Pupil Labs Eye-Tracking system sensors calibration participants were required to focus their gaze onto predefined altering points inside the VR space. Finally, the BinaryVR system required participants to maintain the lower part of their face in resting position for at least three (3) seconds, to ensure appropriate capture and production of blendshape values. Upon completion of the suggested calibration process, and as mentioned in Sect. 2.1, additional manual calibrations were necessary for facial expressions to be captured properly. Our solution included the manual adjustment of float coefficients, multiplied with the corresponding blendshape values produced by BinaryVR, to adjust any incorrect facial expressions offsets. That process required participants to smile, close and open their mouth, move their jaw to the left and right, and finally smirk on their left and right side. For each facial expression the respective float coefficients were being adjusted. This process took about forty (40) seconds to complete.

The calibration process lasted approximately 4 min per participant, including short duration of all equipment mounting, the task load of which was reported to be low by both participants.

As mentioned, the two remotely located participants interacted with one another in a shared virtual space for about ten (10) minutes. They chatted, discussing mostly the overall experience, and pointed to one another aspects that were perceived as impressive or interesting to one another. They also walked around the virtual space and examined both each other virtual bodies and expressions, as well as their own through the virtual mirror. They tested out several hand gestures and body postures at random enjoying the matching of their real movements onto their avatars. In addition, they also both examined motion tracking responsiveness in general, but particularly that of facial and finger tracking; that of each other's avatars, as well as their own. They performed a virtual handshake and a high five. The overall interaction was reported to be natural since all features being tracked in real-time were responsive with no noticeable latency issues reported. No cybersickness episode occurred either. Participants felt comfortable and expressed desire for additional shared tasks.

Nevertheless, an issue relating to the Pupil Labs Eye-Tracking add-on and BinaryVR systems arose during the evaluation process. Since both systems are adjacent to the HMDs, each time participants touched their displays to fix placement, both systems would briefly decalibrate and produce wrong measurements. Tracking inconsistencies were minor, and brief given the miniscule adjustments of the HMDs and the overall short duration of the session. Greater user activity however, as well as prolonged sessions could gradually lose initial calibration measurements and require re-calibration.

4   Conclusions

This study presents the development process of a SVR platform, incorporating remote interaction and communication, full-body motion, finger tracking, gaze direction, and facial expressions, using off-the-shelf technologies and commercial VR application development frameworks. Preliminary usability evaluation results substantiated that the equipment calibration process is of low task load, while both local and remote reconstruction of user's body motion (including finger tracking), eye tracking and facial expressions is of increased speed and accuracy, allowing seamless interaction and communication between remotely located interlocutors.

Future work ought to put the system through greater stress by enhancing computational strain (e.g., increased polygon count, added animations, multiple lights and so forth) and prolonging sessions. A thorough usability evaluation with a statistically significant sample is required. Finally, a greater number of participants may provide a more sustainable solution to the decalibration issues caused by accidental HMD adjustments. More specifically, collection of a great number of blendshapes coefficient data can allow investigation for BinaryVR calibration automation via mediation of blendshape coefficient values.

Acknowledgement. The research work has been supported by the Hellenic Foundation for Research and Innovation (H.F.R.I.) under the "First Call for H.F.R.I. Research Projects to support Faculty members and Researchers and the procurement of high-cost research equipment grant" (Project Number: ΗΦΡΙ-ΓΜ17–1168).

References

1. Maloney, D., Freeman, G., Wohn, D.Y.: Talking without a voice understanding non-verbal communication in social virtual reality. In: Proceedings of the ACM on Human-Computer Interaction, pp. 1–25 (2020)
2. Bekele, E., Zheng, Z., Swanson, A., Crittendon, J., Warren, Z., Sarkar, N.: Understanding how adolescents with autism respond to facial expressions in virtual reality environments. Trans. Visual. Comput. Graph. **19**(4), 711–720 (2013)
3. Kasapakis, V., Dzardanova, E.: Using high fidelity avatars to enhance learning experience in virtual learning environments. In: Proceedings of the International Conference on Virtual Reality and 3D User Interfaces, Abstracts and Workshops, pp. 645–646 (2021)
4. Dzardanova, E., Kasapakis, V., Gavalas, D., Sylaiou, S.: Exploring aspects of obedience in VR-mediated communication. In Proceedings of the 11th International Conference on Quality of Multimedia Experience, pp. 1–3 (2019)
5. Roth, D., et al.: Technologies for social augmentations in user-embodied virtual reality. In Proceedings of the 25th Symposium on Virtual Reality Software and Technology, pp. 1–12 (2019)

Skill Level Monitoring Applied to AR Assisted Maintenance

Grégoire Mompeu(✉), Frédéric Mérienne, Florence Danglade, and Christophe Guillet

Institute Image, Chalon-sur-Saône, France

Abstract. This paper present a work in progress experiment about AR assisted inspection for maintenance. The purpose of this experiment is to define a set of indicators that could help to evaluate the skill level of a user during the inspection task while using AR assistance system.

Keywords: Adaptive assistance · Augmented reality · Assisted inspection

1 Introduction

The evaluation of skills is a main issue regarding the formation of new specialized workers in the industry. This is particularly important in sector like aircraft maintenance considering the tasks complexity and high level of quality expected in such activity. More over with the high variability of cases and situations encountered during the process that is higher than what we can find in production.

With the development of digital systems and technologies such as Augmented Reality, Virtual Reality, computer vision or bid data dedicated to training or assistance for workers we need to be able to evaluate more precisely the interactions between that kind of systems and the worker's skills level. Indeed, we need in the first place to measure the efficiency of the workers on a maintenance task (we will stuck with inspection task for this study).

2 Literature Review

The most used key indicators to reach that first goal are the learning time, the process time and the number of mistakes made. Questionnaires are also useful tools to catch the feeling of the user at the end of the process and try to improve it [1].

Some studies go further placing various sensors on the user in order to get the most detail data to analyses his behavior during the task. [2] present a localization system attached the user's wrists in order to track it and the tools manipulated. The system record the time spent in pre-defined working areas and compare it to a reference time in order to determine the efficiency on the task.

Concerning the way to display the information to the user, Augmented Reality can afford a better visual representation of content than the traditional textual instructions

© Springer Nature Switzerland AG 2021
P. Bourdot et al. (Eds.): EuroXR 2021, LNCS 13105, pp. 158–163, 2021.
https://doi.org/10.1007/978-3-030-90739-6_11

used in maintenance today. Some studies worked to convert that kind of basic information into more intuitive format such as images, pictograms [3] or 3D models [4].

Even if many studies have already demonstrated the benefits of Augmented Reality for maintenance [5, 6], other directions have been explored to improve further the involvement of the user in the task using audio instructions or haptic feedbacks [1]. That kind of systems afford a better understanding of the environment and ease the interactions within it.

Even if it has been demonstrated that AR provide a clear and efficient help for maintenances tasks, this technology can also represent an additional workload of information for expert profiles. We can also observe that the task complexity has a great impact on the contribution of such assistance. Indeed AR based assistance systems can reduce the time spent on a complex task but also increase it on simple task as the system itself can add complexity [7]. To address this issue some studies started to work on adaptive assistance system. The user skill level is sometimes supposed to be known [8]. In this case the user identification in the system associates data describing his skills and can load the best scenario. Others go further trying to evaluate these data in real time to adjust the instructions level of detail during the process [9].

Skills are often evaluated punctually using questionnaire and skills grids or tables [10]. Auto evaluation remains the traditional way to qualify operators' skills in many fields of activity, particularly for those requiring high-qualified workforce such as maintenance or surgery. The high subjectivity of this kind of method requires a huge amount of data and participants to be enough reliable. However nowadays the trend is to exploit data provided by more digital processes in order to characterize each individual [11]. The monitoring of skills evolution is also an approach investigated by researchers. Indeed today the knowledge of skill level of an individual is most of the time evaluated every trimester or every month.

3 Experiment

3.1 Goals and Objectives

The main objective of our experiment is to record different indicators that could translate the skill level of an expert on an inspection task and determine which are the most representatives. The next step will be to use this information to create area of interest directly on the inspected equipment 3D model. This constitutes the first step for the creation of a system able to capture and restitute knowledge automatically from and for the user.

The different indicators studied should also allow us to provide the most personalized and proportionate help to the user based on the deduced efficiency and ease to complete the task.

3.2 Overview

The user follows an inspection process applied to a simple numerical model presenting some damages on its surface. The goal is to identify efficiently and correctly all the damages on the little assembly. The user uses a tablet displaying AR information on the model to help him localize damages. A picking module allows him to add markers on the models where he finds a damage.

During this process, the behavior of the user is recorded through different parameters. We expect these parameters to provide some information on the user's attention evolution when going through the task.

In order to provide a better access to our solution and to capture more easily the parameters we want to analyze we design this experiment as a simulation using virtual reality. So the tablet constituting the AR assistance system is also represented in the virtual environment (Fig.1).

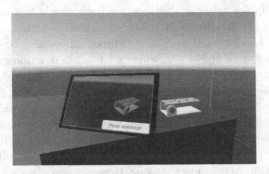

Fig. 1. Model to inspect and tablet in the virtual environment.

3.3 Material and Environment

The model used is a little assembly designed specifically for the experiment. The top part of the model is textured with damages (little rust stains). The experiment takes place in a virtual reality simulation. The hardware used for the VR is a first generation HTC Vive head mounted display and its controllers. The application was developed on Unity Engine and run on a desktop computer with a GTX1080 Ti GPU.

The VR scene includes the model to inspect, a workbench and a tablet. A main menu is also displayed and allow the user to switch between right-handed and left-handed mode and to skip the tutorial. At the beginning of the scenario, the model and the tablet lay on the workbench.

Tow version of the scenario have been designed: one including the AR help while the other one no. The AR help correspond to visual information in the form of little patches overlaying the model. These represent areas to inspect. They are containing at least one damage each to pick up. This help can be deactivated by clicking on the corresponding button in the tablet interface if the occlusion caused by the AR layer become a problem to clearly identify damages. The user can still reactivate the help later by clicking on the same button.

3.4 Participants

Fourteen participants participated to the experiment. Ten among them took part to the AR assisted scenario while the four remaining did not have access to this assistance. We had a variety of profiles such as students, teachers or administrative staff.

3.5 Procedure

Before the experiment, the user fills a short questionnaire detonated to better understand his background with VR technology as a previous contact with it could help him to understand quicker how to interact with the virtual environment.

The experiment starts with a tutorial phase in order to give some time to the user to better understand how to interact with its virtual environment and what we expect form him. During this phase, the model to inspect is a simple cube with two faces textures with damages. The user can manipulate the cube or the tablet with his hands. To pick up a damage the user film the cube with the tablet, align the tablet sight with the damage and click on the "place damage" button in the tablet interface. Then a little spherical marker is placed on the location aimed on the model. The user can undo this action by aiming to the marker and clicking on "delete damage" button. The user is free to end the tutorial phase when he has picked up at least one damage on the cube.

After the tutorial, the core experiment begins. The little assembly described previously replaces the cube but the task remain the same, the user must to pick up all the damages he can identify. There is total of sixteen damages to pick up on the model but the participant doesn't know that and is free to stop whenever he estimates that he have picked every damage up.

4 Preliminary Results

4.1 Parameters Recorded

The different parameters recorded during the experiment are the following:

- Position and rotation of the head, both hands, the tablet and the model
- The time spent manipulating the model and the tablet (independently)
- The time spent looking the model or the tablet
- The time spent aiming the model with the tablet
- The time spent using the AR help
- The number of picked up damages
- The location of each picked up damage
- The time of the core experiment (so that doesn't include the time spend on the tutorial phase)

4.2 Attention and Performances

The preliminary analysis of data already shows that participants manipulated the tablet most of the time. On average, they spent more than 90% of time using it. We expected that as the tablet is used to view AR information but also to pick up damage.

Half of the participants spent approximatively the same amount of time looking to the model or looking to the tablet. For the other half we observe a greater amount of time spent looking directly to the model. They spent between 10% and 25% more time of the global duration of the core experiment.

The number of damages the participant had to identify was sixteen. Eight among them were located on the top of the model and were visible directly without the need of any manipulation whereas the eight remaining were located under the top part of the little assembly so the participant needed to do some manipulation to access them. We observe that participants spent around 15% of their time to manipulate the model but only three of them were able to find at least 80% of the damages. The average number of damages identified is 10.7 that represent .67% of the total. We also observe that participants who spend equally their time looking to the model and to the tablet could find only 40% to 60% of the damages when those who spent their time looking more n of the two items were able to reach more than 90% of the damages.

4.3 Discussion

The recording of the time spent looking the different elements in the scene seems promising as it allowed to distinguish two types of behavior. Moreover, these two group of presents very different results in terms of performance.

However, other indicators as the time spent using AR could not really bring more information about the participant profile and other need to be analyzed. More information that is detailed could be extracted from the speed evolution of the moving elements present in the scene (user, tablet and model) as other studies suggest it.

5 Conclusion

This experiment is promising, as some indicators have already allowed us to identity different behavior in a population including mixed profiles. Some data remain to be analyzed more in detail to describe even more precisely the profiles identified. We also want to point out that we still need to find an equivalent set up to move from the VR simulation to the real AR environment.

Finally, it could be interesting to measure the most relevant indicators in a population with skill levels already known and containing some expert on the task evaluated in order to check if these indicators can really be used to categorized skill levels.

References

1. Webel, S., Bockholt, U., Engelke, T., Gavish, N., Olbrich, M., Preusche, C.: An augmented reality training platform for assembly and maintenance skills. Robot. Auton. Syst. **61**, 398–403 (2013)

2. Siew, C.Y., Ong, S.K., Nee, A.Y.: A practical augmented reality-assisted maintenance system framework for adaptive user support. Robot. Comput. Intergrated Manuf. **59**, 115–129 (2019)
3. Scurati, G.W., Gattullo, M., Firorentino, M., Ferrise, F., Bordegoni, M., Uva, A.E.: Converting maintenance actions into standard symbols for augmented reality applications in Industry 4.0. Comput. Ind. **98**, 68–79 (2018)
4. del Amo, I.F., Erkoyuncu, J.A., Roy, R., Wilding, S.: Augmented reality in maintenance: an information-centred design framework. Proc. Manuf. **19**, 148–155 (2018)
5. del Amo, I.F., Erkoyuncu, J.A., Roy, R., Palmarini, R., Onoufriou, D.: A systematic review of augmented reality content-related techniques for knowledge transfer in maintenance applications. Comput. Ind. **103**, 47–71 (2018)
6. Schmiedinger, T., Petke, M., von Czettritz, L., Wohlschläger, B., Adam, M.: Augmented reality as a tool for providing informational content in different production domains. Proc. Manuf. **45**, 423–428 (2020)
7. Deshpande, A., Kim, I.: The effects of augmented reality on improving spatial problem solving for object assembly. Adv. Eng. Inf. **38**, 760–775 (2018)
8. Mourtzis, D., Xanthi, F., Zogopoulos, V.: An adaptive framework for augmented reality instructions considering workforce skill. Proc. CIRP **81**, 363–368 (2019)
9. Syberfeldt, A., Danielsson, O., Holm, M., Wang, L.: Dynamic operator instructions based on augmented reality and rule-based expert systems. Proc. CIRP **41**, 346–351 (2016)
10. Bonnard, G., et al.: Évaluation multicentrique de la reproductibilité et de la validité d'un carnet d'évaluation des compétences professionnelles des internes de médecine interne. Rev. Med. Inter. **40**, 419–426 (2019)
11. van Laar, E., van Deursen, A., van Dijk, J., de Haan, J.: Measuring the levels of 21st-century digital skills among professionals working within the creative industries: a performance-based approach. Poetics **81**, 101434 (2020)

Immersive Serious Games for Learning Physics Concepts: The Case of Density

Iuliia Zhurakovskaia[1]([✉]), Jeanne Vézien[1], Cécile de Hosson[2], and Patrick Bourdot[1]

[1] Université Paris-Saclay, CNRS, LISN, 91400 Orsay, France
iuliia.zhurakovskaia@u-psud.fr
[2] Université de Paris, LDAR, 75205 Paris, France

Abstract. Training students in basic concepts of physics, such as the ones related to mass, volume, or density, is much more complicated than just stating the underlying definitions and laws. One of the reasons for this is that most students have deeply rooted delusions and misconceptions about the behavior of objects, sometimes close to magical thinking. Many innovative and promising technologies, in particular Virtual Reality (VR), can be used to enhance student learning.

We compared the effectiveness of a serious immersive game in teaching the concept of density in various conditions: a 2D version in an embedded web browser and a 3D immersive game in VR. We also developed a specific questionnaire to assess students' knowledge improvement. Primary results have shown an increase in learning efficiency using VR. Also, most students were able to see the shortcomings of their initial theories and revise them, which means that they improved their understanding of this topic.

Keywords: Density · Virtual reality · Science education

1 Introduction

Density can be derived as a unitless number, being the ratio of the volumetric mass of a (homogenous) body over the one of a reference object (usually water at 4 °C, of density equal to 1 g/cm^3).

In order to teach density, Smith [1] mentioned that it is important to show early on the correct connection between density and flotation (an object denser than water will sink while it will float if less dense). If the learned materials do not fit the students' intuitive framework, they tend to distort the learning to accommodate their beliefs. Also, they can assimilate the new material as a separate system without any relations to the real world. Consequently, they "learn" the material as it is without understanding it, will pass exams, but fail to get a clear understanding of the underlying concept [1].

Strike and Posner [2] argued it is important to *show* students that their current concepts are wrong and do not stand up to serious scrutiny, and based on this, provide them an experimental path to the correct framework.

Recent STEM education research [3] reported that students who used VR for education and students using a regular desktop version exhibited similar results. Moreover, the

© Springer Nature Switzerland AG 2021
P. Bourdot et al. (Eds.): EuroXR 2021, LNCS 13105, pp. 164–170, 2021.
https://doi.org/10.1007/978-3-030-90739-6_12

results of immersion (3D) and desktop (2D) learning gave better results than actual field trips [3]. Based on these findings, and because current sanitary conditions encouraged remote teaching, we decided to evaluate teaching the concept of density in two conditions: in 2D (remotely: keyboard/mouse interaction on a 2D web-based simulation) and in 3D (in person: immersive VR experiment using a run-of-the-mill HMD).

Following a didactic approach, the main tasks we have identified are: (i) to provide a good understanding of different aspects of density for students; analyze and assess this understanding; (ii) to clarify the distinction between density, weight, and volume in students' understanding; (iii) to examine the effectiveness of the serious game approach in teaching density and compare the results with traditional didactic approaches.

This study leverages three separate tools: VR, Serious Games, and Didactics. VR technology allows generating a previously unavailable experience by interacting directly with simulated content that reproduces existing physical phenomena of all sorts. Serious games, also known as game-based learning, consist of any game that aims to enhance the player's knowledge. Such games use pedagogy to influence the learning experience [7, 8]. The purpose of didactic research is to study the questions raised by teaching and the acquisition of knowledge in various scholarly disciplines.

One should note that, at this point, VR has never been used to teach the concept of density. Because this classic concept is addressed early in most teaching curricula, we selected it as a good candidate to evaluate the efficiency of VR to comprehend physics in a classroom setting.

2 Online Questionnaire

To establish a reliable baseline of knowledge regarding the subject of density, we first designed a dedicated online questionnaire based on [4]. The questionnaire contains 13 basics questions about the density concept, each with a 4-step confidence level.

Analysis of the a priori responses to the questionnaire showed that most of the students shared identical misconceptions on the subject (e.g., most students have not integrated the idea that the density of a solid is formally defined in relation to water) and that the knowledge regarding density was largely incomplete.

3 2D Game

The second part of the research consisted in creating a 2D game designed as a web browser experience (Fig. 1). Participants used a regular screen (a laptop or PC) and mouse interaction to play within a 2D simulation, organized as a game with several "levels". This game was developed on the Unity engine [6].

The game is decomposed into several stages: a pre-test evaluates the current knowledge of students, followed by a training session introducing the main objects and possible interactions to familiarize the user with the environment of the game, followed by three different game stages, described below. A bonus level completes the game for extra fun, followed by a post-test questionnaire, which consists of the same questions as the pre-test but in another order.

We designed three sequential gaming conditions: Condition 1 (C1) - All objects have the same volume but not the same mass; Condition 2 (C2) - All objects are with the same mass but not the same volume; Condition 3 (C3) - Two tanks filled with different liquids (water and oil) and two sets of the objects, same ones as in C1. The bonus level is a simple version of C3 (no game score, no predictions, quicksilver instead of oil).

All cubes have individual characteristics: size (volume), texture (dots, with varying spacing), and weight (mass). The texture is indicative of the density: the more dots, the higher the density [1].

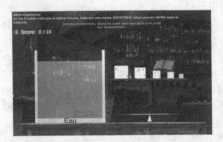

Fig. 1. 2D game.   **Fig. 2.** 3D game.

The main task consisted of placing cubes in a tank full of liquid (water); the user then had to make a prediction about the objects' behavior in the water before observing the experimental outcome. Also, C1 introduced the Roberval Balance as a metaphor to compare cubes according to their mass.

4   Immersive 3D Game

The third part of the experiment consisted in using the same game as in the 2D part, but this time interacting within an immersive VR environment (Fig. 2).

Affordable price and reasonable quality of immersion hardware and software were paramount to this project. We selected the Lenovo Explorer VR headset with two controllers and the Unity game engine as an adequate setup.

All the interaction techniques exploited in this setup are based on the common "simple virtual hand" metaphor. Cubes could be picked up with both virtual hands, manipulated freely, and dropped (not thrown).

One of the main differences between 2D and 3D games was the possibility to manage the actual gaming conditions around participants. Aside from dimension and interaction modes, the main difference between the two versions of the game was the availability of sound. We didn't use audio in the 2D game because we could not control the audio conditions in the users' environment (some users could have muted the sound). In contrast, this was possible in the 3D VR on-site experiment. To provide more immersion and convey additional information (e.g., mass) about objects, each participant was equipped with headphones and binaural sound rendering was provided.

Representing weight in VR is a major problem because although force-feedback devices do exist, such haptic interactors are very expensive, cumbersome, and tend to be fragile. Using sounds to convey mass information to students seemed, therefore, a promising alternative approach [5].

Experimental Procedure. The local ethical committee approved the following experiment, and proper sanitary procedures to prevent Covid-19 contamination were applied [9]. For better immersion and to avoid additional device manipulations, users passed the pre-test in the virtual environment.

Then the students underwent a training session. This initial phase consisted of presenting the setup in a sandbox "no-task" configuration. General instructions were given on how to grasp cubes and place them in different locations.

During experiments, participants read all instructions on a virtual blackboard placed in front of them. In each trial, they could manipulate the cubes at will, with no time constraint. Participants performed a sorting task and, when a tank was present, made a prediction (correct answer +2 points, wrong answer −1 point) about the behavior of the cube in the liquid (sink, stay in the middle, float), before they could observe the actual behavior. The game stages were identical to those of the 2D game.

The final post-test was a copy of the pre-test but with a reordering of the questions.

Following the VR experiment, participants were asked to undergo a 15-min semi-directed interview. The objective was to collect some data relative to subjective perceptions regarding the general quality of the environment and the interaction, the task itself, perceived object affordance, perception of weight, and overall satisfaction with the experiment.

5 Results

5.1 Online Questionnaire

After analyzing the online questionnaire, we exploited the R factor to structure the profiles of our respondents' answers. R computes the similarity of a set of answers and group them into similarity clusters. The questionnaire was made available on a website to freshmen physics students at the University Paris Diderot. There were 44 complete responses. Two respondents stood out strongly from the rest, and all the others were divided into three groups with similar misconceptions. Most students do not correctly understand how density, mass, and volume are related, to the point that some of them will consider one of these physical characteristics as independent from the others. Only one participant provided a correct answer to all the questions. Thus, the analysis confirmed that most of the students shared identical misconceptions, and knowledge is lacking in the specific field of density.

68% of the participants went over the 50% rate of correct answers. The average success rate among all participants was 60,31%.

5.2 2D Game

This experiment was performed on a sample of nine participants, all future physics teachers in the first year studying at the University Paris Diderot. Eight of them had a scientific background, and one of them had a background in literature. Also, we asked them when they last studied the properties of matter: three of them answered "This year during my studies", three others "During my graduate studies", the remaining three said "During my high school studies".

Participants spent an average of 28 min. on the game, with a minimum time of 11 min. and a maximum time of 1 h (see Table 1).

Regarding results of pre- and post-test, the efficiency of participants decreased by 4,27%, but the level of confidence increased by 11,5%: some participants made more mistakes after the experiment than before, but they also gained subjective confidence. This shows that a self-assessed feeling of success is not always the result of successful teaching.

Analyzing answers from tests makes it clear that students still do not correctly interpret how mass, volume, and density are related. Also, a problem arose from the relationship between volume and density in conjunction with a flotation situation. Thus, we see that the concept of density remains challenging to apply to certain practical cases and that the initial misconceptions of students are not easily dispelled.

Despite the inefficacy of 2D games, some students commented that they positively describe such a gaming experience in learning, and their impressions were very good.

Table 1. Time for 2D game (unit: minutes)

Sections	Min t	Max t	Average t
Pre-test	3,62	33,04	10,15
Training	0,51	6,37	2,44
Scenario 1	1,15	5,59	2,86
Scenario 2	0,94	3,20	1,66
Scenario 3	0,84	3,45	2,22
Scenario bonus	0,14	1,40	0,64
Post-test	1,98	16,65	5,31
Total game time	11,52	60,02	28,41

Table 2. Time for 3D game (unit: minutes)

Sections	Min t	Max t	Average t
Pre-test	4,54	9,92	6,62
Training	0,33	2,80	1,06
Scenario 1	2,76	6,99	4,34
Scenario 2	1,03	3,96	1,80
Scenario 3	2,03	3,58	2,89
Scenario bonus	0,29	2,91	1,28
Post-test	3,32	7,97	4,65
Total game time	16,23	37,30	24,07

5.3 3D Game

Because of the prevailing sanitary conditions, only preliminary tests could be conducted on seven participants (Mean age = 23, SD = 2.6) from the laboratory. None of the participants was involved in the design or in the research of the experiment. Almost all of them have a scientific background and play video games every day. Also, 4 of them mentioned that they last studied the properties of matter while in high school and others in middle school.

Playing the density games increased test accuracy from 73,62% to 81,31%, so we can hypothesize that actual 3D manipulations, even with virtual objects, carry more sense and provide more benefits than simple observation in 2D. Similarly, as in the 2D game, the participants increased their confidence by 11,25%. Thus, the actual manipulations were also helpful to bring awareness of some delusions and dispel them, building a correct understanding of the concept of density.

Participants spent 6,62 min. on the pre-test and 4,64 min. on the post-test on average (see Table 2). Analysis answers of tests clearly shows that students have become better at understanding the ratio of density, mass, and volume, but relative flotation remains a more complex concept to grasp.

The average playing time decreased compared to a 2D game. Interestingly, time increased for the Bonus level: Students were more interested because they never tested quicksilver in real life (it is banned from classrooms due to its dangerosity), and the behavior of the cubes surprised them (all objects float in this high-density liquid, and if placed in the middle of it and released, a cube seems to "shoot" out of it).

Also, the salient facts we uncovered were the following:

- General VR scene settings and manipulation procedures were considered satisfactory. Subjects unanimously positively valued all conditions, finding them fun, easy, and they felt confident during the games.
- Most of the participants evaluated sound effects as valuable, giving them additional information and allowing them to focus on a task, and not memorizing which cube is which. Also, 3D sound helped them to get involved in the game.
- Regarding learning, most users established the relationship between the number of points on cubes and density and mass. They were able to apply this in the experiment, but the absence of a similar metaphor for the liquid was sometimes perceived negatively.
- The participants also highly appreciated the proposed learning opportunities by VR (e.g., playing with quicksilver) and found them helpful.

6 Conclusions

Students routinely experience difficulties when trying to apply theoretical knowledge in practical situations. They know which formula to use, but they do not develop a deep understanding of the topic of density.

Although it has never been used for the theme of density, VR has repeatedly proven its ecological validity and usefulness in other contexts (such as procedural learning). The results presented in this study showed that immersive serious games could, if not eradicate students' false conceptions on this issue, at least shake them and help look at it from a different viewpoint, allowing them to reconsider their view on the physical phenomenon.

Comparison of 2D and 3D gaming conditions showed the inefficiency of the former and the benefits of immersive games for learning. The 2D game does not provide a sufficient learning experience. On the contrary, the association of VR, serious games, and didactics led to much better results. We have proven that actual manipulation of virtual objects is more beneficial than just observing or interacting with a computer mouse.

It is difficult to force a student to study well without motivation. The students highly appreciated the use of VR for teaching, leading to more motivation. The use of VR associated with traditional teaching models can be a significant impetus for better learning and in-depth understanding of certain physics phenomena.

References

1. Smith, C.J.S.: Using Conceptual models to facilitate conceptual change: the case of weight-density differentiation. Cogn. Instruc. **9**(3), 221–283 (1992)
2. Strike, K.A., Posner, G.J.: A conceptual change view of learning and understanding. In: West, L., Pines, L. (eds.) Cognitive Structure and Conceptual Change, pp. 211–231 (1985)
3. Zhao, J., LaFemina, P., Carr, J., Sajjadi, P., Wallgrun, J.O., Klippel, A.: Learning in the Field: comparison of desktop, immersive virtual reality, and actual field trips for place-based STEM education. In: 2020 IEEE Conference on Virtual Reality and 3D User Interfaces (VR), pp. 893–902. IEEE, Atlanta (2020)
4. Hashweh, M.: The complexity of teaching density in middle school. Res. Sci. Educ. **34**(1), 1–24 (2015)
5. Clark, R.C., Mayer, E.R.: E-Learning and the Science of Instruction: Proven Guidelines for Consumers and Designers of Multimedia Learning. Pfeiffer, San Francisco (2008)
6. Unity Homepage. https://unity.com. Accessed 13 Sep 2021
7. Jeon, K.Y., Almond, R.G., Shute, V.S.: Applying evidence-centered design for the development of game-based assessments in physics playground. Int. J. Test. **16**(2), 142–163 (2016)
8. Shute V., Ventura M.: Stealth Assessment: Measuring and Supporting Learning in Video Games. The MIT Press, Cambridge (2013)
9. Posselt, J., Gosselin, R.: Protocols of use for immersive platforms under Covid-19. In: Proceedings of the Virtual EuroVR Conference, pp. 19–21 (2020)

Author Index

Printed in the United States
by Baker & Taylor Publisher Services

Printed in the United States
by Baker & Taylor Publisher Services